WHY USUALLY HONEST PEOPLE STEAL

Understanding, Treating And Stopping Nonsensical Shoplifting And Other Bizarre Theft Behaviour

Will Cupchik Ph.D.

ISBN 978-1-896342-10-8

Published by Tagami Communications, 2528 Bayview Avenue, P.O. Box 35532, Toronto, Ontario, Canada M2L 2Y4.

Manufactured in the United States. 2nd Printing.

BookLocker.com, Inc. 2013

Library and Archives Canada Cataloguing in Publication

Cupchik,Will,1940-
Why usually honest people steal [electronic resource] : understanding, treating and stopping nonsensical shoplifting and other bizarre theft behaviour / Will Cupchik.

Includes bibliographical references.

1. Shoplifting—Psychological aspects.
2. Shoplifting--Prevention.
3. Theft--Psychological aspects.
4. Theft--Prevention.
5. Behaviour modification.
6. Kleptomania.

HV6652.C863 2013   616.85'842   C2012-908322-4

Issued also in electronic format; ISBN 978-1-62646-300-4

Will Cupchik Ph.D.

Formerly *Psychologist-in-Charge, Forensic Outpatient Psychological Services Clarke Institute of Psychiatry, Toronto*

Author of *Why Honest People Shoplift or Commit Other Acts of Theft: The Assessment and Treatment of 'Atypical Theft Offenders'*

DISCLAIMER

This book details the author's clinical investigations, personal experiences with, and opinions about the atypical theft behaviours of usually honest and ethical individuals.

The author and publisher are providing this book and its contents on an "as is" basis and make no representations or warranties of any kind with respect to this book or its contents. The author and publisher disclaim all such representations and warranties, including for example warranties of merchantability and healthcare for a particular purpose or individual. In addition, the author and publisher do not represent or warrant that the information accessible via this book is accurate, complete or current.

The statements made about products and services have not been evaluated by the U.S. Food and Drug Administration. They are not intended to diagnose, treat, cure, or prevent any condition or disease. Please consult with your own physician or healthcare specialist regarding the suggestions and recommendations made in this book.

Except as specifically stated in this book, neither the author or publisher, nor any authors, contributors, or other representatives will be liable for damages arising out of or in connection with the use of this book. This is a comprehensive limitation of liability that applies to all damages of any kind, including (without limitation) compensatory; direct, indirect or consequential damages; loss of data, income or profit; loss of or damage to property and claims of third parties.

You understand that this book is not intended as a substitute for consultation with a suitably trained and experienced licensed healthcare practitioner. Before you begin any healthcare program, or change your lifestyle in any way, you will consult your physician or other licensed healthcare practitioner to ensure that you are in good health and that the examples, exercises and recommendations and/or suggestions contained in this book will not harm you.

This book provides content related to physical and/or mental health issues. As such, use of this book implies your acceptance of this disclaimer.

WHY USUALLY HONEST PEOPLE STEAL

Understanding, Treating And Stopping Nonsensical Shoplifting And Other Bizarre Theft Behaviour

Dr Will Cupchik, C. Psych.

**Formerly *Psychologist-in-Charge*,
Forensic Outpatient Psychological Services,
*Clarke Institute of Psychiatry, Toronto, Canada***

Table of Contents

LIST OF CASES

CASE #	NAME	DETAILS
1	Victor	A retired businessman and Holocaust survivor whose theft was seemingly very bizarre and nonsensical indeed!
2	Melanie	The Frequent Employee-of the month Who Had Stolen From Her Employer – for Years
3	Brenda	The Politician's Wealthy Wife Who Stole A Pair Of Shoes in full view of a clearly marked security camera
4	Florence	A middle-level manager who pocketed many thousands of dollars of cash from relatives, co-workers and close friends over a period of several years
5	James	A major fundraiser who stole a lot!
6	Gerald	The professor who stole $1,000,000 from his siblings
7	Margaret	The case of the childless obstetrician/gynaecologist who repeatedly stole items from children's specialty stores
8	Georgina	A remarkable case of the breakthrough into conscious awareness of maternal feelings that had been 'repressed' in a young professional woman's unconscious.
9	Alice	The woman who stole whenever her husband had another bout of cancer
10	Robert	The physician who was brought up in a home with a violent, alcoholic father who also happened to be a senior circuit court judge
11	Charlene	A senior accountant with very low self esteem who repeatedly - and in clearly obvious ways - stole over $380,000 from three successive employers in the same (highly visible) type of business, in a city of less than 300,000 citizens.

About the Author

I have been a member of the American Psychological Association, Canadian Psychological Association and Ontario Psychological Association for over three decades and am now a 'life member' of them all. For nearly four decades I have been providing assessment and treatment for *usually honest* persons who live in the USA, Canada and elsewhere who have committed seemingly bizarre or nonsensical shoplifting and/or other acts of theft, activities that threatened their good names, their working/professional lives and in some cases, even their freedom. Having specialized in the area of atypical theft behaviour for over 39 years, I have developed a highly effective and efficient program that allows genuinely willing and ready clients to work with me from their own homes and to make considerable progress towards *understanding* - and more importantly - *stopping* their ultimately self-destructive atypical theft behaviour. My contact information is as follows:

- for snail mail, 2528 Bayview Avenue, P. O. Box 35532, Toronto, Ontario, Canada M2L 2Y4 Ontario, Canada
- cellphone # is 416 928-2262
- landline # is 416-485-8064
- my email address is *wcupchik@aol.com*, and
- my Skype address is Dr.Will.Cupchik1

I previously held the position of *Psychologist-in-Charge, Forensic Outpatient Psychological Services (1984-86)*, at the Clarke Institute of Psychiatry in Toronto. My clinical investigations of atypical theft behaviour began at the Clarke Institute in 1974. I was senior author of the 1983 article titled <u>Shoplifting: An Occasional Crime of the Moral Majority</u> published in the major, peer-reviewed *Bulletin of the American Academy of Psychiatry and the Law, Volume 11, No.4*. I was also the senior author of a similarly titled chapter that appeared in the book, <u>Clinical Criminology: The Assessment and Treatment of Criminal Behaviour</u>, published by the Clarke Institute of Psychiatry and the University of Toronto, in 1985. My previous book on this topic, ***Why Honest People Shoplift Or Commit Other Acts Of Theft***, has consistently been one of the best sellers in its field, and is currently available in paperback as well as in an ebook edition from Amazon.com, BarnesandNoble.com, Chapters.ca, Booklocker.com and other online bookstores.

I have been awarded Diplomate status by the American College of Forensic Examiners. I also hold full membership in the Canadian Registry of Health Service Providers in Psychology and am a Registered Psychologist with the College of Psychologists of Ontario.

I have been granted a *Certificate of Professional Qualification in Psychology (CPQ)* and an *Interjurisdictional Practice Certificate (IPC)* by the Association of State and Provincial Psychology Boards (ASPPB). Currently, the psychology boards of all fifty states of the United States, the District of Columbia, the U.S. Virgin Islands, Puerto Rico, Guam and all ten provinces of Canada are members of ASPPB.

I obtained my Ph.D. in Counseling Psychology from the University of Toronto in 1979. I acquired my M.Ed. degree in Counseling and Guidance from University of Toronto in 1970, and my B.A. degree with a major in psychology from Carleton University in Ottawa in 1963.

I also earned a Bachelor of Engineering (B.Eng.) degree in electrical engineering from McGill University in 1961 and worked in the aeronautical field as a Systems Design Engineer, designing navigational guidance systems for the then-next generation of American, Canadian and other NATO countries' military aircraft.

I was also listed in the first edition (1984) of *Who's Who in Frontier Science and Technology.*

Additional information about myself and up-to-date materials about the subject of this book, the **webcam-enabled Atypical Theft Offender Intensive Intervention Program** that I offer and the training programs that I can provide for suitable professionals are all available on the *www.WhyHonestPeopleSteal.com* website.

Acknowledgements

My clinical investigations into the phenomenon of essentially honest people who shoplift were initiated in 1974 while I was working on the forensic service of the **Clarke Institute of Psychiatry**, in Toronto. **Dr Don J. Atcheson** (at the time, a senior psychiatrist on the same forensic service) and I began focusing upon these unusual cases when we recognized that certain commonalties seemed to exist. I again gratefully acknowledge his colleagueship, integrity, good humor and friendship throughout our employment at the Clarke Institute and afterwards.

In fact, now more than 27 years after Don and I stopped collaborating, I am even more appreciative of the exceptionally gentle nature, professionalism and kindnesses he extended to me during our work together, and later on as well. As an example of the quality of the man, I would like to share that when we were ready to submit our first article, *Shoplifting: An Occasional Crime Of The Moral Majority*, for publication, Don came to my office door and said that while he thought the article was excellent, there was one important correction that needed to be made. He pointed out that I had put his name before mine at the top of the article, effectively suggesting that he was the senior investigator. I had done that out of respect for the fact that Don was by far the more senior of the two of us. He said that while he was "honoured to ride on (my) coattails" the fact was, he emphasized, that most of the time and effort, as well as most of the original insights into atypical theft behaviour, were mine, and so he insisted that I should have my name in the position of the senior investigator. Those who have worked in the academic and/or clinical worlds, particularly in the field of the social sciences and humanities (and/or elsewhere in the corporate, legal and other lines of work) will immediately recognize, I am sure, how frequently such demonstrations of complete honesty, professional integrity and kind generosity may - or may not - occur.

I also want to thank the then staff of the forensic service of the Clarke Institute of Psychiatry, where I worked for twelve years, from 1974 through 1986. The period from 1974 through 1982, in particular, was highlighted by great interdisciplinary camaraderie, professional enthusiasm and mutual support. I also thank the patients who attended our forensic service and shared with us their personal stories and the facts of their atypical theft behaviour.

I am grateful to the **clients** I have worked with from all over the USA, Canada and elsewhere who have given me the opportunity to work with them to help uncover and deal with those issues that had helped precipitate their theft behaviour. Doing so always requires courage and determination, and a willingness to visit those invariably uncomfortable and possibly painful places that must be addressed in order to assist them to stop stealing.

I am grateful to the late **Dr Jack Birnbaum**, an excellent psychiatrist, multi-published author and dear, dear friend, for his oft-voiced enthusiasm for my clinical and authoring endeavours in the area of atypical theft behaviour. His own enthusiasm has continued to motivate me to investigate this truly fascinating area of clinical interest. I miss Jack, his wonderful wit, worldly wisdom and close friendship, dearly.

Also gone but not at all forgotten is the late **Dr Robert Goulding,** an exceptional psychiatrist, a great teacher, major mentor and at the end, a wonderful friend from whom I gained so very much over many years, and still do.

My very dear friends, **Dr Jack Lin**, a remarkable intellect, Jungian-oriented Psychologist, fellow engineer and the co-founder of National Technical Systems, headquartered in Calabasas, California, and **David Martin**, architect truly extraordinaire of Monterey, California, have given me a great deal of support over the past more than two decades, and have motivated me to do even better. We 'three amigos' are truly blessed to have met and deepened our friendships over the time we have known one another.

Denis Dean, a very dear friend and the editor of my novel, *The Avro Arrow Manipulation*, offered his sage advice in regard to the title, and front and back covers of this book. As usual, his kind suggestions were 'spot on'!

My very close friend, **Judith Rockert**, has been a constant support for all my personal and professional endeavours for so many years. We have shared a great deal these last three decades, and I have always benefited from her most humane and wise input. As importantly, we have shared countless moments of great laughter, a salve at any time, and especially whenever I have spent many hours at the computer.

I want to recognize the excellent support that I have received from **Drs Caldwell Esselstyn, Mark Minden** and **Barry Simon**. Their assistance has helped me in many ways during the completion of this book and all of our contacts have been very much appreciated.

I am truly blessed to have exceptional children **(Jeff, Matt** and daughter-in-law, **Sorelle**) and superb grandchildren **(Shia, Essie, Levi** and **Nechama**). I am also proud to be **Uncle Will** to **Melanie, Daren, Logan** and **Eden Levitt**. Each of these young people has outstanding talents and qualities and they enrich my life every day by simply being part of it! I love you all; our times together give me the greatest pleasure and happiness.

I thank my sister, **Nina**, and brother-in-law, **Tom**, for their continued support and my nephew, **Howie**, for his input as well.

Lastly, let me acknowledge the superb assistance of my wonderful wife, **Barbara**, who has provided me with her unflagging encouragement for this as well as all my other projects. Her steadfast support and keen insights have made working on this book that much easier. Furthermore, Barbara, an excellent published writer in her own right, closely reviewed and helped to edit this book. Nevertheless, any failings it may have are unquestionably my responsibility alone.

Dedication

This book is dedicated to those individuals who I acknowledged on the previous pages, as well as to the many colleagues and clients who have helped me gain an increasingly deeper understanding and insight into the workings of usually honest persons who have stolen in some fashion or another - either once, occasionally or perhaps often, even though, by doing so, they have violated their *own* usual moral and ethical codes.

I especially dedicate this book to the clients (mostly from all over the USA and Canada) who came to my office in Toronto to take the very concentrated multi-day Atypical Theft Offender *Intensive Intervention Program* that I offered for some fifteen years.

I am also most grateful to those other, more recent clients from all over the USA, Canada and elsewhere with whom I have worked online (usually via Skype) for more than five years as of the publication of this book. They have assisted me to develop and refine a highly efficient, much less expensive, and even more beneficial means of providing a viable and robust 20-session long, assessment and treatment *Intensive Intervention Program for Atypical Theft Offenders*, while at the same time causing minimal disruption to their daily lives.

I also dedicate this book to my beautiful, loving and talented wife, Barbara, with the deepest gratitude for her nourishing love, unflagging commitment and positivity, and to our remarkable children and our exceptional grandchildren. You fill my life with great joy and so much pleasure. I love you all!

PREFACE

The Classic Case Of An Honest Man Whose Dynamic Unconscious Revealed Itself By Precipitating Seemingly Nonsensical Shoplifting

Over the past nearly four decades I have often been interviewed by representatives of the print and electronic media who wanted to better understand why a celebrity or very financially well off individual would risk so much (in terms of personal reputation, professional standing, etc…) for usually, so very little in terms of monetary gain. On these occasions I have usually provided the basics of the understanding I have gained from dealing with such persons. At the same time I have often provided real (yet very camouflaged, of course) cases from my files of over 700 such cases, often including the case of this gentleman I shall call Victor.

To begin this discussion of atypical theft behaviour let me offer for your consideration the case of Victor, a wealthy retired business owner from Los Angeles, who committed a totally unnecessary, single act of theft in 1995. His story has much to inform us about life, the lingering effects of early trauma and how the mind works, via his own remarkable acting out theft behaviour. I reported on this case in my previous book, yet it bears recalling again, for it offers what I believe is a truly classic example of the folks I have termed Atypical Theft Offenders. [In interviews I have held with the print and electronic media from various countries over the years, I have often referred to this case, as it seems to be among the most readily appreciated by laypersons, and is, as well, one of the most moving and dramatic examples of atypical theft behaviour I have ever encountered.]

Case # 1: Victor: A retired businessman and Holocaust survivor whose theft was seemingly very bizarre indeed!

Victor was apprehended in the city of Los Angeles where he lived, in the spring of 1995, for shoplifting $15 worth of goods. What made the offence seem particularly bizarre was the fact that Victor was a very wealthy person.

As is true of many Holocaust survivors, Victor was an individual who had overcome incredible odds and horrific personal tragedy, had strived and succeeded in becoming successful (in his own business and personal life) yet remained one for whom existence was permeated by a lingering aura of poignant pain, horror and sadness.

Everyone in Victor's family, including all four grandparents, both his parents and his four younger siblings, had been exterminated in the Nazi concentration camps. He recalled for me with deep emotion how, after they had tumbled out of the cattle car which had stopped just inside the gates of Auschwitz, his best friend had physically held him back from joining the line into which the Nazi soldiers had herded the rest of his family, including his siblings, and had told him to "stand up straight and look strong", so the German soldiers might think him potentially useful. And indeed that is exactly what happened. Because he appeared to be a sturdy young boy his life was saved so that he could do his captors' bidding. After the war was over and Victor was liberated, he was accepted for entry into the USA and began his life anew.

Victor had worked hard his entire adult life, eventually building his own successful business as he married and became the father of three wonderful children; now all accomplished adults in their own right. Having been subjected to such depravity and injustice during his adolescent years in the camps, he afterwards consciously chose to honor his dear parents and other family members by living a highly ethical and moral life. He was, therefore, more shocked than anyone else when he offended against his own code of what was right and was caught and charged for shoplifting in Los Angeles on April 12, 1995. A few weeks later he was referred to me by a psychiatrist who was himself a Holocaust survivor and who knew of my earlier work on the forensic service of the Clarke Institute of Psychiatry with perpetrators of seemingly bizarre shoplifting behaviour.

When I interviewed Victor, at the time a senior citizen, he could not provide me with any reason or excuse whatsoever for his theft behaviour. He only recalled having entered a drugstore and then having placed an item in his coat pocket, at which point he proceeded to walk out of the store and was immediately apprehended.

Later on in our interview, as I was taking his early history and he was describing his years in the concentration camps, he recalled for me his day of liberation. All the prisoners had been awakened in the middle of the night, and marched off in the dark outside of the camp's perimeter and along a rock-laden rail line vaguely lit by a crescent moon. They were sure that they were being marched to their deaths, probably to be shot in the woods and buried in a prepared pit, as had so many other tens of thousands before them. He recalled that virtually none of the inmates were wearing shoes or any other foot-coverings as they had been so quickly rushed out of their barracks, and that his own feet were deeply bruised and bleeding as he staggered along. He recounted for me, almost matter-of-factly, that during more than three hours of forced walking, those prisoners who fell down and were slow to get up, were immediately shot. Victor stayed on his feet and kept moving.

He said that after those horrifying hours of staggering along the rail line, they were suddenly and without ceremony informed that the war was now over for them, that they were free and that they should stay where they were as the Red Cross and Allied soldiers would soon arrive. Their Germans guards then ran away. Red Cross-marked trucks appeared near dawn and the prisoners' immediate needs were attended to, including the application of salves and bandages to their injured feet.

The date of liberation, he mentioned in passing, was April 12, 1945. A few minutes later, I realized the import of what he had said and interrupted his continuing description of these events to ask, "When did you say you were liberated?"

"April 12, 1945," he said. And then, as he heard what he had said, an expression of shock followed by one of amazement flashed across his face. "Why, it's the same date that I stole!" he exclaimed, and he began to sob heart wrenching tears. "Now," I inquired, "can you guess why it was that on April 12, 1995, you entered a drug store and stole a package of Dr Scholl's insoles when you say that you had no need for the product, and could have easily paid for it - or for entirely new shoes for that matter - had you needed them?"

After another minute or more of now quieter sobbing, Victor softly replied, "For my feet, I suppose. My feet that were hurting so much... in 1945!"

Victor later said that ever since he arrived in the United States after the war, he always made certain that he had more-than-adequate footwear; he bought the best shoes he could afford, and prided himself on the fact that he always kept his shoes is excellent repair. He would never have required the item he stole, at least not in 1995!

Incidentally, Victor expressed his certainty that he had not consciously recalled on the morning of his act of theft that it was the fiftieth anniversary of his day of liberation. He claimed to never allow himself to "waste time" thinking about his war experiences, and he never, ever discussed them with either his family or friends.

It is virtually certain, in my clinical opinion, that Victor's unconscious had recognized the date on which he stole as the 50th anniversary of his liberation and that he had had a severe 'anniversary reaction' which manifested in an act of (definitely *atypical*) theft behaviour, on April 12, 1995.

Some readers may recall that in 1995 there were very many commemorative events in the USA and elsewhere around the world, related to the end of World War II, and in particular, of the Holocaust. Victor told me that he avoided being exposed to these proceedings as best he could; he did not want to have his memories aroused. But, while the memories of the horrors he experienced had been kept out of his conscious awareness, I believe it is virtually certain that his unconscious mind was fully aware of the significance of the date (April 12th) and was likely preoccupied with those memories at that time.

****

Most readers, I believe, will agree that the story of Victor offers very powerful evidence that his act of atypical theft behaviour warranted compassionate consideration before concluding that 'since he did the crime, he should do the time'.

It has been my clinical experience that, while many of the more than 700 cases of atypical theft behaviour that I have assessed and/or treated were not necessarily as dramatic, nevertheless there exists very similar psychodynamics among them; i.e., many of the usually honest persons I have assessed and treated, have likely acted out by stealing in response to their unconscious minds having been stirred by some deep, traumatic and/or otherwise painful memories and/or external events. As we will return, again and again in this book, to the stories of

seemingly atypical theft behaviour by usually honest and ethical persons, I believe that you, the reader, will likely come to agree that the theft behaviour of usually honest persons, when closely and appropriately examined, make a very strong case for accepting the hypothesis that there does indeed exist an <u>unconscious</u>, and one that is very <u>dynamic</u>, in the sense that it helps to drive overt behaviour in ways that are often dramatic and even dangerous to the theft offender's personal reputation, interpersonal relationships, working life and even, in some instances, his or her very freedom.

INTRODUCTION

Over the last nearly four decades I have assessed and treated many hundreds of basically honest, frequently well educated, sometimes prominent and/or even wealthy individuals who have shoplifted items usually worth an insignificant amount (often, in the order of $2 to $100) in comparison with their then readily available assets. As mentioned above and as I will describe in detail on the pages that follow, such *atypical theft behaviour* by *usually honest* adults offers some of the strongest (and frequently very dramatic) inferential evidence of the existence of a dynamic unconscious mind.

How my educational, academic and work background prepared me for this area of clinical investigation

My first professional career was as an electronics engineer. I graduated from McGill University in 1961 with a Bachelor of Engineering degree and acquired at that time, in the middle of what was often referred to as the 'cold war', a most enviable job for a newly minted engineer, designing navigational guidance systems for the then-next generation of American and other NATO countries' military aircraft.

I well recall, even now, more than fifty years later, a conversation I had with one of my best friends at the time when we university students were walking from the Engineering to the Physics building for our next classes. Jon was in civil engineering while I had opted for the electrical engineering option. He asked how I could possibly look forward to spending my professional life having to rely on the *assumption* that there were supposedly atomic particles called *electrons*, <u>which we were told even then we could never actually hope to see one</u>. He thought that depending upon the actions of a hypothetical atomic particle that only *supposedly* existed was far too ambiguous a concept upon which he was willing to base his working life.

Now, more than a half-century later, of course, we take for granted the use of a truly amazing array of electronic devices from televisions to smartphones to laptop computers and tablets, and so on. As a result, we now have enough inferential evidence that electrons probably do exist, even though it *still* remains true, according to physicists, that we cannot hope to ever *see* even one of them.

I have always been aware that my approach to psychology, human conduct in general and atypical theft behaviour in particular, has been informed by having had the benefit of a very vigorous academic background in science and scientific methods. To put the matter simply, if something looks, sounds and behaves like a duck, then we should be prepared to accept the distinct possibility that the being in question is indeed a duck – at least as a temporary hypothesis. We could be wrong, of course, but it is surely reasonable to *assume* that, if substantial evidence has been accumulated to suggest that the existence of a duck is probable, then most of us would agree that we should consider, as a distinct likelihood, that we are indeed probably dealing with a duck.

I offer the above two notions, that of electrons and ducks, to suggest that when there exists compelling indications for the existence of a hypothesized *something*, then unless and until at least equally compelling - and contrary- evidence suggests otherwise, most of us will be satisfied enough to accept the working hypotheses as very possibly valid.

My early professional familiarity with the dynamic unconscious
As a psychotherapist in the 1970s I was often aware of the input from my clients' unconscious minds provided by their recollections of disturbing night dreams, and the occasional appearance of so-called 'Freudian slips' as whenever someone used a very different and highly revealing word or phrase than that which he or she had *consciously* intended to say. (As an example, one person whose role was to thank and compliment a speaker who had just been, in fact, quite boring, 'goofed' by, instead of saying "Well, that talk certainly *capped* off our conference!" uttered the following; "Well, that talk certainly *crapped* off our conference.") *Yes, Virginia, such things really do happen!*

The fortunate 'aha' moment that occurred to me while conducting a therapy group: inventing the 'Rope Trick'.
What proved to be a highly instructive introduction into the power of the dynamic unconscious minds of ordinary people occurred while I was in the doctoral program in counselling psychology at the University of Toronto. At the time I was also working part-time as a group therapist for a prominent psychiatrist in Toronto and one day I happened to be dealing with a member of a therapy group who was attempting to fathom and verbalize the dynamics at play in her marital relationship. Unfortunately for her, she was at that time quite 'stuck' and unsure what to make of, let

alone how to describe, her marital relationship. As she spoke she was becoming more and more frustrated and less articulate. In order to help her deal with this issue, on the spot I intuitively created a mental imagery exercise that I thought might be of assistance. As this was a therapy *group* I invited the other members present to also close their eyes while I presented a so-called 'seed image', i.e., one that provided a few key elements for the individual to imagine (in this case, the client, a 'Significant Other' with whom the client was having 'issues', and an object that I simply referred to as 'a rope'). I asked everyone to 'see' the three distinct elements in their minds' eyes and to 'watch' what happened next.

Well, I could hardly be more surprised at the group members' responses! Firstly, every single one of the individuals present imagined scenes and events that seemed to be very much representative of the status and dynamics of the relationships they themselves were considering. The woman who had been so frustrated and confused when attempting to grasp the nature of her relationship with her husband, actually laughed out loud, and said, *"That's it! That is what our relationship is about!"* When I asked her to elaborate, she replied, *"Well, I see the two of us climbing a steep hill, up to our bums in deep snow. I am in front, with a heavy rope over my shoulder, holding onto it with both hands as I pull my husband along behind me. He is a dead weight; the rope is tied around his waist at his belly button, and he is not doing anything to help me climb the hill. And that is what I see clearly now as the essence of our relationship. The rope is like a thick umbilical cord, he is acting like a helpless child, and I am having to do all the heavy lifting to move us forward. Yep, that's it, alright!"*

When I asked the other members of the group to share their own imagery experiences, every one of them had had a unique imagery sequence and most stated that they had experienced some insights into what was happening in their relationships. Furthermore, each also felt some relief, a virtual internal 'shift', however slight, in regard to how the relationships were now viewed, post-exercise - and what to do about them.

Now, a thorough consideration of this exercise, including why it might work and how to employ it to gain insight and perhaps even modify one's relationship, is entirely outside the scope of the book you are now reading. In fact, when I gave the exercise, which I started to refer to as 'the Rope Trick', to literally hundreds of other individuals over the following years, I was so intrigued as to why and how it worked so well that I spent more than five years of doctoral level work conducting a detailed clinical examination of the Rope Trick from within a vigorous experimental design. In fact, this effort became my doctoral thesis and will be the subject of another book that I am hoping to complete in the near future; it is certainly long overdue. Suffice to say at this time that the Rope Trick has showed itself to be very helpful to hundreds of clients over the years when they were dealing with the troubling relationships in their lives.

The main reason I have mentioned the Rope Trick is to make the point that it has shown itself to help ordinary folks bring forth, from their unconscious minds and without attempting to force matters, sequences of images that have come into their conscious minds and that have often been shown to be very meaningful. How is this possible, that ordinary persons frequently produce such insightful and relevant images? Where do they come from, these relevant imagery sequences? Their unconscious minds, is the most likely answer.

I should point out that I am hardly the first clinician to delve into, and attempt to describe, the existence and meaningful value of our unconscious minds. In fact, at the beginning of my doctoral thesis that I titled *Clinical Imaginative Imagery*, I quoted the famous psychiatrist, Carl Jung, who, in The Collected Works of C.G. Jung, Volume 18, The Symbolic Life (1975) stated, *"When you concentrate on a mental picture, it begins to stir, the image becomes enriched by details, it moves and develops. Each time, naturally, you mistrust it and have the idea that you just made it up, that it is merely your own invention... it is not true.... Therefore I am convinced that we cannot do much in the way of conscious invention. And so, when we concentrate on an image, and when we are careful not to interrupt the natural flow of events, our unconscious will produce a series of images which will make up a complete story."* (p. 172).

One of the most important of my own contributions to the field of clinical psychology and psychiatry is the fact that these four decades and many hundreds of cases of atypical theft behaviour that I have assessed and treated have made it abundantly clear, that **when usually honest persons shoplift or commit other acts of seemingly bizarre theft, such behaviours are often the overt behavioural manifestation of the individuals' unconscious minds.** By carefully considering what was stolen, when it was stolen, and what events or circumstances just preceded the acts of theft, the answers clearly and powerfully point to the actions having been triggered by memories, emotions and/or thoughts that resided in the individuals' unconscious minds. In this book, and in my earlier one, *Why Honest People Shoplift Or Commit Other Acts Of Theft*, there are numerous examples of such cases.

The case for the long-standing notion that there exists, within the human psyche, what is usually referred to as the 'unconscious' mind.
In this book I will offer many examples that strongly suggest that observable theft behaviours have very likely been precipitated, at least in part, by the individuals' unconscious minds. In fact, I believe that the examples I offer - like that of the case of Victor, already presented - drawn directly from my own clinical investigations, are so powerfully obvious, that most persons, even the most non-psychologically inclined folks among us, will consider accepting the likelihood of the existence of a vital, dynamic unconscious mind.

As a further example, let me mention another of my clients, a lawyer from the U.S. northwest who usually earned more than $800,000 per annum. She had experienced a most traumatic pregnancy during which she was repeatedly told that the fetus might not survive, or that if it did, then there might be very serious, life threatening problems ahead. Fortunately the child was successfully born, although with a relatively minor physical defect – an unusually small big toe on his right foot. Thereafter, whenever another one of her friends gave birth, this woman would insist on buying extravagant dresses and toys for her friends' newborns, and yet would frequently also sneakily place an article of children's clothing or a small toy into her purse or bag. She had stolen items on more than twenty occasions, but only since the birth of her own child. Usually the items she stole were worth less than $20, and given the bylaws of her profession she was clearly likely risking a devastating consequence if she were ever found guilty of theft in a court of law.

The reason she had sought my help was that she had recently been stopped by a store employee and while she was able to talk herself out of being charged by claiming that she had absentmindedly placed the item in her purse while reaching for her credit card to pay for the $280 worth of items she was going to pay for, the experience had profoundly shaken her and she wanted to deal with her stealing behaviour before she was actually charged -and possibly convicted- of theft. As we identified and worked through the various issues that came to the fore when discussing her personal background (including her parents' oppressive pressure that she be the 'perfect' child) and the (for her) traumatic experience of giving birth to a child who was not 'perfect', it became clear that every time she bought a present for one of her friends' seemingly healthy and physically faultless children, she felt envious, frustrated and guilty that she had failed to produce a 'perfect' child of her own. Her stealing was, in part, a way of compensating herself for her self-defined failure.

For Whom This Book is Intended

This book is primarily intended for a readership that includes usually honest and ethical individuals who have exhibited seemingly bizarre and/or nonsensical *atypical* theft behaviour, as well as for a larger audience of laypersons, students of the human condition, mental health professionals, lawyers and judges who are interested in learning more about the inner workings of the mind that can precipitate apparently bizarre or nonsensical stealing behaviour by usually honest and ethical persons. These are individuals who, in 1985, my original co-investigator, psychiatrist Dr Don Atcheson and I termed "**Atypical Theft Offenders**" (ATOs).

And, as is true of my earlier book, *Why Honest People Shoplift Or Commit Other Acts Of Theft*, this book will be of interest to the following individuals:

- **clinicians** whose task it is to provide effective assessment and/or treatment for such theft offenders;
- **lawyers** whose role it is to defend or prosecute them;
- **judges, probation and parole officers** who must deal with these cases;
- **loss prevention personnel** who often are the first professionals to encounter the Atypical Theft Offenders immediately following their acts of theft;
- **police officers** who arrest and charge Atypical Theft Offenders;
- **EAP (Employee Assistance Plan)** and **HR (Human Resources) personnel** who may need to deal with usually reliable and honest employees who have been charged with theft, including of their employer's property,
  as well as
- **students of psychology, psychiatry, social work and criminology** who are curious about the aberrant behaviour of generally 'normal' and upright persons
- **the theft offenders' so-called Significant Others** (i.e., spouses, parents, grown children, etc...), and
- **all those who are interested in understanding why usually 'good' people sometimes do the 'bad' thing we call stealing** and learning about the very strong empirical evidence that honest

DR. WILL CUPCHIK

persons' unconscious minds can help precipitate entirely inappropriate acting out theft behaviour.

Various pen-and-paper instruments provided in this book, including the *Cupchik Theft Offender Spectrum*, the *Cupchik Theft Offender Questionnaire* and the *Free Brief Screening Interview Questionnaire*, are all valuable tools for the possible Atypical Theft Offenders to fill out and provide to me and/or their local therapists and lawyers in order to increase the likelihood that they will get the psychological and legal help they require. By purchasing this book the owner is hereby permitted to make one copy only of any of these tools for his or her own personal use.

Warning and Disclaimer

This book is designed to provide general information in regard to the subject matter covered. It is sold with the understanding that the publisher and author are not engaged, in this book, in rendering clinical, legal, or other professional services about any particular case. The contents of this book may not be relevant or applicable to every -or even any particular-theft offender case that the reader may have in mind. If clinical, legal or other expert assistance is required, the services of a competent professional should be sought. The theft offenders themselves and the professionals who arrest, assess, treat, and/or represent them and/or determine the disposition of their court cases, must take responsibility for the uses made of this book.

It is not the purpose of this book to reprint all the information on the subjects covered that is otherwise available to the author and/or publisher. You are urged to read all the available material on the subjects, learn as much as possible about the subjects referred to in this book, and to tailor the information to your own personal or professional needs. The book you are now reading and my earlier book on this subject, *Why Honest People Shoplift Or Commit Other Acts Of Theft: The Assessment And Treatment Of Atypical Theft Offenders* (2002), share some common ground and even some cases. Both are available in paperback and ebook formats. Indeed, for the fuller understanding of this subject, the reader is encouraged to read both books, as in places they emphasize different elements of the topics covered. You may consider my earlier book to be 'Volume 1' and the book you are now reading to be 'Volume 2'. Nothing in Volume 2 contradicts anything in Volume 1; rather, their materials complement one another. Be advised, however, that this latest book has more refined and revised versions of the *Cupchik Theft Offender Spectrum* and *Cupchik Theft Offender Questionnaire*.

Theft behaviour is an exceedingly complex human activity. Its motivations are frequently 'multi-determined,' that is, there are often a number of reasons why the individual atypical theft offender has stolen a particular item (or items) at a particular time. No claim is made or intended that the cases presented have described all possible motivations of atypical theft offenders.

Furthermore, please note that all the case examples offered in this book are composites and have been significantly altered as far as identifiers are concerned. Therefore they cannot and should not be construed to represent any one actual person only, his or her behaviour or motivations, and should not necessarily be used to come to any firm conclusions about any particular case with which the reader may be familiar. Any similarities between the cases presented and the one the reader is familiar in, will invariably be merely coincidental.

Every effort has been made to make this book accurate in regard to the nature of the data that is presented. However, there may be mistakes both typographical and in content. Therefore, this text should be used only as a general guide and not as the ultimate source of information on the subjects discussed. Furthermore, this book contains information only up to the printing date. New data, insights and knowledge are always being derived and are, of course, not necessarily represented in this book.

The purpose of this book is to educate and inform and to provide information that may assist an Atypical Theft Offender to curtail or even stop his or her theft behaviour altogether. The author and the publisher, Tagami Communications, shall have neither liability nor responsibility to any person or entity with respect to any loss or damage caused or decisions arrived at directly or indirectly by using any of the information contained in this book. Ultimately the individual, together with his or her health provider, must accept responsibility for any decisions made or actions taken as a result of reading or taking into account any materials presented in this book.

The **Cupchik Theft Offender Questionnaire** and **Cupchik Theft Offender Spectrum** are two pen-and-paper instruments that are the copyrighted intellectual properties of the author. The versions offered in this book are more recent and comprehensive versions than were provided in my earlier book. Nevertheless, no claim is made or intended that these devices are other than meant to be of supplementary and suggestive (not definitive) assistance to a competent and suitably trained mental health professional, who will need to arrive at his or her own determination, and only after completing a thorough and appropriate assessment, whether the theft offender being dealt with should be considered to be an Atypical Theft Offender (ATO), a Typical Theft Offender (TTO), or of the Mixed ATO/TTO type.

Readers will also find the **Cupchik Rank-Ordered Summary Of Shared Personal History, Qualities and Experiences of Atypical Theft Offenders**, is offered in this book so that Atypical Theft Offenders and those who are interested in understanding such behaviour can see what percentage of the 30 cases in the 2013 study shared these features, and compare such with the actual case(s) they have in mind.

Individual purchasers of this book are hereby granted permission to use these three pen-and-paper devices once each only. No additional copies of these devices are to be made, stored or transmitted in any form without permission of the publisher. Permission to use the **Spectrum, Questionnaire** and **Rank-Ordered Summary Of Shared Personal History, Qualities and Experiences** may be purchased from the author by suitable professionals and/or organizations, as indicated later in this book – see Appendix C.

A Further Caution Regarding The Applicability Of The Material Contained In This Book To Any Specific Cases Of Interest To The Reader

In no way can I know what may be clinically appropriate for any individual case in which I have not been formally and fully professionally involved. Much of the material in this book reports upon the findings of clinical investigations, assessment procedures, treatment modalities and exercises that I have developed and have found to be useful when dealing with Atypical Theft Offenders. Such information may or may not be relevant or useful in any specific case that the reader has in mind. The responsibility for successful clinical assessment and treatment, legal representation and professional involvement by loss prevention personnel, police forces and others must lie with the client himself or herself and the clinicians, lawyers and other professionals involved in any particular case. Nothing in this book can or should be construed to indicate necessarily appropriate or applicable approaches in regard to any particular case the reader may encounter or have in mind.

Regarding Confidentiality And The Privacy-Preserving Modifications of The Cases Presented In This Book.

In order to assure the confidentially of the persons from whom the data and details are drawn, actual names, ages, gender (sometimes) and other identifying details of the 'cases' presented in this book have been substantially altered. It has thus been possible to effectively disguise the identity of those clients from whom these composite cases were formulated.

It should also be noted that care has been taken to make the sample 'cases' no more dramatic than those upon which they were based. Indeed, *all* of the case descriptions have been 'toned down'. Therefore, the reader can be assured that, as remarkable as the 'cases' presented in this book may appear, the original cases from which they were derived *were even more so!*

An Orientation To Some Terms

Throughout this book references to "*our* investigations" are meant to refer specifically to those that I carried out over a seven-year period, from 1979-1986, with my co-investigator, senior psychiatrist Dr D.J. Atcheson, while we were both working on the same clinical team on the forensic service of the University of Toronto-affiliated Clarke Institute of Psychiatry, and where from 1984-86 I held the position of *Psychologist-in-Charge, Forensic Outpatient Psychological Services.*

References to "*my* investigations" are meant to refer to those I have carried out since leaving the employ of the Clarke Institute some 27 years ago (in 1986), and which I have conducted from within my own private practice as a Registered Psychologist in Toronto. I have attempted, for the sake of clarity, to indicate which of these two phases of my clinical work with Atypical Theft Offenders particular materials in this book refer. My apologies for any errors that may occur or be inferred in the body of this book in these regards. Any errors or erroneous inferences are unintentional.

Also note: The thirty cases that together comprised my most recently completed (2013) study are referred to throughout this book as 'cases', Subjects or Ss.

Our initial formal investigations (1979-1983) involved only shoplifting events. However, as we stated in a chapter that I co-authored with Dr Atcheson[i], in a book entitled <u>Clinical Criminology: The Assessment and Treatment of Criminal Behaviour</u> [ii](1985), *"the authors and certain colleagues have noted the similarities between some shoplifters and certain perpetrators of other acts of theft. (We have coined) the term 'Atypical Theft Offenders' (ATOs) to refer to those usually honest perpetrators of acts of shoplifting, fraud and other sorts of theft who seem to share the same psychodynamic qualities."*

Defining the 'Atypical Theft Offender'

An *'Atypical Theft Offender'* (or ATO) is primarily an honest, often hard-working and ethical individual; his or her illegal theft behaviour is essentially an aberration from -and at odds with- the ways in which the person usually conducts himself or herself in the world. This person is invariably markedly uncomfortable with the theft behaviour, and frequently reacts with feelings of shame, guilt, remorse and/or a genuine sense of humiliation in response to the acts of theft that he or she has committed. At the same time, however, the individual may be aware that he or she has difficulty stopping the theft behaviour, and is at a loss to fully understand the reasons for such seemingly bizarre and nonsensical conduct.

The stealing is primarily *not* carried out for reasons of either need or greed.

My Live, Online *Intensive Intervention Program* for Atypical Theft Offenders

The live, online **Atypical Theft Offender** *Intensive Intervention Program* that I have developed and have provided to suitable theft offender clients for the past five years represents the culmination of my nearly four decades of clinical investigations into atypical theft behaviour. This Skype-based Intervention Program is aimed at: (1) uncovering, over a period of twenty clinical sessions (each 50-minutes long), the underlying factors that are likely responsible for precipitating the client's atypical theft behaviour, and (2) making major psychotherapeutic headway in moving the client towards dealing with those issues that have helped precipitate his or her self-destructive theft behaviour. By the end of the Program we have usually not only determined the main reasons for the stealing and have also done much, and in some cases perhaps all, of the therapy required to minimize the likelihood of the individual ever stealing again.

I first used Skype in 2008 to work with a theft offender and his wife who at the time was living in California. Since then I have worked with many clients using this technology and have determined that it is indeed a highly effective and efficient way of working with people from our respective homes (mine in Toronto, Canada and theirs just about anywhere else in the world where the client has adequate access to the Internet). By doing so we are usually able to achieve at least as good results as would have been attained were they to have physically worked with me in my office.

Since June 1, 2011, I have worked exclusively via Skype, utilizing the 20-session Intensive Intervention Program that incorporates the best features of my previous *in-office* program, together with other elements enabled by the fact that clients are able to stay in their own milieu and carry on with their own lives throughout the now-extended program. As the reader may be aware, there are now alternatives to using Skype. (We can usually find the most convenient live, online audio-video tool for us to employ).

For sincere inquiries about becoming a client of the Program, by all means first read this book as well as the webpages on my *www.WhyHonestPeopleSteal.com* website. For specific and most up-to-

date information about the Skype-based 20-session long Intensive Intervention Program, please go to its dedicated webpage at
http://www.whyhonestpeoplesteal.com/live_interactive_video_enable d_Intervention_Program.htm

After reading these materials, to inquire about whether it would be worthwhile our working together, request a *Free Brief Screening Interview* by emailing me at *wcupchik@aol.com*; just be sure to include my initials...(WC)... in brackets in the subject line.

Once engaged in the Program we usually work together for one or two consecutive 50-minute clinical sessions at a time, once a week, for a total of 20 sessions, at times that we mutually agree upon. Over the course of the approximately 2-1/2 months it takes to complete the Program, the client has ample opportunities to do the 'homework assignments' that I provide and thereby make real changes in his or her day-to-day life.

PREFACE

In 1974 I began my clinical investigations of shoplifting by usually honest and successful individuals while on staff of the Clarke Institute of Psychiatry, in Toronto. And I have been very pleased, over the past nearly four decades, to have been contacted by many major North American and other countries' print and electronic media organizations to discuss my clinical findings in regard to this seemingly bizarre and nonsensical theft behaviour. For example, when actress Winona Ryder was apprehended for allegedly shoplifting in 2002, ABC television network's *Good Morning America* invited me to New York City to discuss the likely reasons that an essentially honest, possibly religious and/or wealthy and/or famous person would risk *so much* (in terms of personal reputation, job prospects, professional standing, etc...) for what is (usually) relatively *so little* in terms of monetary or material gain.

At the time of Ryder's sentencing a few months later, I was once again flown to New York, this time to appear on CBS television's *Early Show* to discuss this fascinating subject. I was gratified that when the *New York Times* did an extended piece on Ryder's alleged actions and the subject of shoplifting by usually honest persons in general, I was the *only* expert to whom the piece referred by name. The same was true when PEOPLE magazine did an article in 2003 centred upon the alleged theft behaviour of actress Shelley Morrison (of the sitcom *Will & Grace*); the article included a sidebar that referred exclusively to my clinical work.

It is now sixteen years since my first book on this subject, *Why Honest People Shoplift Or Commit Other Acts Of Theft*, was originally published (in 1997). That book remains entirely relevant and is available in both paperback and as an ebook formats from major online bookstores; indeed, it is an excellent complementary book to this one. Since that book first appeared I have continued to gather a great deal of additional information and experience working with this population of theft offenders; as a result of these efforts I have further developed and refined my assessment and treatment approaches in this area. In 2013 I completed my latest major study in this area, based upon a sample of thirty *new* cases that involved, not only instances of seemingly nonsensical shoplifting behaviour, but in a few cases, also fraud and other kinds of theft (including one that involved stealing over $1,000,000), all carried out by persons who

li

were at least sufficiently financially well off, and some of whom were deeply religious and/or held responsible or even high profile positions in their working and/or social lives.

New Information That This Book Provides

The book that you are now reading provides for the first time a good deal of additional data about *which personal issues the individuals with this problem of atypical theft behaviour often have in common,* and the latest clinical approaches that I have developed to assist these persons to stop their theft behaviour. It also includes my latest (2013) study's findings regarding the possible mistake of prescribing antidepressants with the stated purpose of helping to stop the stealing; in fact, my clinical findings clearly indicate that not only may the use of antidepressants *not* decrease the likelihood of further theft behaviour, but on the contrary, such medications may actually *increase* some of these Atypical Theft Offenders' stealing. Furthermore, a few of the persons in this study reported that they *never* stole until *after* they began using antidepressants!

I also will address what I believe to be the misleading use of the term *behavioural addiction* in regard to Atypical Theft Offenders.

Readers who discover through reading this book that they are likely among the group of individuals whom my original co-investigator, psychiatrist Dr Don J Atcheson and I termed Atypical Theft Offenders, are invited to share their stories by emailing me at *wcupchik@aol.com*. Please include my initials in brackets *(WC)* in the subject line of your emails so that I can recognize that your email is truly meant for me. I am the only person who reads these emails and will keep what you have written confidential. And please note that while I may not directly respond to your email, be assured that I *will* read and consider what you have written. Finally, if you find that you are interested in working with me to cease your theft behaviour via the webcam-enabled Intensive Intervention Program that I personally conduct, by all means contact me at the same email address.

THE HONEST THIEVES AMONG US: WHAT'S GOING ON?

- In January 2012 California Assemblywoman Mary Hayashi (D), wife of Dennis Hayashi, an Alameda County Superior Court judge, allegedly left a Neiman Marcus store without paying for items of clothing worth nearly $2500. She pleaded no contest to misdemeanour shoplifting, was sentenced to three years probation and less than $200 in fines.

- In 2007 one of Brazil's most prominent and internationally respected rabbis, Henry Sobel, an individual recognized for his unquestioned courage and unblemished conduct, was arrested on charges that he shoplifted neckties from stores in Palm Beach, Florida.

- In 2006, lawyer Claude Allen, President George W. Bush's Domestic Policy advisor, resigned after he was charged with defrauding a Target store of a high-end stereo, when he allegedly bought the item, put it in his car, then returned to the store, picked up an identical stereo and took it to the customer service desk, claiming he decided to not keep the item and requested his money back, using the receipt for the one he had previously purchased and that was, at that very moment, still in his car. (Incidentally, a reporter for a local newspaper in the Washington D.C. area called and interviewed me shortly after Allen's arrest, in an attempt to gain some understanding regarding the question of why someone in as valued and unique a position as Allen, would risk so much in terms of reputation, job and the ability to practice law, for so little as a few hundred dollars. We had a lengthy discussion of my findings in the area of Atypical Theft Offenders. Interestingly, this same reporter later contacted me to let me know that his editor had told him that he actually was not at all interested in 'understanding' Allen's conduct, but instead wanted a newspaper article that would take a very hard line stance in regard to this and similar cases.)

- In 2002, actress Winona Ryder was arrested after allegedly walking out of a Saks department store in Beverly Hills without paying for more than $4000 in merchandise.

- In 1993 the Acting Secretary of the U.S. Army, John W. Shannon, was charged with stealing $30 worth of goods, including a blouse, from a store on the Army base.

- In 1991, actress Hedy Lamarr (a highly intelligent person who co-held U.S. patent #2,292,387 for the design of a new kind of guidance system for torpedoes), was arrested for stealing eye drops and laxatives from a drugstore in Florida. She had previously been arrested in 1966 for shoplifting in Los Angeles.

- In 1988 a former Miss America and the then New York City Cultural Affairs Commissioner, Bess Myerson, reportedly stole less than $50 of merchandise from a department store.

Cases that didn't make the national headlines
- An experienced state police officer entered a department store and stole two pairs of gloves in full view of the hidden surveillance cameras that he knew were there (because he had previously been called by the loss prevention personnel of the very same store to lay charges of theft against other individuals, and had seen the videotaped footage of shoplifting committed in front of the very same concealed camera).

- A prominent physician was apprehended after a series of thefts of jewellery and cash from his fellow surgeons' lockers while the latter were working in their operating rooms.

- An award-winning public school teacher was apprehended for shoplifting several items from various establishments, including supermarkets and clothing stores.

Misuse of the term 'kleptomania'

Laypersons can be excused if they are inclined to use the term 'kleptomania' when referring to some of the individuals mentioned above in regard to their theft behaviour. After all, that is the label that is frequently -and, as I believe will be amply demonstrated in this book- *erroneously* applied by clinicians.

In fact, the word 'kleptomania' probably ranks with 'paranoia' among the psychiatric terms that are most often employed by laypersons when referring to persons who exhibit certain problematic thinking and/or behaviour. How many times in your own life have you heard someone (you?) say to another person who expressed some strong concern or suspicion about someone or something..., *"Oh, don't be paranoid!"*

Likewise, whenever someone we know, or have heard of, who has more than enough funds, has been charged with stealing one or more items worth only a relatively few dollars, many will be inclined to think or say, "Ah, that person must be a kleptomaniac!" In fact, over the nearly four decades that I have been clinically dealing with such cases, people in the media have repeatedly contacted me, saying something to the effect of, "Hey, the stealing that (actor, politician, wealthy and/or prominent person) carried out must be a case of kleptomania; right?" *Well, actually, no: in that that's virtually always likely to be an erroneous statement!*

In this book we will examine these kinds of theft behaviour from within the context of the more than 39 years of clinical investigations that I have carried out, including during the dozen years, 1974 through 1986, when I was employed on the forensic service of the Clarke Institute of Psychiatry, in Toronto. Since 1986 through to the present day, I have continued my clinical assessment and treatment of Atypical Theft Offenders from within my own private practice. To this point in time I have personally *assessed*, and in most instances *treated*, more than 700 such cases.

Note # 1: Who this book *is* –and is *not*- about

Most thefts are carried out by persons who are quite content with, and perhaps even proud of, their frequent theft behaviour. They steal primarily simply because they choose to; they are satisfied with their illegal conduct and experience virtually no shame or remorse whatsoever in regard to their stealing. Indeed, they are often very pleased with their prowess in seldom getting caught, and may even brag about their successful exploits to their friends and/or relatives, some of whom (not uncommonly) may likewise be involved in theft behaviour. These so-called **Typical Theft Offenders or TTOs** (a term that I and my original co-investigator, psychiatrist Dr Don Atcheson coined over a quarter-century ago) are most assuredly *not* the sorts of theft offenders that this book is concerned about.

This book is focused on **A**typical Theft Offenders, *not* **T**ypical Theft Offenders, i.e., not those persons such as, *perhaps*, financial advisors Bernie Madoff of New York City and Bert Jones of Montreal who, for literally decades, evidently deliberately, and according to various reports in the media, possibly without any profound sense of conscience, shame or remorse, defrauded a great many persons of many millions (as did Jones) or *billions* from investors both large and small (as did Madoff). These two individuals are, perhaps, examples of classic, prominent **T**ypical Theft Offenders, and any further discussion of *their* conduct and underlying motivations is beyond the scope of this book.

The aim of this book, as was the case with *Why Honest People Shoplift Or Commit Other Acts Of Theft: The Assessment and Treatment of 'Atypical Theft Offenders'*, is to help you to understand why usually honest persons, individuals who themselves are often disgusted by, ashamed of, remorseful about, and are at a loss to explain (even to themselves) their atypical theft behaviour, nevertheless, steal, and thereby place in great jeopardy their personal reputations, their standing in society and among their peers, and perhaps, as well, their jobs, their right to continue to practice their professions (e.g., of law, medicine, nursing, teaching, law enforcement, etc…) and/or even their right to remain living in the country in which they currently reside (in the cases of non-citizens).

DR. WILL CUPCHIK

In contrast with Typical Theft Offenders, these **Atypical Theft Offenders** (or ATOs) almost never tell their friends or relatives of their theft behaviour, and would be mortified if their stealing were to be learned of by these persons or by their community at large. Their feelings of shame and remorse are hallmarks of their responses to their own stealing.

As a psychologist for over three decades, and probably not unlike yourself, I am *not* very surprised when apparently clearly corrupt or abusive persons commit acts of dishonesty or aggression. To put the matter simply, when apparently 'bad' people do bad things - well, that is not exactly shocking. However, like most members in society, I *do* find extraordinary, those cases of persons who are 'straight shooters', i.e., reputable, hard working, and ethical individuals, persons who *don't* usually act out inappropriately, yet who have done so, either for the first time, or even more fascinatingly, again and again, by stealing -mostly, but not always, via acts of shoplifting.

These Atypical Theft Offenders are often upstanding, contributing members of our society – and yet, they offend against not only society's mores, but their own value systems as well. As a high profile and very wealthy lawyer (and senior partner of his firm) told me when he arrived in my office several years ago; *"I am only here because my (law) partners told me I had to see someone, and the Dean of the Department of Psychiatry at the University of Toronto recommended that I see you. But be assured, Dr Cupchik, that I am not interested in any 'psychobabble' that you might be inclined to spew in my direction to explain away my theft of that tube of toothpaste from the drugstore section of the department store (located in the office tower that housed many of the city's most prominent law firms, including his own).*

"But my problem is that I don't know why I stole that darn tube of toothpaste. It makes no sense. I have never done such a thing in my life. Furthermore, I have always believed that 'if you do the crime, then you do the time'. So I haven't got the slightest idea why I would steal anything, let alone something like that. But I know I did it and I have to find out why!"

After a very careful assessment I and my colleagues on the forensic service of the University of Toronto-affiliated Clarke Institute of Psychiatry concluded that the fact that this highly reputable and prominent lawyer stole from the drugstore on that particular occasion, most likely had *something* (actually, probably nearly everything!) to do with the fact that, at the very moment of his theft, his extremely sick young child was undergoing chemotherapy at the Sick Children's Hospital a few blocks away, and he was understandably emotionally distraught at that time as he and his wife thought they might be losing their child to cancer. In this book I will explain the underlying dynamics, based upon three separate clinical studies that I have conducted over a span of nearly four decades, that probably helped to precipitate the atypical theft behaviour of this exemplary lawyer and so many other Atypical Theft Offenders.

From reading this book you will learn:

- Why some usually honest and ethical people shoplift or commit other acts of theft;
- Why *(perceived) unfair personally meaningful losses,* such as of one's health, job, marriage, child etc..., might help trigger theft behaviour;
- Why the occurrence, or anticipation of the occurrence, of cancer in an individual or in that person's close relative or friend, might promote atypical theft behaviour;
- That the term 'kleptomania' is frequently erroneously applied to atypical theft behaviour;
- About the *Cupchik Theft Offender Spectrum,* and where the person you may be concerned about fits along the Spectrum, and whether that person should be viewed primarily as either an Atypical Theft Offender, Typical Theft Offender, or a Mixed-type Theft Offender;
- Why wealthy and/or prominent persons may risk so much in terms of their personal and professional reputations, for (usually) so little, by stealing;
- About the three main layers of the human mind and how they are involved in atypical theft behaviour;
- Of numerous case examples that will help illustrate the factors that can promote atypical theft behaviour;
- A simple yet decidedly helpful model of personality and interpersonal interaction that has particular usefulness when considering the theft behaviour of usually honest persons;

- Why the use of prescribed antidepressants to help curb atypical theft behaviour likely not only doesn't help, but may actually make the problem worse;
- Why some individuals only started to shoplift after they had begun taking antidepressants;
- How some instances of *other* kinds of theft (fraud, embezzlement, etc…) may also be committed by usually honest persons;
- About the predominance of physicians, nurses, police officers, and firefighters among Atypical Theft Offenders, and why that may be the case;
- About the prevalence of long-term anger, low self-esteem, inadequate assertiveness, highly disturbed and/or traumatic early childhoods amongst Atypical Theft Offenders;
- That anger and/or a desire for vengeance is almost universally present in Atypical Theft Offenders;
- About the errors of clinicians who focus upon the thoughts and feelings of theft offenders primarily or exclusively *while* the latter were engaged in the act of stealing, and/or *just before* and/or *immediately after* their theft behaviour, without considering what else was happening in their lives around the time that they stole;
- Research studies that bring into serious question the clinical findings of investigations funded by the pharmaceutical companies whose medications (including antidepressants) are being tested;
- About the assessment and treatment programs I have developed over the past decades, *and*
- The current (15-step) live, online Intensive Intervention Program that I now use and that enables me to work with theft offenders who reside virtually anywhere in the world, without either of us leaving our homes. (It is hardly a surprise that the marvellous invention of Skype is usually involved.)

Note # 2: A comment on my earlier book, and how best to use it together with this book for your benefit

As mentioned earlier, the book you are now reading was published sixteen years after the original edition of my earlier (and somewhat more formal) book on the subject. The previous book, titled *Why Honest People Shoplift Or Commit Other Acts Of Theft: The Assessment and Treatment of 'Atypical Theft Offenders'*, was revised more than a decade ago, in 2002, and remains "a resource for professionals and laypersons", just as is stated on its cover. Indeed, the book you are now reading is intended for the same audience.

Since my earlier book's publication I have acquired a great deal of additional experience in dealing with usually honest persons who have stolen, and I recently completed a comprehensive study of some 30 new cases drawn from the additional hundreds I had seen in the interim. I decided that I wanted to present the information that I have gathered from the totality of my clinical investigations in a format aimed primarily at laypersons, while at the same time being of much assistance to the ATOs themselves and the professionals who deal with this interesting forensic population. I decided, therefore, that I would write *this* book in a somewhat more personal, and slightly less formal, format.

In cases where a theft offender is facing a court hearing, that person might be well advised to *also* obtain a copy of *Why Honest People Shoplift Or Commit Other Acts Of Theft*, read it, and provide a copy to his or her lawyer along with a copy of this book. Over the years since my earlier book has been available, I have been informed by many theft offenders that the original book was very helpful, not only to themselves, but to their therapists, their lawyers and the courts as well. I understand that many defence lawyers have not only read the book, but have also provided the prosecution and judges with copies so that *they* might make more informed judgements as to *whether* and *how* to proceed in regard to taking the cases to trial, and what form of sentences might be most helpful to the individual theft offender and to the society in which they reside.

You might consider the book you are now reading together with my earlier one, as an excellent one-two combination that might best assist you and the professionals involved in the case of atypical theft behaviour about which you are concerned. While there is some minor repetition of findings and a few cases in this book that were drawn from the earlier one, by and large each of the two books also contain valuable and unique items of information. For example, in *Why Honest People Shoplift Or Commit Other Acts Of Theft*, I included (see Chapter 31 in that book) what I termed *"An open letter to the Atypical Theft Offender's 'Significant Other'"*; I believe this 'letter' can be of considerable assistance in helping the theft offender's spouse to better appreciate the role that he or she can usefully play in assisting the partner to stop stealing. As well, my prior book contains thirty-three composite cases of atypical theft behaviour that offer a broad range of examples of such conduct. Four of the twelve cases presented in the book you are now reading have been drawn from the earlier book and are offered here as well, because they have so much to teach us about atypical theft behaviour.

The findings of my latest (2013) study that I present in this book for the first time, involved some 30 new cases drawn at random from the additional hundreds I have assessed and treated since my earlier book was published. While most of these cases involved primarily or exclusively instances of shoplifting, a few involved acts of theft of very substantial sums of money and/or goods - in one case, of over $1,500,000. These additional cases are included to help broaden the scope of our understanding of possible atypical theft behaviour.

As mentioned above, I decided that I would write this book from a more personal perspective, as well. I hope that you will find this style of presentation to be a welcome approach to presenting and discussing the topic of the atypical theft behaviour that is carried out by usually honest persons.

THE MEDIA COMES A-CALLING

Ever since our first article, titled Shoplifting: An Occasional Crime of the Moral Majority, was published a full thirty years ago in the major peer-reviewed professional journal, *The Bulletin of the American Academy of Psychiatry and the Law* (1983), I have frequently been contacted by media outlets, especially when yet another prominent citizen or celebrity has been apprehended for shoplifting. (For an abbreviated listing of media who have contacted me over the years, just check out the 'Media Contacts' webpage on my WhyHonestPeopleSteal.com website: http://www.whyhonestpeoplesteal.com/Media_contacts.htm .)

I am always pleased to speak with reporters since my experience is that most of them seem genuinely interested in gaining an understanding of such seemingly nonsensical behaviour. I usually stress that my clinical findings clearly indicate that the apprehended persons most likely do *not* suffer from so-called 'kleptomania' (a label that is far too frequently applied in such cases). I believe that among the dangers implicit in labelling these persons as 'kleptomaniacs' are that: (a) the designation is almost never valid (for reasons we will address later on, in detail), and (b) it is important to consider that, until and unless the most likely *real* reasons for their theft behaviour have been determined, it is extremely unlikely that these theft offenders will receive proper treatment, and therefore they may very well re-offend!

Over the years I have appeared on literally dozens of television and radio programs, including ABC's *Good Morning America*, CBS's *Early Show*, MSNBC *Investigates*, and British and Canadian nationwide radio. I have also been quoted in the pages of the New York Times, Denver Post, L.A. Times, San Francisco Chronicle, the Globe and Mail, and PEOPLE, SELF, HEALTH and READER'S DIGEST, doing my best to help the general public gain a better understanding of the atypical theft behaviour of usually honest persons.

I have also become accustomed to the likelihood that whenever another prominent person is caught for allegedly shoplifting, I may shortly afterwards be contacted by reporters from the print, electronic or cyber media. In fact, a week before writing this paragraph I was interviewed by a senior writer for a major U.S. television network's news website who was interested in learning about the possible reasons behind the seemingly bizarre theft behaviour of someone she happened to know personally, someone who was a litigation lawyer who earned close to a million dollars a year, but who apparently enjoyed stealing pieces of expensive silverware virtually every time he ate at some of the most exclusive and priciest restaurants in his hometown of Miami. I mentioned to the reporter that one of the reasons I was writing the book you are now holding is because there still exists a need for a clear, comprehensive explanation, one actually based upon decades of rigorous clinical investigation, of the reasons for this sort of seemingly bizarre and ultimately potentially self-destructive behaviour.

Most of us know or have heard of someone who has no objective need to steal anything, yet who evidently has done so, perhaps than once or even often. You may even know that this person has been caught and perhaps even convicted more than once, and yet still continues to steal, risking so much in terms of his or her professional reputation or working situation, and their standing among family members, relatives and friends. In fact, *you* may even be the usually honest and ethical sort of person I am referring to and so I am very pleased to assure you that, if you will read this book thoroughly, I am confident that you will likely gain a great deal of knowledge and insight about your atypical theft behaviour and how to help stop it!

(Incidentally, I am always interested in hearing from persons who wish to share their stories about having a problem with acts of shoplifting or other apparently nonsensical theft behaviour. By all means, email me at *wcupchik@aol.com* if you wish to share your personal experience.)

Meanwhile, I believe you will benefit from reading this book, including by realizing that there are, virtually always, entirely understandable reasons why such atypical theft behaviour happens. If *you* are the person with this problem, you will also hopefully gain some relief from realizing that you are certainly not alone in this kind of behaviour, and will come to realize that you are not a 'bad' person either, but rather, like the vast majority of my clients, you are very likely an essentially good and valuable individual, and someone whose theft behaviour *can* be dealt with in such ways as to help ensure that you will be less likely to repeat such conduct.

My clinical investigations, as indicated by the results of my latest (2013) study, have uncovered several common themes in the atypical theft behaviour of usually honest persons, and these are themes that laypersons are usually able to easily grasp and readily appreciate. Indeed, there is often an "aha!" reaction on the part of interviewers and laypersons alike when they recognize the possible reasons for these theft offenders' seemingly irrational acts of stealing.

<u>PART I</u>

An Initiation

Into The World

Of

Atypical Theft Offenders

Chapter 1

SOME SHOCKING EXAMPLES OF SHOPLIFTING PERPETRATED BY PROMINENT PEOPLE

At least several times a year, local and/or national media will headline articles about acts of shoplifting that have evidently been carried out by persons whom most of us know - or know of - and who would be among the last individuals we ever expected would have been arrested for stealing (especially items worth a relatively minor amount compared to those persons' readily available assets).

Frequently the items have allegedly been taken from supermarkets, department or specialty stores and we can be forgiven for thinking or saying aloud to our family or friends something like, *"Can you believe it? On the news it just said that _____ has been charged with stealing items that he (or she) could so easily have afforded to buy! Why, for heaven's sake, would he have done that? It will wreck his reputation, and perhaps he will even lose his license to practice his profession or get another job. He isn't stupid! In fact he is very bright and has more than enough money. So, what gives?!"*

To put the matter even more succinctly, we might ask, *"Why would someone risk so much for so little gain?"* That is the very question that this book aims to answer.

Some startling examples of alleged shoplifting carried out by persons who would seem to be the last folks we would expect to behave in such a manner

In early August of 2010, Rudy Giuliani's 20 year old daughter, Caroline, at the time a Harvard University student, was arrested for allegedly shoplifting several items worth about $100 from a cosmetics store in New York City. Later that month she evidently struck a deal in court to get her shoplifting charges dismissed by being given 'an adjournment in contemplation of dismissal' in exchange for serving a day of community service and avoiding any further problems with the law for six months.

And consider the case (also mentioned previously) of President George W. Bush's former domestic policy advisor, Claude Allen, who resigned his position in February 2006, after having been apprehended for allegedly stealing from Target and Hecht's stores. In August of 2006 he pled guilty to one misdemeanour count of theft. Allen, a married man with four children and an evangelical Christian, was at the time apparently earning over $160,000 a year.

I have previously mentioned the case of Winona Ryder, a prominent actress who was charged with shoplifting in 2002.

Older readers may recall that in 1988, media personality (and former Miss America) Bess Myerson pled guilty to shoplifting items worth about $44 from a department store in Pennsylvania.

Several years ago I was contacted by two American television networks to comment on the case of the former attorney general (married at the time to another prominent lawyer), who attempted to get the valuable paintings she had stolen, *insured!* To do so required, of course, that she list the artists' names and the titles of the paintings. This she did, although she surely must have known that those exact works of art would likely be listed somewhere in a database of stolen paintings. So why would she have done something that virtually guaranteed she would be caught?

One could go on and on, recounting instances of prominent citizens who have apprehended for shoplifting. In my practice over the years I have interviewed all manner of reputable and usually honest individuals who have stolen, including even some deeply religious individuals, among them a distinguished Catholic priest, a prominent member of a large Jewish congregation, and a highly respected and religiously observant Muslim, each of who admitted to seemingly bizarre theft behaviour.

Now, of course, for every case of a usually honest individual who has committed an act of shoplifting or some other kind of theft, there are very likely dozens of other persons whose acts of stealing were carried out with the primary motivation being to not pay for the item, <u>and without the slightest feelings of remorse or shame</u>. As I have already mentioned, over 25 years ago, my colleague, psychiatrist Dr Don J Atcheson and I termed this latter group of individuals, who most of us would readily consider 'common thieves', *T*ypical Theft Offenders. **In this book we shall focus**

upon those individuals who truly are usually honest and law-abiding, who almost invariably detest the very idea of people stealing, but who, nevertheless have themselves committed acts of theft.

Before going on let me state that I have chosen to mention cases of relatively prominent people who have shoplifted primarily because those are the cases that tend to make the headlines. When very wealthy or members of prominent families are apprehended for shoplifting we are taken aback, shocked or even disgusted. However, I can assure the reader that my clinical investigations clearly indicate that their acts of stealing are almost invariably due to the same kinds of underlying issues that have prompted less well known -but no less honest- persons to act out.

Chapter 2

WHY I BECAME INTERESTED IN THE THEFT BEHAVIOUR OF USUALLY HONEST ADULTS

Like many of the readers of this book, I have always been interested in how *things* and *people* work. In fact, as a young teenager, when I was trying to decide whether to go into psychology or engineering, I decided that I would attempt *both* professions. By age sixteen, I correctly concluded that engineering would likely be a harder path for me, and so, if I was going to try both professions, I should probably do engineering first. And so, the summer prior to my final school year in the five-year electrical engineering degree program at McGill University, specializing in electronics, in 1961, I did take my very first university course in psychology at what is now called Concordia University.

After graduation as a newly minted professional engineer, I was fortunate to obtain a job with an exceptional engineering company in Ottawa, Ontario called Computing Devices of Canada (CDC). This firm designed and built navigational guidance systems for the then next-generation of mostly military (NATO, including USA) aircraft. In my time at CDC I designed three alternate systems for ship-based, submarine-seeking helicopters, and I was, and remain, proud that all three designs were actually accepted and CDC remained at the forefront of such system designs for decades. At the same time, however, given that it was in the midst of the so-called Cold War (the Cuban missile crisis was only months away), and since my plan had been all along to also further my studies in psychology, after one year at CDC I decided to return to university full-time and completed my Bachelor's degree with a major in psychology at Carleton University, in Ottawa, in 1963.

In retrospect, it is clear to me that I have always been interested in the relationship of one thing to another, one person to another, and/or even one person to an *object* or *machine* or *activity* (think *shoplifting*).
As a professional engineer, I was focused on how to help a helicopter carry out its anti-submarine patrol, all the while keeping track of exactly where it was in relation to its mothership *and* the other helicopters that

were carrying out their own parts of the search pattern. Years later, as a doctoral student in counseling psychology I was vitally interested in gaining an in-depth understanding of the status and dynamics of an interpersonal relationship between two people.

In my forensic work as a psychologist, I was intrigued by the relationship between a theft offender and the items that he or she had shoplifted. This particular interest came about largely as a result of having been accepted, in 1974, as a psychology intern, on the forensic service of the University of Toronto-affiliated, Clarke Institute of Psychiatry. It was mere serendipity that, during that time period (1974-86), our outpatient forensic unit was having referred to it for clinical assessment and possible treatment, a very wide variety of primarily responsible (and even a few relatively high-profile) individuals, who had been charged with seemingly nonsensical acts of shoplifting. These individuals included a prominent lawyer, a senior engineer, an experienced nurse, a Dean of Law at a major university, elementary and high school teachers, business owners, a house-cleaning person and some homemakers, among others.

As I was at the time assigned to the team of professionals led by senior psychiatrist Dr Don Atcheson, he and I had occasion to commiserate about the slowly emerging, curious commonalities among this broad assortment of accused shoplifters. Over the years from 1976 through the early 1980s we collected and collated a good deal of data about these individuals and had our resulting article titled, *Shoplifting: An Occasional Crime Of The Moral Majority,* published in the prestigious, peer-reviewed professional journal, the <u>Bulletin of the American Academy of Psychiatry and the Law,</u> in 1983.

A significant political and scientific event that occurred while I was in engineering at university and that impacted the ways in which I would come to contemplate the ways of the world.

As I mentioned, my first profession in the early 1960s was as an electronics engineer. Actually I was in second year engineering at McGill University on October 4, 1957 when two momentous events occurred. One was the flight of the CF-105 Avro Arrow, at the time the most advanced fighter-interceptor aircraft in the world, designed and built in Toronto. The second event was by far more world-shaking, namely the flight of the first Sputnik satellite that was launched by the then Soviet Union and that proceeded to circle the earth in a low orbit. As happened at most science and engineering departments at universities all over the so-called Western World, McGill's engineering faculty was shaken to its core. Soon afterwards, many universities' engineering programs were rapidly modernized, including in my chosen field of electronics, as we were introduced to numerous courses in so-called 'atomic physics' and 'semiconductor theory'.

I well recall that the following year our physics professor introduced the first so-called 'atomic physics' course we were to encounter, by saying that some of us might find it a very uncomfortable subject because, in ways, it would not appear to 'make much sense'. He said that the basis of atomic physics was mathematical, not what we had been brought up to consider as 'logical'. For example, while the 'old' Newtonian model of physics maintained that the weight of a pound of matter stays constant, no matter what, the newer 'atomic physics' proclaimed, in Einstein's famous formula $E=MC^2$, that if one could hurl a unit of matter at the speed of light, the pound of matter would be transformed into energy.

This same professor also told us a very interesting story that still has relevance today for all of us who would like to better understand the workings of the human and material worlds. He said that in the early 1900s, there was a most remarkable philosophy professor who taught at one of the prestigious Ivy League universities in the eastern USA. Evidently this professor relished in taking his first year students (all males, most of whom had been brought up in upper class, firmly religious Christian homes), and by the force of his profoundly rational and philosophical mind, he would essentially help his students *de*construct their religious beliefs to the point that, by the time they went home for Christmas vacation, many of these students were no longer certain of what they believed, including whether there was a God, if 'he' was a *Christian* God, etc... . (No doubt it made for very interesting conversations at their families' Christmas dinner tables that holiday period!)

The philosophy professor evidently also had the further, perhaps even more impressive, knack of helping his students *re*-construct their own, relatively thoroughly thought through, religious beliefs to the point that, by the *end* of the school year, they were well on their way to once again having firmly held, yet highly idiosyncratic beliefs about religion in general, and their own in particular.

One year, however, when the professor's students returned from Christmas vacation, they learned that their professor had died. As a result, many of them were left only with questions and uncertainties about their religious beliefs as well as many other issues. The 'punch line' of this story, according to our physics professor, was that these students, upon graduating, went on to produce more leaders in American business and other walks of life, than any other comparable graduating class from any other Ivy League university during that period. They had been left, upon graduation, with more questions and fewer answers. This state of ambiguity, of not-knowingness, can be a difficult one to tolerate, although it can open one up to vistas hardly imagined when one believes that one already has the major answers to life's mysteries as one enters adulthood.

I am convinced that this early intellectual training in atomic physics and allied subjects has allowed me to keep my mind open to alternate, even seemingly opposing, facts and ideas. The reason I have recounted the above story is to suggest, to the extent that you are comfortable in so doing, that *you* also keep *your* own mind open as we proceed to explore the data and ideas that will be presented throughout the remainder of this book. If you are able to do so, you will find that seemingly bizarre and nonsensical acts of shoplifting can indeed be understood and 'made sense off' as we come to realize that such behaviour usually stems from the perpetrators' responses to key issues and/or events in their lives.

My years on the staff of the forensic service of the Clarke Institute of Psychiatry

Without a doubt, among the most interesting dozen years of my working life were spent working on the forensic service of the University of Toronto-affiliated, Clarke Institute of Psychiatry. We regularly received for assessment and treatment, perpetrators of all manner of criminal activity. The more seemingly sensational or bizarre the case, the more likely it was that, sooner *than* later, these offenders would appear, either on the *out*patient unit (for those who were deemed less dangerous, to themselves and/or others) or on the *in*patient unit (where individuals who had been charged with serious physical or sexual assaults, and all manner of other major crimes, including murder, were confined during their assessments). In fact, it is literally true that I and other staff members would read the morning newspaper and/or hear the news on the radio on the commute to work, and accurately predict that the more seemingly remarkable or strange the crime, the more likely it was that it would be only a matter of time until the alleged perpetrator appeared on our unit for assessment and, perhaps, treatment.

While it is true that many of the cases of rape, assisted suicide and murder that arrived at the Clarke Institute of Psychiatry's forensic unit were intriguing from a professional point of view, nevertheless for me, it was the seemingly outlandish *acts of theft* (usually but not always, shoplifting) by supposedly intelligent, relatively financially secure and professionally successful persons, that most drew my attention. I was fascinated to learn why it was that these particular individuals had risked *so much* (in terms of their personal reputations and working lives, ability to continue to practice their professions, etc…) for, frequently, *so very little* in monetary terms). Most of them, in fact, had shoplifted items worth a miniscule amount compared to their own readily available financial assets.

Consider, for example, the award-winning high school teacher with a Masters degree who deeply loved his job, yet who repeatedly risked being fired for stealing items usually worth less than five dollars from a store within two blocks of his school. Another example was the emergency room physician who occasionally stole pens and blank CDs from a local office supplies box store. A third case was that of an experienced nurse who worked in a long-term rehabilitation facility, who truly enjoyed going to work each day, and yet risked losing her nursing licence because of her repeated acts of shoplifting from a nearly department store. A fourth case involved a prominent physician who stole over-the-counter medications from his neighbourhood drug store. A fifth case involved a deeply religious individual who worked for his church's major charity but who made off with over $500,000 from the church's coffers.

At the Clarke Institute we received them all, theft offenders who knew better, had no financial need to steal, and yet had admittedly committed these acts of theft -often in a remarkably blatant fashion- as if either they were either quite inept or very poor – neither of which was the case!

My own heritage piqued my interest in understanding illogical conduct

Born during the early part of World War II yet safely ensconced in a small city in the province of Quebec in Canada, I was quickly made aware of my Jewish heritage, in part by some of my school chums and 'good friends' who occasionally issued anti-Semitic insults as easily, and often as innocently, as if they were sitting at a dinner table saying, "Pass the butter!" One might forgive them because, in at least some cases, they assuredly knew not the import of what they were actually doing.

Of course, it was not only in my hometown of St. Jean sur Richelieu, some twenty-five miles from Montreal, that I encountered anti-Semitism. When I was a student in engineering at McGill University in 1956, I well recall the nearby fraternity house whose president informed us that his members were vehemently against holding a joint 'open house' with our members following an upcoming football game, given that we were "not of the same religious persuasion." As well, at the time it was widely believed that many universities in both Canada and the USA had a 'quota system' that applied to Jewish applicants to their medical and other professional faculties. As a result of these situations I was left to wonder why so many obviously intelligent people and members of institutions of higher learning could hold such prejudiced opinions and manifest such bigoted behaviours.

The Holocaust also influenced my professional interest in atypical theft behaviour
Decades ago the University of Toronto was the site of a conference at which the main speaker was, as I recall, the chairman of the U.S. President's Commission on the Holocaust. The most powerful point he made, as far as I was concerned, was that the Holocaust, surely one of the most diabolical, immoral and cruel events ever perpetrated upon other human beings, had been designed, orchestrated and carried out by some of the most educated and accomplished members of the professional classes (judges, lawyers, doctors, engineers, etc...) in German society. They were in a sense, some of the best and brightest citizens of Nazi Germany.

Furthermore, the 1961 trial of ex-Nazi SS Lieutenant Colonel Adoph Eichmann in Israel turned out to be, in part, an exercise in the study of 'the banality of evil' (a poignant term that was part of the title of German-American political theorist Hannah Arendt's book on Eichmann's trial). **In this trial, a very ordinary member of society (Eichmann) showed that he was capable of carrying out immoral acts of the worst and most far-reaching kinds.** He was considered a major functionary in arranging the transport of Jews from their homes, first into ghettoes, and then to the concentration camps.

I also became aware of the January 20, 1941 so-called Wannsee Conference, which was a meeting of some of the key personnel in the Nazi Germany heirarchy aimed at coordinating the capture, transport and extermination of Jews. The 1984 German television film *Wannseekonferenz* (*The Wannsee Conference*), produced as a recreation of the meeting, and ran 85 minutes—exactly the length of the conference itself, with a script derived from the minutes of the meeting.

[For further information about this grotesque, organized gathering I would recommend that readers find one of the films made about this 'conference' and/or read the detailed summary of the meeting as described on Wikipedia: http://en.wikipedia.org/wiki/Wannsee_Conference. Again, it was the shear 'ordinaryness' and bizarreness of the meeting that made it clear that intelligent, educated and high functioning individuals were fully capable of orchestrating and carrying out the most heinous acts imaginable.]

From the above facts and experiences I came to be particularly interested in instances where intelligent, presumably thoughtful people do seemingly stupid, thoughtless things. It was, and remains, intriguing for me to attempt to understand why usually moral, ethical persons would offend against their own standards, and in particular when they themselves would be quite unable to reasonably explain or justify their misdeeds.

During my twelve years on the staff of the forensic service of the Clarke Institute, it hardly surprised me that relatively disadvantaged individuals who had been brought up in environments of deprivation and/or violence, and/or were living on the fringes of society, would act out in criminal ways. **But it was most unexpected to find an ample supply of educated, successful persons who committed acts of theft that even they and their associates would undoubtedly find abhorrent, were they to have been committed by someone else, perhaps one of their own friends or colleagues.** And between 1974 and 1986 (the years when I worked on the forensic service) many of the acts of shoplifting that had been perpetrated by members of this latter, privileged group, led to them arriving at our forensic unit for assessment and treatment, allowing my colleague, senior psychiatrist Dr Don Atcheson and myself to examine this phenomenon and the perpetrators particularly closely.

After having developed a reputation as a specialist in uncovering and being able to articulate plausible and probable explanations for atypical theft behaviour, after I left the Clarke Institute of Psychiatry in 1986 to go into full-time private practice I continued to receive very many referrals of reputable (and sometimes quite prominent) individuals who, nevertheless, had placed themselves in considerable personal and professional jeopardy as a result of committing their seemingly nonsensical acts of theft.

I am, at this time, usually in a position to offer an comprehensive, detailed list of non-mutually exclusive, but highly probable explanations, for the atypical theft behaviour of the usually honest individuals whom I have thoroughly assessed. And as important, I have developed powerful approaches to effectively treating many of these persons. It is important to appreciate that the aim here is most definitely <u>not to excuse</u>, but rather to <u>uncover</u>, <u>understand</u> and, in laypersons' terms, <u>explain</u> why the individuals in question have committed their acts of theft – and to assist them to <u>stop</u> their ultimately self-destructive behaviour.

Chapter 3

WHY THE SHOPLIFTING BEHAVIOUR OF PROMINENT AND/OR WEALTHY AND/OR RELIGIOUS PERSONS INTRIGUES US ALL

What so grabs our interest when an supposedly deeply religious, professionally successful, financially well off, and/or prominent person shoplifts (especially items worth a relatively paltry sum compared to that individual's readily available assets) is the fact that there is no blatantly obvious need for that person to have bothered stealing the item(s) in question. We are astounded that someone who has so much -and so much *to lose*, if caught- would potentially risk it all, especially for so little in monetary gain. And some of us might understandably experience resentment or even anger when it appears that someone who already has a great deal, seems to be reluctant to part with a relatively small sum in order to acquire an item that most of the rest of us would feel obliged to *purchase*, were we also to want to have the item(s) in question.

When we learn that persons who know better, nevertheless attempt to get away with something by disreputable means, we are offended. We may think, *"It is not fair; it is downright wrong, and I hope they get their comeuppance!"*

The most common sort of theft (i.e., shoplifting) has likely always intrigued us.
A recent Internet search of the word 'shoplifting' produced nearly *ten million* results while a search for the word 'paranoia' was about 7 million and the word 'stomach-ache' produced only 4 million. An Internet search of the *New York Times* database likewise results in a listing *hundreds* of articles when using the keyword, 'shoplifting'.

What happens when the wealthy try to get away with more (especially if it is just a *little* more)
Over a century ago, in its December 2, <u>1904</u> edition, the *New York Times* published a most interesting article that recounted the appearance in court of a woman "known as Mrs. Hobert," who appeared before a Magistrate Whitman in Jefferson Market Court. Unfortunately for Mrs.

Hobert, when the manager of the store in which she was arrested himself asked for the charge of shoplifting to be withdrawn, on the grounds that he had learned, after an investigation, "that this woman is a member of one of the best families in the city, and moreover, that she has been suffering from severe illness" for three years, the Magistrate refused.

The stated grounds upon which the Magistrate refused to have the case withdrawn were interesting in and of themselves. On the one hand he is quoted as saying that "I can't see that this case differs from any other that has come before me.... I have a duty to perform as a public officer. There should be no discrimination, and there will be none in this court whether the accused be poor or which, socially prominent or unknown." While holding such a view appears to speak to an equality before the court that most might consider admirable, the very next sentence uttered by the Magistrate (assuming the newspaper article reported and quoted him accurately) suggests that he was, in fact, going to hold Mrs. Hobert to a *markedly different standard* than a less financially well off shoplifter would have been. Magistrate Whitman is quoted as saying, immediately after he spoke of the admirable quality of "blind justice", that "The fact of this woman being wealthy and socially prominent only makes her crime the more flagrant, and she should be punished in the most severe manner."

Magistrate Whitman would certainly find many individuals in current day America and elsewhere to be very simpatico with his 'double standard' of treating the rich more severely than the poor, for the very same crime of theft. Some of us can at least appreciate, if not entirely concur, with the Magistrate's views of over a century ago. After all, it may irk us that someone with so much already (in monetary or social terms) would attempt to get something more 'for free', even if it is only a 'little more'.

So, why do they do it?
At the same time, we are left with our questions as to why Mrs. Hobert did it? At the least it piques our curiosity and, not knowing the answers to the questions that we have, we are left to contemplate the most seemingly obvious facts; here is someone who already has 'a lot' yet apparently tried to get away with a little more. Does it remind us of the sibling, co-worker, or acquaintance who was always trying to get a bigger slice of the pie than us, literally or figuratively? Perhaps it is not uncommon for some to still have lingering resentment in regard to the

perceived unfair pieces-of-the-pie distribution of love, affection, attention, etc…, that was doled out by one or both parents. (Older readers may recall the Smothers Brothers television program, where Tom Smothers would often accusatively say to his brother, Dick, "Mom always liked you best!")

Another reason the topic of shoplifting may interest us is that, after all, most of us have to *work* to earn money and we *pay* for the things we get. We call this latter activity, 'buying'. 'Buying' something means paying for that which we wish to acquire. Of course, buying something that is 'on sale', i.e., paying less for the same item than if it were not on sale, is also entirely acceptable in our society. Witness the shopping tradition called Black Friday that occurs the day after American Thanksgiving, or the so-called 'Boxing Day' sales that take place in Canada the day after Christmas day.

On the other hand, 'shoplifting' is stealing, getting something for *nothing*, and it is not only illegal but, according to the ten commandments and most other religions' tenets, it is morally wrong.

The difficult-to-comprehend inherent complexity of some corporate crimes
Most laypersons don't fully understand the details of the sorts of deceptive or illegal practices that some businesses employ, except in the broad strokes. When companies and/or their executives use various complex nefarious means (devious accounting practices, inappropriate expense account filings, etc…) to underhandedly acquire funds, we have the impression that something wrong has been done, but many of us do not truly comprehend the exact nature of what was done.

Remember the 'credit default swaps' that were part of the 2008 financial crisis? The following is from Wikipedia (retrieved on October 26, 2012, from http://en.wikipedia.org/wiki/credit_default_swaps) and describes a 'credit default swap' (CDS) as being *"a financial swap agreement that the seller of the CDS will compensate the buyer in the event of a loan default or other credit event. The buyer of the CDS makes a series of payments (the CDS "fee" or "spread") to the seller and, in exchange, receives a payoff if the loan defaults. In the event of default the buyer of the CDS receives compensation (usually the face value of the loan), and the seller of the CDS takes possession of the defaulted loan.*

However, anyone can purchase a CDS, even buyers who do not hold the loan instrument and who have no direct insurable interest in the loan (these are called "naked" CDSs). If there are more CDS contracts outstanding than bonds in existence, a protocol exists to hold a credit event auction; the payment received is usually substantially less than the face value of the loan."

How many lay readers fully understand what the above description of a credit default swap really means? Probably, not many!

But *shoplifting!* Now *there* is an act that is seemingly entirely obvious (especially as compared to a credit default swap!) and we can usually easily comprehend the details of *what* was taken, by *whom* and as importantly, *how.* As a result, we can follow the consequences of a simple act of shoplifting with ease, and dare I suggest, perhaps even satisfaction – especially when the guilty party gets his or her due.

Most of us have a keen sense of fairness versus unfairness, of right versus wrong, of good versus bad. And acts of shoplifting can stir these senses and elicit strong feelings. We are, after all, dealing here with one of the Ten Commandments; in fact, number eight: "Thou shall not steal." That is a very clear and unequivocal injunction. While the shenanigans that led to the 2008 stock market and housing mortgage meltdowns might be complicated and make it difficult to ascribe clear and definite blame, an act of shoplifting is usually much more straightforward and blame and responsibility can easily be laid.

I have often told reporters for various media who have contacted me that it is very interesting that, given the choice, say when having friends over for dinner, between inviting someone with a known drinking problem and has had convictions for driving while inebriated *or* inviting an individual who was been convicted of stealing, a substantial proportion of hosts would be more inclined to invite the 'drunk' than the 'thief'.

In this book I reveal the several non-mutually exclusive answers to the following question: <u>Why is it that some usually honest, ethical persons shoplift?</u> These answers have been gained from decades of my own clinical investigations into atypical theft behaviour, and I offer a number of examples, using composite cases garnered from my own files. Of course,

18

to preserve confidentiality, I have altered possible identifying features and details. At the same time, however, as dramatic as the examples I will offer will be, I want to assure you, the reader, that the true facts in these cases were even more remarkable than those that I present for your consideration.

From reading this book you can expect to gain considerable insight into the reasons why some acts of shoplifting (and other kinds of theft) are committed by those persons who usually live their lives with honesty and integrity, who should and do know better, and who really have no objective reason to steal, but do so anyway – sometimes, time and again.

Atypical Theft Behaviour by Usually Honest Persons
To continue our investigation of atypical theft behaviour, I have already offered for your consideration the case of Victor, the wealthy retired gentleman from Los Angeles, who committed a totally unnecessary, single act of theft. I have already pointed out that his story has much to inform us about life, the unconscious mind and atypical theft behaviour.

Most readers, I believe, will find that the story of Victor offers very powerful evidence that his act of atypical theft behaviour warranted at least some compassionate consideration before concluding that 'since he did the crime, he should do the time'.

It has been my clinical experience that, while many cases were not necessarily as 'pure' or dramatic, there exists very similar psychodynamics; i.e., most of the usually honest persons I have assessed and treated, have acted out by stealing in response to having their unconscious or subconscious minds stirred by some external events or circumstances.

****

Let me offer you another example of atypical theft behaviour, this time carried out by a usually outstanding member of her working community.

Case # 2: Melanie: The Frequent Employee-of the month Who Had Stolen From Her Employer – for Years

Melanie had been a seemingly dedicated employee of a high-end specialty store for over fifteen years – until the day her theft behaviour was exposed and she was fired. Just over 38 years old at the time she contacted me, she had great difficulty talking about her problem without crying wrenching tears of shame, and could not explain to me how it was that she had stolen from the employer who, she stated, she greatly admired and personally liked. A clearly highly intelligent and intuitive individual, she had, within three years after she began her employment at the store, been put in charge of selecting and ordering the more high-end items that her company sold. Since taking over that job, the company's profits had greatly increased, and Melanie's salary had steadily improved, as well. She was a very highly trusted, valued and well-paid employee.

Brought up in an upper middle class home with a mother she described as extremely fragile and a father who had great difficulty expressing emotion (she could not remember him ever once having hugged her or told her that he loved her), she could not explain to me why she had, over a period of seven years, stolen from her employer a great many specialized items that were worth, usually, anywhere from a few dollars to over $500 each. She kept the items (worth over $15,000 in total) in her apartment; they were never sold, given away, used or worn, but Melanie said that she felt gratified at merely having them in her possession. Since her parents were very generous financially, she was certain that they would have given her the funds to purchase all the items she had stolen, without a moment's hesitation - but she had never asked them.

Another remarkable feature of this case was that, over a period of a few sessions, it became abundantly clear that Melanie was truly exceptionally bright and verbally highly proficient. She often used highly apt metaphors to describe her thoughts, feelings and experiences, and it was obvious that she had a great facility with visual imagery (a subject with which I am especially familiar, given that it had been a major part of the topic of my doctoral dissertation). Week after week, when she came into my office, she would take out her 3-ring binder and share with me the powerful insights she had gained since our previous session, in words and images that were, at one and the same time, brilliantly simple and profoundly elegant.

Melanie had informed me in an early session that she dropped out of university just prior to the final exam of her final year in economics. In sessions that followed it seemed that she had a long-time habit of not completing studies, projects or relationships. In reference to the latter, Melanie told me that as soon as a promising relationship was on the verge of becoming sexually intimate or otherwise close, she would find some excuse to stop seeing the individual. Our in-depth investigation of this pattern revealed a strong sense of very low self-esteem. Melanie was continually afraid that she could not satisfactorily 'finish' almost anything!

At the beginning of our eighth session, Melanie entered my office with an expression that could best be described as highly vulnerable, terribly embarrassed and very angry. She seemed on the verge of 'exploding' verbally and emotionally. Instead, she slowly and quietly began to share with me something that she had never told another person, namely that, beginning when she was twelve years old, an uncle had repeatedly sexually molested her. She said that, on the one hand, she had been terrified, but on the other she found that she craved physical 'affection' as that was something her parents had never given her, but that her uncle began to provide for her. Given that her mother had more than once been institutionalized for a 'nervous breakdown', Melanie was certain that she could never cope with being told of her brother's sexual misconduct. At the same time, Melanie's father was so remote and punitive that she was terrified that he would blame and punish her for her sexual encounters with her uncle.

Over a period of several months in therapy Melanie was able to deal with her complex feelings towards her (by now, deceased) uncle, and she came to understand why she so feared letting anyone else physically or emotionally close to her. She also slowly came to appreciate that her avoidance of completing tasks were a means of keeping herself 'stuck' in a job that was considerably below her intellectual capacities. As she continued to examine her thoughts and feelings, and to allow herself to consider what kind of work she might like to do, she started to crystallize an image of herself becoming a nurse. She investigated what courses she would need to take to complete her Bachelor's degree, took them, and then entered a Masters of Nursing program.

In considering this case in detail, my own conclusion was that Melanie's theft behaviour was the means that her own unconscious had of moving her out of the dead-end job she had been in for years, and of prompting her to deal with her earlier sexual abuse and other emotional issues. For all of her working life she had simply gone to work, come home and then spent very many hours watching mindless television programs until she was tired enough to go to bed. When she was not either working or watching TV she exercised fanatically and became a competitive marathon runner – all activities that she used to keep her from getting in touch with her feelings and contemplating her future.

The unconscious mind may help trigger atypical theft behaviour as a means of forcing the offender to seek help in dealing with important unresolved or undealt with personal issues

It has been my observation for many years that acts of atypical theft behaviour have sometimes likely been perpetrated from the unconscious level of the individuals' psyches as a means of forcing major changes in their personal or working lives, as well as in acquiring professional psychological help. Many Atypical Theft Offenders have stolen in order to force changes, or at least focus attention on, their unsatisfactory vocational, interpersonal or marital situations. It is almost an truism that when a *very intelligent* person commits a seemingly *very stupid* act, attention should be paid to the possible underlying reasons *why*! Of course, many of us are likely able to avoid uncomfortable facts or situations that might disrupt the current state of affairs in our lives, for a very long time. However, if the 'help' we eventually acquire is not sufficiently expert, we might continue to avoid identifying and facing those aspects of our lives that need to be addressed, thereby eventually possibly emboldening our unconscious minds to trigger increasingly blatant, bizarre and/or nonsensical acts of theft and/or other inappropriate behaviours.

It bears noting that a substantial minority of the Atypical Theft Offenders I have assessed over the years had experienced sexual and/or other kinds of abuse during their childhoods. Being children, they were not able, on their own, to process these traumatic experiences. One might appropriately say that these children had their innocence *stolen* from them. It has been my clinical experience over more than four decades of conducting psychotherapy, that *some* adults who had their innocence 'stolen' from them would turn to stealing as if they were attempting to compensate themselves for that which they had so unfairly lost.

****

Case # 3: **Brenda: The Politician's Wealthy Wife Who Stole A Pair Of Shoes in full view of a clearly marked security camera**

Brenda was a beautiful woman in her early fifties whose husband's twenty year long political career at the state level seemed destined for national heights, until she brought his ascension to an at least temporary 'hold' after she was arrested while leaving a store in a high-end shopping mall in Bal Harbor, Florida, with a pair of unpaid-for $800 shoes in her large handbag.

Her theft seemed particularly bizarre, given that she was the sole heir to the $10,000,000 fortune her recently deceased father had left her. Given her occasional tendencies to act out rather bizarrely at political and social functions over the years, many in her home state had become almost desensitized to hearing of yet another one of her apparently 'weird' capers. And many more silently sympathized with her husband, Rob, who soldiered on despite his wife's many efforts that appeared aimed at derailing his political ambitions.

While Brenda was let go with a warning and a small fine for stealing the shoes (since this was her first criminal offence in the state) her other antics continued unabated for another two years, until a woman whose name was 'Carol Smith' (about twenty years of age) came forward and claimed that Brenda's husband was in fact her father! Furthermore, she exclaimed, Rob had been carrying on a decades-long affair with her mother. While such claims are not that unique for celebrities to endure, the fact that Carole looked remarkably like Brenda's husband when he was about the same age, left little doubt in many people's minds but that the younger woman was possibly speaking the truth.

It turned out that Brenda had not been consciously aware of her husband's 'second family', but it would appear highly probable that at some deeper level within her psyche, she was responding to her husband's long-time and however well hidden duplicities. Brenda's bizarre behaviour over the years could now be seen in a much different light - not as those of someone who necessarily had major psychiatric issues, but rather as reactions to however faint realizations that something was indeed deeply wrong in her marriage. Having failed, for many years, to gain her husband's agreement to enter marital therapy, Brenda's anguish and anger had led her to act out in ways that he could scarcely continue to dismiss or ignore.

What might be considered, at least in part, attempts at retribution or vengeance, are not infrequently aspects of atypical theft behaviour. The spouses or children of law enforcement officials, religious leaders and other prominent individuals recognize, at least unconsciously, that if they commit acts of theft, such behaviours would not reflect well upon those whom they would embarrass. Several years ago I appeared on a network television program about shoplifting along with a young man who was the son of the police chief in his hometown. Needless to say, 'advertising' on television the fact that his father had a thief for a son, likely did not play well with the local citizenry, who would soon be voting on whether to re-elect his father to another term.

****

The above three examples, of Victor, Melanie and Brenda, offer important glimpses behind the curtain regarding acts of atypical theft behaviour. Our initial interest may have been piqued by the fact that these persons (or their relatives) were supposedly exemplary and/or prominent persons; a closer examination of the reasons for their theft behaviours has made clear that we should perhaps not be too quick to form 'a rush to judgement' in viewing atypical theft behaviour as always deserving the harshest condemnation. Instead, it is worthwhile asking, over and over again, "Why *would* someone risk *so much* for (usually) *so little* gain?" After having finished reading this book I am confident you will very likely agree with me that acts of seemingly bizarre and nonsensical theft behaviour usually have entirely understandable (though, of course, not entirely 'justifiable') reasons. **Just keep in mind that the purpose here is not to excuse, but rather to *understand* and *explain* the reasons behind such seemingly strange theft behaviour.**

Chapter 4

THE TERMS 'ATYPICAL THEFT OFFENDER' AND 'TYPICAL THEFT OFFENDER' AND HOW TO DISTINGUISH BETWEEN THEM

It will help you to better understand the findings presented in this book if we recall the definitions of the terms 'Atypical Theft Offender' and 'Typical Theft Offender'.

Recalling the definition of the term 'Atypical Theft Offender'

An *'Atypical Theft Offender'* (or ATO) is a theft offender who is primarily an honest, frequently hard-working, and ethical individual; his or her illegal theft behaviour is essentially an anomaly from -and at odds with- the ways in which the person usually conducts himself or herself in the world. This person is invariably markedly uncomfortable with the theft behaviour, and frequently reacts with feelings of shame, guilt, remorse and a genuine sense of humiliation in response to the acts of theft that he or she has committed. At the same time, however, the individual may be aware that he or she does not seem able to stop the theft behaviour, and is at a loss to fully understand the reasons for such seemingly bizarre and nonsensical conduct. The stealing is not primarily carried out for reasons of either need or greed.

In this book you will encounter many cases of theft that have been carried out by Atypical Theft Offenders. The following is such a case.

I would remind you that in all 'cases' presented in this book, the most important identifiers (age, gender, marital status, actual items - number or value- stolen, etc...) may have been altered to preserve confidentiality. Be assured, however, that in every case, the data as presented is actually less remarkable than that of the actual cases from which it has been drawn.)

****

Case # 4: Florence (Flo), a middle-level manager who pocketed many thousands of dollars of cash from relatives, co-workers and close friends over a period of several years

Florence was a 55-year old middle manager who worked for the state government. Her husband, Jack, also worked for the government, and between them they earned over $250,000 a year. They owned their own home outright, had a cottage by the ocean that was fully paid for, and their children had been accepted to university on almost full scholarships. Unbeknownst to her husband, Flo had, since she was a young teenager, been stealing from her well-off parents -- sometimes hundreds of dollars at a time. Furthermore, Flo informed me that, for the previous few years, on weekends she frequently helped out one of her friends who owned a successful retail business. This 'free' help she offered came to an abrupt end when she was confronted with taped closed circuit videos that showed her putting cash into her own pockets when she was ringing up sales at the cash register. In all, her friend accused her of being responsible for an estimated $15,000 shortfall in the store's sales over the previous two years.

Flo sought my help after being referred by a clinical social worker to whom she had confided her acts of theft. Given her own ample financial assets, her secure job, the fact that she had stolen from an individual who she described as her BFF ('best female friend'), clearly seemed, on the surface, very bizarre – to say the least! It was during our fourth interview that she also informed me that she occasionally even stole $20 bills from the purses of some of her co-workers.

Flo was unable to provide me with any reasons whatsoever to explain her theft behaviour. She did recognize that she often stole when she was feeling agitated, but again, did not know what she had to be agitated about. She loved her work, her home, her husband, and her children; she had several close friends and attended church regularly. In other words, she had a very good, debt-free upper-middle class life and was more than content. So, why did she steal?

[Usually, by the third or fourth session, if not sooner, my client and I have uncovered some of the likely reasons for that individual's atypical theft behaviour. In this case, however, Flo's answers to my questions about her childhood ("Did she ever experience any sexual, physical or emotional abuse?"- Her answer, "No!";... "How did her parents, siblings and

friends treat her?" - Her answer, "Very Well,", and so on) had been uniformly positive. As well, questions about her relationship with her husband invariably brought forth positive answers as well: they loved each other, their sexual relationship was fine, they had many mutual friends whom they both enjoyed, etc....]

On our sixth interview (an 'emergency' one that she had called and asked for, "As soon as possible, PLEASE!"), Flo arrived at my office in an extremely emotionally upset state. She told me that she had not been entirely truthful in some of her previous responses to my queries. For example (and now she became very soft spoken and hesitant) she informed me that she was about to tell me something that she had "never, ever, told another living person." She said that when she was a child her parents would often send her to spend one or both days of a weekend at her unmarried uncle's farm, and that the uncle had, over a period of years, from the time Flo was seven until she was thirteen, carried on a secret sexual relationship with her, until Flo finally insisted to her parents that she would not go to her uncle's home, ever again. When her parents inquired why she was so determined to not visit her uncle, Flo said that she tried to tell her parents that 'bad' things would happen on those occasions, but her mother, in particular, became quite incensed and would hear none of it! Instead, her mother severely beat Flo for being so disrespectful of, and lying about, her uncle, but never again insisted on further weekend visits to Flo's uncle's home.

It took Flo most of the session to reveal her story, between tears, silences and periods of violent trembling. Flo said she was relieved that she had told me but felt it was somehow wrong for her to have done so. She assured me that she held no animosity towards her parents for not protecting her from her uncle, even though she had learned in later years that two of her cousins had been subjected to similar sexual encounters with the same uncle and that their and her parents had been so informed – again without any of them taking precautionary actions. Flo also acknowledged that her sex life with her husband was not entirely satisfactory, especially as, whenever he touched her in an intimate fashion, she would invariably tense up, stay "frozen", and remain so during the rest of their 'love-making'. Orgasms were a phenomenon she had never experienced. Not surprisingly perhaps, it turned out that Flo's stealing from her parents began shortly after she began spending weekends at her uncle's home.

In our very next session Flo began to tell me about her husband, Jack's, extremely caring and protective attitude towards Flo's best friend, Sally. In fact, Flo informed me, when Sally's husband was away on business trips (a nearly regular monthly occurrence), Jack was so kind as to go over to Sally's house and keep her company for dinner. These 'dinners' had gone on for many months as of Flo's telling me about them. When I inquired why it was that Flo and Jack didn't invite Sally over for dinner to their home, she said that indeed, Sally and her husband often did come over to Jack and Flo's home for the evening, but that Jack seemed to think that Sally shouldn't be alone in her own home and that he should keep her company for just a few hours on those evenings that her husband was away.

Inasmuch as Flo's rendition of Jack and Sally's frequent dinners together while the latter's husband was out of town seemed markedly unusual at best, I asked Flo whether she was quite secure in the belief that Jack and Sally had a strictly platonic relationship. Flo expressed surprise at my question as it had never crossed her conscious mind - or so she assured me; Flo and Sally were dear friends, she said, and even though Flo's and Jack's own sexual relationship did have some issues, she was nevertheless certain that Jack was sexually content and that he had no interest of that nature in Sally.

It was about three weeks later that Flo called me once again in great distress and asked for an emergency appointment. She arrived with a half-inch stack of email exchanges between her husband, Jack, and her good friend, Sally. Flo said that she had used some software she had purchased to hack into her husband's email account in order to search for and retrieve any questionable emails. While none of the emails specifically stated that they had engaged in sexual intercourse, they did repeatedly refer to the pleasures that each experienced while hugging and kissing, laying in bed together after dinner, and how much they missed each other and could hardly wait for the next time that Sally's husband would be out of town so that Jack might come to her home.

As Flo read the emails to me, she understandably became more and more distressed. However, she told me that when she had confronted her husband with the emails the previous evening, he flew into a fury that his confidential email account had been hacked, and told Flo that since there was no statement regarding any act of sexual intercourse, Flo was simply overreacting to Jack's and Sally's "totally appropriate acts of mutual affection." Flo assured me that she was mostly satisfied with Jack's explanation and she was certain that, while some of their actions were questionable, they were surely not involved in anything that could be considered a full-blown sexual affair.

A thorough review of Flo's clinical interviews indicated strongly to me that the way in which she had likely survived her adolescent sexual encounters with her uncle was to emotionally and mentally distance herself from what was happening, and to try to not think about what had transpired when they were together. Now she seemed to be doing something similar in regard to her husband's and her best friend's relationship. While such 'distancing' may have served some useful function to the pre-teenaged and teenaged Flo, undoubtedly there had been consequences; her stealing from her parents had likely been a way of getting back at her parents for not protecting her and her more recent theft behaviour at her friend Jane's retail establishment was likely an acting out response driven from her <u>un</u>conscious, in reaction to her husband's possible sexual liaisons with Sally.

Flo's theft behaviour was that of a classic Atypical Theft Offender. The stealing was clearly not carried out of need or greed; Flo was risking losing her job as a manager earning more than $150,000 a year when she stole $20 at a time from a co-worker. And stealing from her friend's retail store was likely yet another indication of Flo's misdirected anger and frustration.

****

It has been true that, with many of the Atypical Theft Offenders whom I have assessed and treated, in order to avoid confronting the painful issues in their lives, they simply avoided consciously thinking about such matters. They tended to distract themselves with overwork, excessive exercising, drink or drugs, compulsively watching television, and/or other activities that kept them from addressing the matters that were likely to be so disturbing to them.

Incidentally, Flo's difficulty in accurately perceiving the likely goings-on between her husband and her best friend, Sally, is not entirely unheard of. Indeed (and this is actually true!) I well recall a former client who told me that when she happened to return to her and her husband's retail establishment one evening, she opened the front door to find her husband and one of their attractive sales clerks having sexual relations on the store's floor. When she flew into a rage and denounced her husband for his extramarital involvement, he vehemently denied the accusation. In fact, his exceptionally arrogant and breathtakingly brassy response to her accusation was to actually say, *"Who are you going to believe; me or your own eyes?!* This experience became the final blow to her marriage as she chose to believe what she had witnessed with her own eyes.

****

Let's now consider another fascinating example of a classical Atypical Theft Offender. James was a deeply religious individual with a very powerful conscience who had great difficulty understanding and coming to terms with *his* atypical theft behaviour.

Case # 5: James: A major fundraiser who stole a lot!

James, a very religious, 45 year old husband and father, had been arrested after an audit showed that, while working as a senior fundraiser for a major religiously affiliated hospital, he had siphoned off more than $500,000 for his own purposes over a three-year period. Further investigations uncovered that James had, during that same period, treated himself to several trips to New York City and Los Angeles, where he splurged on upscale hotel accommodations, limos and the best tables and meals at expensive 'in' restaurants. He had been the top fundraiser for his institution for several years running and had frequently worked sixty-hour-plus weeks. He was an active member of his church, the assistant conductor of the church choir, and had been awarded several commendations for his high-profile volunteer work in the community.

Shortly after he was finally arrested for stealing, a psychiatrist-friend of his had evidently recommended that he seek a professional consultation with me in advance of his trial, in order to perhaps provide himself with a Psychological Report that could be used by his lawyer to speak to the possibility of an at-least- reduced sentence. True to his usually high principles, however, James refused to do so, saying that he did not want to 'cop out' of suffering the full -and in his view- completely deserved punishment for his theft behaviour.

Incidentally, when first confronted with the auditor's report of probable wrongdoing, James had immediately confessed his guilt and initially refused to even be defended by a lawyer. He said that while he didn't understand <u>why</u> he had carried out his theft behaviour (which was an egregious affront to his personal code of conduct and religious beliefs), he reiterated that he nevertheless believed he <u>deserved</u> to be severely punished.

James first contacted me only <u>after</u> he had served his full term in penitentiary. When we met in my office at the Clarke Institute of Psychiatry James told me that, now that he had served his full sentence, he believed that he had repaid some of his debt to society, and was now ready to undertake an examination of his conduct. He said that he was actually very confused and frightened by what he had done, as he had always believed he was an honest and ethical individual, had prided himself for not being a clock-watcher, and had thought of himself as a person who regularly gave "more than full and fair value" for his wages. He believed the hospital did marvellous work in his community and it placed highly in a list of U.S. hospitals' top medical facilities. James believed he was fortunate to be able to work for them and prided himself on his skills in eliciting large donations from some of the wealthiest and most prominent members of the community.

*<u>What scared him most, he said, was that he didn't have the slightest idea **why** he had defrauded his employer of $500,000 dollars, and **why** he had acted out by living such an extravagant and bizarre life-style, which was so out of keeping with his upbringing and usual mode of modest middle-class living. Furthermore, he was afraid that unless he dealt with this matter fully, that he might do a similar thing again at some time in the future.</u> (His fear was likely entirely justified since, as my clinical experience has shown, until and unless an Atypical Theft Offender uncovers and deals with the underlying reasons for the theft behaviour, the likelihood of recidivism can remain high, even if a considerable amount of time passes between the acts of stealing.)*

During our early sessions I learned that James and his mother had been abandoned by his father, without any financial resources whatsoever, when James was 14 years old. He had very fond recollections of his father although he admitted that he still at times experienced brief, almost overpowering rages when he thought of his father having left him and his mother in such dire straits. They had been forced to live with his grandparents for several years until his mother remarried when James was 19 years old.

James' biological father was an accountant who had held a very responsible managerial position with a manufacturing company. He was also an authoritarian individual with a major drinking problem, and when drunk he would mete out brutal punishment to James for his youthful misdemeanours. James remembered only too well the sounds and sights that accompanied his father's weekend binges, and the beatings with a belt that he had endured. His recollections included painful images of his mother trying to get his father to stop his drinking, and father's violent reactions to her pleadings. Finally his father chose to leave rather than change, and shortly afterwards his mother heard through mutual friends that her husband had moved to another city with a woman he had met months before he left the family home. James never forgave his father and he never saw him again, other than once at a relative's funeral a few years later: James said he did not acknowledge his father's calling out to him on that occasion.

James' anger towards his father remained largely un-dealt with, although he had often prayed for guidance regarding how to handle his feelings of hurt and rage. When he received a promotion at work to the post of chief fund-raiser a few years earlier, he found himself reporting to a vice-president who was much older and also a severe alcoholic. The boss seemed to be continually berating James over an unending number of petty matters, in spite of his obvious competence and success in fund-raising. It was after barely a year of working under that supervisor that James' stealing began.

During his clinical treatment with me James had to learn to deal in more appropriate ways with his anger generally, and towards authority figures in particular. He also had to confront his unresolved feelings regarding his father. Once he had faced these issues and other related matters in the course of several months of therapy, he became much more appropriately assertive with peers as well as those in authority, and learned to get his needs met through means that gave him greater feelings of satisfaction and contentment than he had experienced in a long time.

In his new job he was once again confronted with a supervisor who was rather authoritarian in his manner. This time James requested and eventually received a transfer to another department with a supervisor who, he perceived, was both fair and welcoming. During the interval when he was waiting for the transfer to happen, James dealt with his troublesome supervisor in a very assertive and mature fashion - and he did not steal.

****

You will have noted that while Flo's theft behaviour involved shoplifting and stealing from relatives and friends, James' stealing was of a whole different order, involving approximately one-half million dollars. Both individuals were carrying great wounds from their childhood; both acted out, not out of need or greed, but in response to deep-seated and unresolved anger related to having been abused. This sort of dynamic has been a common theme in a substantial number of Atypical Theft Offender cases that I have assessed and treated over the years.

It is worthwhile stating, of course, that most people who suffered greatly as children do not end up stealing. However, in perhaps the great majority of cases, persons who experienced deep wounds as children may manifest other behaviours that will seriously and adversely impact at least some of their personal and working lives. We all have our own ways of handling difficulties that we have experienced in our lives. Some of the more fortunate of us will emerge relatively unscathed. Many of us, however, will carry the residuals of these earlier wounds with us into adulthood and they may well seriously affect our lives, until we finally turn and face them, and deal with them in healing and growth-producing ways.

At the same time and on the other hand, there are persons who may - or may not- have had such difficult early experiences, but who, in contrast to Atypical Theft Offenders, also act out via theft behaviour, but *without* feelings of remorse or shame. These individuals belong to another category of theft offender, one that Dr Atcheson and I came to refer to as **Typical** Theft Offenders. Let's consider one of these cases next.

****

Defining the term 'Typical Theft Offender'

A *Typical Theft Offender* (TTO) is an individual who is comfortable with his or her theft behaviour. This individual experiences neither shame nor remorse in relation to such actions, and, in fact, considers it to be an entirely acceptable means of acquiring goods or money. This person's stealing *is* primarily carried out for reasons of greed, however the individual may rationalize his or her motivations.

To assist in highlighting the contrasts between *Atypical* and *Typical* Theft Offenders, let's consider the case of Gerald, a classic Typical Theft Offender.

Case # 6: Gerald: The professor who stole $1,000,000 from his siblings

Gerald was a psychology and history of art professor at a major university in the Southwest. He was reasonably well regarded in his academic department although, according to his wife, his attitude often seemed to many of his colleagues to be rather self-centered and even at times, quite rebellious. Also, it turned out, Gerald lived a shadow life.

Gerald began selling street drugs to university acquaintances while a graduate student and seemed to enjoy the notoriety he had acquired among those who knew of his sideline. He continued to sell drugs to his friends and acquaintances even after he obtained tenure at the university where he was employed at the time he came to see me (at his wife's insistence). He readily acknowledged that he had used marijuana almost daily for over four decades when he first presented in my office. As well, he he informed me that he had carried on various extramarital affairs throughout his marriage, including some with former students. He laughed as he reminded me that he was divulging his extramarital activities only because he knew that our communications were confidential.

Gerald matter-of-factly reported that when his father was arranging his estate, about five years before he died, Gerald persuaded him that, as the eldest of five siblings, he would be the logical one to be the executor of father's will. His father, a fairly successful businessperson but a rather socially isolated individual who ran his own high-end mens' clothing store, acceded to Gerald's request.

A year after their father died, and in response to having had distributed to them by Gerald what they considered a surprisingly meagre inheritance compared to what they had been led to expect at various times by their father, Gerald's siblings hired their own lawyer to conduct an independent investigation into their late father's financial affairs. After a substantial search, some key documents surfaced that showed that Gerald had hidden the very existence of several sizeable investments their father had made during his life. These documents included a handwritten note written by Gerald four years before his father's death to his old high school friend who was also the lawyer that handled the preparation of Gerald's father's will, indicating Gerald's clear intention was to acquire most of his father's estate for himself. The amount that he kept for himself and refused to even acknowledge the existence of to his siblings was exposed by the acquisition of a computer printout of the contents of an offshore bank account where he had placed the funds. These documents showed that Gerald had planned for at least those four years prior to their father's death, to abscond with the bulk of his estate.

Gerald evidently had vehemently denied that his actions constituted any wrongdoing until confronted by his siblings with the 'smoking gun' document in which he had outlined, in his own handwriting, his plan to keep most of his father's estate. At that point he changed his story and told his siblings that their father, a month before he died at the age of 88, and when he was very ill indeed, had decreed that Gerald alone should acquire most of his estate. Gerald could not explain away, however, the aforementioned handwritten note to the lawyer that clearly showed his intention to keep the bulk of their father's estate for himself. Nor could he produce any written document to support his claims that his father, shortly before his death, decided to leave most of his estate to Gerald. Faced with the option of going to court, Gerald decided to reach a financial settlement with his siblings. In my office Gerald said, "Dr Cupchik, I am only here to satisfy my wife's insistence that I do so. Be advised, however, that I have no regret or guilt whatsoever for my behaviour regarding securing the bulk of my father's estate for myself. It was simply his dying wish, and I agreed to comply."

Incidentally, in my interview with Gerald's wife, Gertrude, I was informed that he had a habit of weaving a complex web of misinformation and outright lies for his friends and acquaintances alike. For example, apparently when he spent a year at a foreign university as a researcher,

Gerald introduced himself as an only surviving child of Holocaust survivors (while the truth was that his parents had emigrated to the USA more than a decade before the start of the Second World War and he actually had four living siblings). His wife said that when she occasionally confronted Gerald with his inclination to tell outright lies and invent implausible tales, he merely laughed and said that people chose to believe what they wanted and that no harm was done by his 'stories'. This tendency to lie and deceive was truly a long-time pattern that Gerald carried out with nearly psychopathic ease, refusing to stop even when faced with his wife's frequent expressions of discomfort regarding his behaviour. Having Gerald see me was his wife's last-ditch attempt to get Gerald to finally own up to his thieving and lying behaviours, after which, if he did not deal with these matters, she was seriously considering leaving him.

Such an extreme pattern of frequent deception is much more likely to be perpetrated by Typical Theft Offenders than the theft offenders who are the main subject of this book. As mentioned above, the lack of remorse and shame, even when finally confronted with undeniable evidence of their wrongdoing, is a hallmark of Typical Theft Offenders.

****

A closer examination of the cases of James and Gerald reveals major differences in their motivations, behaviours, the ways in which their criminal acts were carried out, and how they reacted to same.

James represents the classic Atypical Theft Offender while Gerald is an excellent example of a Typical Theft Offender.

In both cases the amounts stolen were substantial, and both James and Gerald used the funds for their own pleasures However, James had clearly suffered from mental and emotional anguish in regard to his theft behaviour, had very likely acted out from a resentful state of mind, and he had experienced considerable remorse in regard to his theft behaviour.

Gerald, on the other hand, had coolly planned to steal from his siblings for several years before their father died, and he neither experienced nor expressed any regret or remorse about his theft behaviour.

When apprehended, James not only admitted his guilt immediately, but refused an opportunity to perhaps gain a 'more favorable' forensic assessment; he did nothing whatsoever to escape the court's full punishment. Meanwhile, Gerald had, for years, continued to deny any wrongdoing, and even when caught red-handed by his siblings, he refused to take responsibility for his actions, claiming he was merely serving their father's wishes.

****

As a way of more formally differentiating between Atypical Theft Offenders and Typical Theft Offenders, in 1996 I developed and regularly employed a questionnaire, the **Cupchik Theft Offender Spectrum,** that further highlights the differences between these two types of theft offenders. Most of the hundreds of clients who I have dealt with over the years score at least one or more answers to the Spectrum's statements in each of the two alternate categories. Not surprisingly, I have had the most success in treating clients whose responses indicate that they are primarily aligned with the Atypical Theft Offender end of the spectrum. On the other hand, it is my clinical opinion that the likelihood of success in rehabilitating individuals such as Gerald, above, is miniscule.

In the next chapter I offer the latest and most up-to-date version of the *Cupchik Theft Offender Spectrum.* Some additional questions have been added to the Spectrum since its earlier editions appeared. The point in providing the Spectrum here is to offer any readers who may be dealing with their own theft behaviour, a means of determining an at least 'first-approximation' or 'rough idea' of where he or she likely belongs along the Atypical Theft Offender←→Typical Theft Offender continuum.

My decades of investigating theft behaviour have convinced me that acts of theft, especially of the seemingly bizarre or nonsensical sort carried out by usually honest, ethical individuals, are almost invariably manifestations of quite complex psychological issues at work. Regardless of how an individual might 'score' when employing the *Cupchik Theft Offender Spectrum,* however, pleased be advised that, while usually a reliable indicator of the degree to which a person may be viewed as primarily an Atypical Theft Offender, *only* an appropriate and thorough clinical assessment carried out with the assistance of a suitably trained and experienced mental health professional, is likely to provide an accurate estimation in this regard. In other words, use the *Cupchik Theft Offender Spectrum* only as a rough guide when attempting to determine your true position along the Spectrum.

PART II

Two Original

Assessment Tools

Help Determine Where

A Theft Offender Belongs

On The ATO-TTO

Continuum

Chapter 5

THE CUPCHIK THEFT OFFENDER SPECTRUM

The latest version of the **Cupchik Theft Offender Spectrum** is offered here so that you may make an initial determination as to whether the theft offender you are concerned about is likely to be an <u>Atypical</u> Theft Offender, a <u>Typical</u> Theft Offender, or a so-called <u>Mixed-type</u> Theft Offender. [You may note that an earlier version of the Cupchik Theft Offender Spectrum was included in my earlier book, *Why Honest People Shoplift Or Commit Other Acts Of Theft*. However, the current version of this device has several more items and has been further refined.]

Instructions for using the Cupchik Theft Offender Spectrum
All questions should be answered and the 'totals' noted. The responses to the questions, when tallied, will be suggestive of whether the offender is of:

* the Atypical Theft Offender type,
* the Typical Theft Offender type, or
* the ATO/TTO - *mixed* type of theft offender.

Caution and Disclaimer:
The results gained by employing the *Cupchik Theft Offender Spectrum* should be considered *suggestive* but <u>not</u> definitive. Theft offender cases are often so complex that it is *very unlikely* that a much more reliable and valid pen-and-paper instrument will *ever* be available in the future to provide a *conclusive* categorization as to the theft offender 'type' in any particular case. It will therefore always remain the task of a suitably trained and experienced clinician to make such a determination. However, the Spectrum does provide a quantifiable resource that may assist in making such a determination.

The Cupchik Theft Offender Spectrum (V-9)

Please note: This version of the Theft Offender Spectrum is intended for use by the purchaser of this book *for one case only.* A request for limited permission to duplicate or adapt this questionnaire for clinical research or other professional purposes should be sent to Dr Cupchik at the above address. See Appendix C for more details.

The following 20 questions, if answered in the affirmative, tend to suggest that '*Atypical* Theft Offender' elements were operating in a particular case: if answered in the negative, they tend to suggest that '*Typical* Theft Offender' elements were operating in a particular case

	CUPCHIK THEFT OFFENDER SPECTRUM **(Part 1)** ISBN: 1-896342-10-8 *C.T.O.S., V9 1996, 2002, 2013 © Will Cupchik . All rights reserved.*	ATO-type	TTO-type
Item #	QUESTION	YES	NO
1	Did the theft offender experience any unusual and/or major <u>losses</u> as a child?		
2	Do these early losses <u>remain largely unresolved</u>, as may be evidenced by the severe intensity of the theft offender's emotional state when referring to these matters?		
3	Was <u>cancer</u>, or any other <u>major illness</u>, an issue existing either in regard to the theft offender or a 'significant other' at about the time of the offence?		
4	Did the offender experience any major <u>personally meaningful losses close to the time of the offence?</u>		
5	Was the offender experiencing <u>marked resentment or anger towards his or her 'intimate other', or any other important person in the theft offender's life</u> at about the time of the offence?		

Item #	QUESTION	YES	NO
6	Did the theft offender steal in such an obvious fashion <u>as if to purposely get caught?</u>		
7	Was the <u>monetary value of all that was taken virtually insignificant</u> when compared to the offender's readily available financial resources?		
8	Would a claim of "<u>partial dissociation</u>" be justified in this case? That is, would it be accurate to say that the offender <u>was not fully aware of what she or he was doing</u> at the time of the offence?		
9	Does the offender <u>attend church or some other spiritually directed group functions</u> on a regular basis?		
10	Was the individual under an <u>unusual or excessive amount of stress</u> at the time of the offence?		
11	Was the offence, at least in part, a <u>symbolic act?</u>		
12	Was the offence likely <u>an attempt to embarrass</u> a 'significant other'?		
13	<u>Is the offender uncomfortable</u> with his or her theft behaviour?		
14	Does the offender appear to be experiencing <u>profound shame, humiliation or embarrassment in regard to the fact of his/her having committed the act</u> (as differentiated from such feelings existing merely in relation to having been caught)?		
15	Did the offender experience <u>verbal, physical and/or sexual abuse</u> as a child?		
16	Was the offender <u>taking prescribed antidepressants</u> at the time of the offence?		

Item #	QUESTION	YES	NO
17	Was the adult offender <u>experiencing marked anger towards one or both parents</u> at the time of the offence?		
18	Did one or both parents have <u>serious alcohol and/or drug abuse</u> problems when the offender was a child?		
19	Has the offender <u>stolen from close friends or relatives?</u>		
20	Does the offender usually experience <u>low self-esteem?</u>		
	Number of items answered "<u>YES</u>", thereby suggesting the offender *may* belong to the <u>Atypical Theft Offender</u> category: ===============>	*A:*	-- -
	Number of items answered "<u>NO</u>" thereby suggesting the offender *may* belong to the <u>Typical Theft Offender</u> category: ===============>	-- -	*B:*

44

The following 13 questions, **if answered in the affirmative**, tend to suggest that '*Typical* Theft Offender' elements were operating in a particular case: **if answered in the negative**, they tend to suggest that '*Atypical* Theft Offender' elements were operating in a particular case:

	CUPCHIK THEFT OFFENDER SPECTRUM (Part 2) *C.T.O.S., V-9 1996, 2002, 2013 © Will Cupchik. All rights reserved.*	ATO -type	TTO -type
Item #	QUESTION	NO	YES
21	Was what was stolen <u>desired</u> by the offender?		
22	Was what was stolen <u>needed</u> by the offender?		
23	Was <u>greed</u> a probable factor?		
24	Was there a <u>conscious premeditation</u> in regard to the theft?		
25	Is stealing <u>an accepted or sanctioned mode of behaviour</u> for the offender's intimate other, peers, or social group?		
26	Was the item or items stolen <u>made use of</u> by the offender for his or her own purposes?		
27	Was any stolen item <u>sold</u> by the offender?		
28	Did the offender <u>give the item to a 'significant other'</u>, i.e. a friend, relative or life partner?		
29	Was the offender, while still a child, <u>'initiated' into stealing</u> by a parent of trusted authority figure?		
30	Was a <u>weapon</u> used during the commission of the offence? *		
31	Has the <u>offender previously been convicted of any other kinds of crimes</u>, e.g. crimes against people or property (such as assault, 'malicious destruction of property' or 'driving while impaired', etc...)?		
32	Does the offender acknowledge being <u>proud</u> of the theft behaviour?		

45

33	Is the theft offender <u>comfortable</u> with his or her theft behaviour?		
	Number of items answered "<u>NO</u>", thereby indicating an inclination to perceive the offender as belonging to the <u>Atypical Theft Offender</u> category: ==============>	**C:**_ _	**--** **-**
	Number of items answered "<u>YES</u>", thereby indicating an inclination to perceive the offender as belonging to the <u>Typical Theft Offender</u> category: =============>	**--** **-**	**D:**_ _
	<u>Total number of items checked off in the 'ATO-type' columns</u> (add together the numbers in boxes "A" and "C") and place the sum in Box "E" ==============>	**E:**_ _	---
	<u>Total number of items checked off in the 'TTO-type' columns</u> (add together the numbers in boxes "B" and "D") and place the sum in Box "F" ================>	---	**F:**_ _

*re Question # 30: If a weapon was used in the commission of the offense, this would virtually exclude the possibility of claiming the Atypical Theft Offender category for this offender, unless there are truly extraordinary circumstances or factors to be taken into account. (As an example, a psychiatric breakdown in response to having just experienced the loss of a child might precipitate such behaviour in some rare cases; the use of a weapon in a theft as a means of prompting the police to take lethal action, often referred to as 'suicide by cop', in the case of a genuinely suicidal individual, might be another.)

==

Discussion: a consideration of the client's scoring of the *Cupchik Theft Offender Spectrum*

By comparing the sums located in boxes *"E"* and *"F"* you will likely be able to make an fairly accurate estimation of which category of theft offender the particular case in question represents.

46

There are essentially only three categories of theft offender to consider:
- **Atypical** Theft Offender type,
- **Typical** Theft Offender type, or
- **Mixed** type (i.e. displaying *substantial* aspects of both categories of theft offenders).

****

1. Atypical Theft Offenders: My extensive forensic experience with theft offenders suggests that if *at least 80% (i.e., 26 or more)* of the thirty-three questions above are answered in the ATO-oriented direction, then the individual may be initially classified with some confidence as an Atypical Theft Offender.

The higher the number of answers in the ATO-oriented direction, the greater the confidence with which a provisional diagnosis of 'Atypical Theft Offender' may be justified.

****

2. Typical Theft Offenders: On the other hand, if *at least 80% (i.e., 26 or more)* of the thirty-three questions above are answered in the TTO-oriented direction, the greater the confidence with which a provisional diagnosis of 'Typical Theft Offender' may be justified.

****

3. Mixed-Type (ATO/TTO): If neither the ATO nor TTO categories receive at least 26 answers in their direction, then the client is more likely to belong to the Mixed-Type of theft offender, possessing substantial amounts of *both* Atypical Theft Offender *and* Typical Theft Offender qualities.

****

Note: On occasion, even Typical Theft Offenders may become so disgusted and distressed by their illegal conduct and/or its devastating effects on their lives and those of others, that some of them may eventually genuinely desire to cease their theft behaviour. Experience with some such clients has shown that the prognoses in such cases, while necessarily guarded, are occasionally positive.

Do keep in mind that the Cupchik Theft Offender Spectrum assists us to *approximate* where, along the length of the Spectrum, the individual theft offender falls. And as also indicated previously, most of the theft offenders I have worked with were *not* 'pure Atypicals' but had a minority of Typical Theft Offender characteristics as well. However, the majority of them have been more Atypical than Typical, according to the Spectrum. For example, while it is true that most of the persons I have worked with *do* express shame and remorse (Atypical traits), many of them have shoplifted items that they *wanted*, either for their own use or for the use of Significant Others, or for reselling (and those are usually hallmarks of Typical Theft Offenders). In this book and for practical purposes therefore, while addressing these matters in working with the clients involved, it should be understood that most of the cases I present are *primarily* but not *purely* Atypical Theft Offenders. As I have throughout this book, for the sake of brevity, as long as the individual scored substantially more items in the 'Atypical' than 'Typical' direction (for at least 80% of the items) on the Theft Offender Spectrum, I have referred to them as Atypical Theft Offenders.

****

In order to offer you, the reader, additional valuable material with which to consider the case of atypical theft behaviour that you may be in interested in examining, in the next chapter I present the latest version of the **Cupchik Theft Offender Questionnaire**, a 61-question pen-and-paper questionnaire that, drawing upon my latest clinical findings, asks what I have learned are relevant questions to be considered when attempting to understand and assist possible Atypical Theft Offenders.

Chapter 6

THE CUPCHIK THEFT OFFENDER
QUESTIONNAIRE

I initially devised the **Cupchik Theft Offender Questionnaire** as a practical pen-and-paper instrument that provides a rapid means of gathering potentially important basic information about any particular client. The C.T.O.Q. is organized into areas that may uncover salient aspects of the theft offender's case and that may help determine whether this client should eventually be categorized as (1) an Atypical Theft Offender, (2) a Typical Theft Offender, or (3) of the Mixed Atypical/Typical type. [As was also true of the Cupchik Theft Offender Spectrum, an earlier version of the Cupchik Theft Offender Questionnaire was included in my earlier book. However, the current version of this device as presented below has more items and has been further refined.]

Cautionary notice:

This questionnaire can be used to assist the theft offender at home, in the therapist's office, and/or in court. Therefore its use should be approached with considerable thought and effort. Theft offenders should utilize the services of a competent professional when completing either or both the *Cupchik Theft Offender Questionnaire* and *the Cupchik Theft Offender Spectrum*. No representation is offered for the level of reliability or validity of these two pen-and-paper instruments.

Instructions for completing the C.T.O.Q.

This questionnaire is meant be filled out by the theft offender client, either prior to, or immediately following the first clinical session. In either case *it will be important for the clinician to go over with the client all the answers to all the items*; clients often miss or dismiss potentially relevant materials because they simply are not aware of the possible connections between their answers and the matters that are the main focus of this book.

CUPCHIK THEFT OFFENDER QUESTIONNAIRE (V6)

ISBN: 1-896342-10-8 Copyright 1996, 2001, 2013 Will Cupchik

<u>Mailing address for feedback regarding this pen-and-paper instrument :</u> Will Cupchik PhD, 2528 Bayview Avenue, PO Box 35532, Toronto, Ontario, Canada M2L 2Y4

To the theft offender: Please fill out this questionnaire as fully as you can; then, go over the answers with your lawyer and/or clinician.

SECTION A: CURRENT INFORMATION

Current Date:___/___/___

Your Name:_____

Age:_____ D.O.B.___/___/___

1) <u>What have you been accused of stealing</u> in regard to the current charge(s)?

2) What is the <u>total dollar value</u> of what you have been accused of taking?
Total value = $_____

3) <u>From whom</u> have you been accused of taking these moneys/materials?
(Name of person, company, institution, etc...)

4) <u>When (and over what period of time)</u> did the alleged activities take place?

5) Have you <u>ever been charged with theft before?</u>
Yes ( ) No ( )

6) If you have been <u>convicted</u> of theft before,
<u>how many times?</u> _____ times

7) Please list in the table below ALL the instances you have stolen, <u>whether you were caught, arrested, charged, convicted, or not.</u> If you need additional space simply make another copy of the form to complete.

Event	Date D/M/Y	What was taken? Describe item(s)	From Where?	Dollar value	Were you charged?	If Convicted, what was the sentence?
i						
ii						
iii						
iv						
v						
vi						
vii						
viii						

8) <u>Describe in as much detail as you can, the most recent incident(s)</u> that led to your coming for this assessment. (Use the other side of this page, if necessary)

9) <u>Describe below what was happening in your life at about the time of the most recent offense(s).</u> Mention any stressors, illnesses, marital or other relationship related problems/issues existing at the time, or events such as the actual or anticipated loss of a job, health, family member; also any change of city, country etc...that may have just proceeded the actions which you are accused of having carried out, and which led to you being here today.

10) <u>For whom</u> was the item (or money) <u>intended?</u>
myself ( );
my spouse ( );
my children ( );
other person(s) ( ). _____

11) If the answer to #10 is "other person(s)," <u>what is the relationship</u> of these persons to you?
friend ( )
lover ( )
in-laws ( )
other ( )_____

12) <u>Did you think/know you were being observed</u> while you carried out the offense?
Yes ( ): No ( )

13) If the answer to #12 is 'Yes" then in your own words<u>, state why you went ahead with the act? What did you say to yourself</u> while you carried out the act?

#14) <u>Did anyone among your friends, family or yourself, have a diagnosis of cancer or other serious illness at the time of the offense?</u>
Yes ( ) No ( )

#15) If the answer to #14 is 'Yes', <u>who</u> is it that had that diagnosis? What is that person's relationship to you?

#16) Would you say that you had experienced, or were anticipating experiencing, any <u>personally meaningful loss(es)</u> at around the time of the offense?
Yes ( ) No ( )

#17) If the answer to #16 is 'Yes', please <u>describe the actual or anticipated loss(es).</u>
-
-

18) Are you <u>married</u> or <u>living common law</u> with someone?
Yes ( ) No ( )

19) If married or living common law, how would you <u>describe the current state of your relationship with your 'significant other' at the time of the offence</u>?
(<u>circle</u> one of the following)

Excellent Very Good Good Fair Poor Very Poor

****

SECTION B: BACKGROUND

20) <u>your age:</u> _____

21) <u>Gender:</u> male_____ female_____

22) <u>Are you ... (check all that apply)</u>....
- **married_____**
- **living common-law_____**
- **separated? _____**
- **divorced? _____ If divorced, how many times? _____**
- **single? _____**

23) In what country were you <u>born</u>?
 (i) United States_____
 (ii) Canada _____
 (iii) Other: _____
 (iv) Which country?_____

The following questions deal with your biological or adoptive parents, your childhood, etc...

24) Your <u>father's first name:</u>_____

25) Where was he <u>born?</u>_____

26) Is he <u>still living?</u> Yes ( ) No ( )

27) If your father is still alive, what is his <u>current age:</u>_____

28) If alive, what is the <u>state of his health?</u>

29) Your <u>mother's first name:</u>_____

30) Where was she <u>born?</u>_____

31) Is she <u>still living?</u> Yes ( ) No ( )

32) If your mother is still alive, what is her <u>current age?</u>_____

33) If alive, what is <u>the state of her health?</u>

****

Regarding early separations, losses:

34) <u>When you were a child, were you separated from either or both of your parents for any substantial length of time?</u>
Yes ( ) No ( )

If you have answered "Yes" to this question, <u>please explain:</u>

C.T.O.Q.-V6 copyright Dr Will Cupchik 2013 All Rights Reserved. .

35) Please think back carefully: did you experience any (other) personally meaningful losses or traumatic experiences as a child?
Yes ( ) No ( )

Note: If adopted, at what age were you adopted? _____

If your answer is 'yes' to Question 35, then please describe these losses or trauma below.:
-
-
-

****

Further information about the most recent offense

36) What was your general feeling state at about the time of the offense?
(a) positive feeling state _____
or
(b) negative feeling state_____

37) Were you depressed just prior to the offense?
Yes ( )
No ( )

38) If the answer to #37 was 'Yes', *what* were you depressed about? In detail please.
-
-
-

39) Were you experiencing anger towards anyone in particular at about the time of the theft?
Yes ( )
No ( )

40) If your answer to #39 is 'Yes,' <u>towards whom</u> were you experiencing anger? _____

41) <u>What</u> were you angry about with this person?

_____

42) <u>What stressors were you experiencing at about the time of the offense?</u>

43) What was happening in your life [work-related, personal, familial – i.e., with your life partner, parent(s), or child(ren)], just prior (earlier the same day or perhaps the previous day or so)] to your most recent act of theft? Please also indicate whether you were feeling frustration, resentment, disappointment, sadness, anger or any other negative feelings in regard to any person, circumstances or situation, shortly before you stole? Be specific.
-
-
-
-

44) <u>Did you use a weapon in the commission of the offense, and if so, what was it?</u>

Yes _____ and it was a: _____ *or* No_____

45) <u>Have you previously been convicted of any other kinds of crimes</u>, e.g. crimes against people or property (such as assault, or 'malicious destruction of property') or 'driving while impaired', etc..."
Yes_____ No_____

46) <u>If</u> your answer to question 44 is 'Yes', please describe the charges, and the details regarding these events, below.

47) What else about you, your theft behaviour, or your circumstances would you like your helping professional (clinician, lawyer, etc...) to know, or think that person probably *should* know in order to be of assistance to you in this matter?
-
-
-
-

48) How old are you now? _____ How old were you at the time you *first* stole *anything* (e.g., money, toys, other things)? _____

49) Have you ever used antidepressants that were prescribed for you?
Yes_____   or   No_____

50) At what age did you first use antidepressants? _____

51) What is/are the brand name(s) of the antidepressant(s) you have used?

_____ , _____ , _____

52) Did you ever steal <u>before</u> you began using antidepressants?
Yes___   No___

53) Have you ever stolen <u>while</u> you were taking prescribed antidepressants? Yes_____   No_____

54) Are you <u>currently</u> taking an antidepressant? Yes_____   No_____

55) If you are <u>currently</u> using an antidepressant, what is it called? _____ For how long have you been taking an antidepressant? _____days *or* _____ months *or* _____ years

****

56) <u>If you have been taking an antidepressant for longer than three months, *and* you have also stolen during that period, then check off which of the following statements would you say is the most accurate:</u>

(a) My stealing *frequency*, i.e., how frequently I have been stealing while I have been using the antidepressant, has <u>decreased</u>.
Yes _____ No_____

(b) My stealing *frequency*, i.e., how often I have been stealing, while I have been using the antidepressant, has <u>increased</u>.
Yes _____ No_____

(c) My stealing *frequency*, i.e., how often I have been stealing while I have been using the antidepressant, <u>has been about the same</u> as when I was *not* taking the antidepressant.
Yes _____ No_____ Not Applicable_____

57) Who, <u>in your personal life</u>, knows about <u>any</u> of your stealing?
My life partner: Yes_____ No_____
My parent(s): Yes_____ No_____
My child(ren), if any: Yes_____ No_____
Friend(s): Yes_____ No_____

58) Who, in your personal life, <u>knows about the full extent</u> of your stealing?

_____

59

59. How <u>supportive</u> do you think your spouse/partner would be if he/she knew the full extent of your stealing? *Does* he/she <u>really</u> know the FULL extent of your theft behaviour?

_____

_____

60. As far as you know, has your spouse/partner ever stolen?
Yes _____ No _____

61. If your spouse/partner has stolen, did you both steal on at least one occasion at the same time and from the same place?
Yes _____ No _____

The individual's responses to the *Cupchik Theft Offender Questionnaire* **will frequently suggest a pattern** that may be very useful in helping to understand the theft offender and his or her thinking, feelings, circumstances and actions in relation to the theft behaviour. This information may assist the clinician in determining whether the offender is more appropriately to be viewed as an *Atypical* Theft Offender, a *Typical* Theft Offender, or an ATO/TTO *Mixed-type* Theft Offender. This determination, of course, may be of major relevance to the defence and prosecuting attorneys, to the judges that must deal with the case, and the clinician who may wish to offer appropriate treatment.

PART III

Atypical Theft Behaviour

May Involve

All Three Levels

(Conscious, Subconscious
& Unconscious)

Of The Offender's Mind

Chapter 7

THE CONSCIOUS, SUBCONSCIOUS AND UNCONSCIOUS LEVELS OF THE HUMAN PSYCHE AND HOW THEY INFLUENCE ATYPICAL THEFT BEHAVIOUR

While surely nearly all of us accept that we have a **conscious** mind, and agree with Descartes that there is some sense of validity to the notion of "I think (i.e., I am consciously aware of thinking), therefore I am," I appreciate that there may still be some readers who, even now, in the year 2013, might be reluctant to take for granted the existence -let alone the remarkable dynamic powers- of the **subconscious** and **unconscious** levels of the human psyche.

I offer many examples in this book of instances of theft behaviour by usually honest persons that should assist in making such conduct more understandable by referring to what may have been going on in the different layers of the Atypical Theft Offender's mind. Now, however, let me offer a metaphor that I often provide to my clients to assist them in appreciating and accepting the likelihood that these three major levels of the human mind exist and may be operating to promote their stealing.

The three levels of consciousness: a metaphor and some examples
Imagine if you will, a large iceberg floating in the ocean. As you may recall from your high school science classes, approximately 90% of an iceberg is submerged below the surface of the water. In other words, we only get to see the top 10% of the berg that is above the waterline.

Now imagine then that our minds are also rather like icebergs, in the sense that *most* of their contents and mechanisms are out of sight, i.e., out of our **conscious** awareness. Can I offer some evidence of this appropriateness of this analogy? Yes! If someone were to ask you for your date of birth, could you tell him or her? *Surely!* What about your phone number; could you tell them what it is? *Of course!* But from where did you access that information? Unless you were **consciously** thinking of your date of birth (or cell phone number) at the very moment that you had been asked for it, then it was not in your **conscious** mind at that moment. But you, in effect, 'reached into your <u>subconscious</u> mind' to 'retrieve' that information, and... lo and behold, the date or number appeared in your **conscious** mind.

The 'memory' of your computer or tablet or smartphone operates in a similar fashion. On its screen at any moment may be all that of which you are currently (or wish to be) **consciously** aware. But, if you want to bring another program, file or app up onto the screen, you have only to ask your computer for that which it has in its memory (its **subconscious**, if you will) and sure enough, it will likely display on its screen (i.e., in its **consciousness**), the program, file or app that you want.

You may also be aware that, even if you were not able to momentarily retrieve some item of information (e.g., the name of an acquaintance or of a movie you saw recently), then, assuming you *ever* had that data, it likely still resides somewhere in your mind. Older folks sometimes find that they need to **consciously** concentrate quite deliberately before they can 'retrieve' the piece of information they were seeking from wherever it was 'hiding' (i.e., *not* in the **conscious** part of their minds).

Indeed, even when we attempt to *erase* a file from our computer, tech wizards may well be able to retrieve that very material from the deeper innards of the device. (To minimize the likelihood of such information retrieval from ever taking place, a mechanical engineering friend of mine who is very tech savvy and who also happens to be in the construction business, told me that when he wants to ensure that one of his no-longer-in-use computers or smartphones will not be able to divulge any trade secrets or other confidential information to anyone, he brings it to a construction site and asks one of the bulldozer operators to kindly pass the tracks of the machine back and forth, several times, over the device.)

It is obvious that none of us could possibly hold *all* the information that we have acquired over the years in our **conscious** mind, all at the same instant of time. That would be rather like listening to all available radio stations, all at the same time. Talk about 'information overload'! So, just as your radio has a filter (an analog or digital 'dial' that allows you to access only one station at a single moment, say 102.4 on your FM dial, for example), your **conscious** mind has a filter or gatekeeper that allows only a limited amount of information to be present in the **conscious** mind at any one time. (Incidentally, research has been done that shows that most persons – even including chess grandmasters - can only be aware of a maximum of seven (7) discrete or separate bits of information in their **conscious** minds *at any one instant*.)

To take a third very common example, when you last travelled from home to work or to the mall, it is highly likely that your **conscious** mind 'wandered' from time to time, i.e., your **conscious** mind may have been focused upon a personal or work-related matter, and yet (with any luck) you were able to walk or drive safely from home to work or the shopping mall. *How did you do that?*

Well, at least in part, your **subconscious** mind was ensuring that you got from A to B safely, making sure to pay sufficient attention to traffic signals and signs, and instructing your hands, at suitable times, to turn the wheel of your car and move your feet to operate the accelerator or brake pedal in a timely and appropriate fashion. Of course, if you don't pay *sufficient* **conscious** attention to where and how you are walking or driving, you may be more likely to have an accident, or go past your intended destination. Therefore it is vital that all of us pay *at least just enough* **conscious** attention to get tasks done safely. As we all know, however, many accidents do occur when we are *not* maintaining sufficient **conscious** attention to the task at hand.

The <u>periphery</u> of the conscious mind

Please consider the words you are now reading. As you are reading these words, you are likely **consciously** focusing on only one word or phrase at any one instant. However, you are able to make sense of the meaning of the collection of 10, 15 or more words that are making up this sentence, in part because of your short-term memory allows you to 'hold' onto the other words that are making up this sentence. These other words may be said to be on the *periphery* of your **conscious** mind.

To take another example, the last time you may have driven somewhere, and let us say the traffic light turned red, then for an instant, you may have been focused upon the red traffic light. At the very same moment, however, you were likely also seeing (though not necessarily attending to, in the *focus* of your consciousness) several other things; pedestrians, bicycles and/or cars that were also in your field of vision. Of course, in order to drive safely from point A to point B, you have to be simultaneously aware of many things in your field of vision, as well in your rear and/or side view mirrors.

How do you do it all? By paying attention to all that your senses pick up, even as you may from one moment to another, attend in particular to only one or a few of all the discrete pieces the information you are receiving. For example, while driving, if the driver of the car ahead of you puts on his brakes, for a moment you may pay particular attention to that car's slowing down. A moment later, the person crossing the street at the light draws the *focus* of your attention. The point is, even as you and I may have a lot of information available to us at any moment, we make the *focus* of our attention (i.e., of our **consciousness**) only a portion of all that information. But the rest of information did not go away; rather, the *focus* of our attention is drawn to only *some* of it at any single moment.

Likewise, when an Atypical Theft Offender goes to a mall, soon after, say, having had a particularly upsetting confrontation with his or her boss or spouse, that person's *focus* of **conscious** attention may be drawn towards an item of clothing or some food, and while the individual who had been confronted a while earlier may not now be the *focus* of attention while looking at the clothes or food, the emotional responses to the earlier encounter likely still linger. The theft offender may not, at the moment of choosing to steal an item, be 'attending' (i.e., paying focused conscious attention) to the anger he or she is feeling towards the other individual; yet the anger is likely there. And if only the clinician will inquire, thoroughly, into *what was happening in the theft offender's life just prior to the act of stealing,* the recent argument and the feelings of anger that were still being borne while the theft offender was at the mall, will likely be identified and mentioned. The fact that the person was not necessarily *focusing* upon the anger at the time of the theft does not mean that it was not there. It also does not necessarily mean that the anger was in the individual's subconscious or unconscious – although that is also possible. More likely, in the example being presented here, the feelings of anger may have been, at least at moments, in the **periphery** of the theft offender's **consciousness**.

The *sub*conscious and *un*conscious layers of our minds
Now, the difference between the <u>**subconscious**</u> and <u>**unconscious**</u> parts of our minds is that we can usually rather easily access the information located in our <u>**subconscious**</u> (i.e., out of 'conscious

awareness' but not 'buried and hard to access'). However, if something is in our **unconscious** mind it can be much harder to bring into **conscious** awareness.

A most remarkable illustration of an unconscious mind refusing to give up some of its contents to conscious awareness, even while clearly impacting overt behaviour.
One of the most dramatic examples that I have ever learned about, of important material being 'buried' in the **unconscious** mind yet nevertheless influencing present observable behaviour, was described in an article published (if I recall correctly, in the *British Journal of Psychiatry*) a few decades ago. I came upon this article as I was researching clinical studies that involved the influence of past events upon current behaviour. The article described the curious case of a man (lets call him David) who had been a soldier in WWII, and who, after the war was over, returned to his home and went back to a factory and the work he had done there before the war began. However, he soon began missing work from time to time, and eventually refused outright to return to work.

David would mostly spend his days either on the front porch of his home, or increasingly, inside his home. After another period of time he even seldom ventured outside his bedroom, but could offer his family no plausible reason for not wanting to leave that room. He could only tell them that when he even considered leaving the bedroom or glanced towards the bedroom door, he became extremely anxious; he did not **consciously** know why.

Well, an indication of how different times were then from present day, was that, upon learning of this man's most curious behaviour, not one but *two* psychiatrists from the nearby mental hospital actually made a *home visit* to interview him. Unfortunately, even their highly skilled interviewing techniques failed to extract from David any plausible explanation as to why it was that he wouldn't leave his bedroom. The mere discussion of the topic, however, was clearly extremely anxiety provoking for him.

In a final, desperate attempt to learn why David was behaving in such a curious and self-limiting manner, the psychiatrists asked for permission to administer to him sodium pentothal, a so-called 'truth serum'. David agreed to their request. Once under the influence of the drug, finally, a story emerged from David's **unconscious**, one that was later confirmed as entirely truthful, but one that he had failed to access or recall and bring to his **conscious** mind prior to that time, even when repeatedly asked whether he had ever experienced any particularly disturbing event that might help explain his reluctance to leave his bedroom. It turned out that David's high anxiety, whenever it was suggested that he come out of the bedroom, was related to a truly dramatic, and indeed *traumatic*, experience that he had had during the war.

Here's the backstory that emerged that helped explain David's reluctance to pass through the bedroom door.
David had been a paratrooper during the World War II. During that conflict, the British military sometimes used huge gliders filled with paratroopers that were towed behind bombers, flown into enemy territory, and the soldiers then parachuted down to the ground, regrouped, and went off on their missions. On one particular such mission, however, a typical 'night drop' on a moonless night behind the enemy's lines, David's parachute took him away from the intended landing zone and he was unable to find his comrades.

After two hours of searching for his fellow soldiers through the dense forest, and with dawn's first light fast approaching, David decided that it was in his best interest to find a hiding place before it became fully daytime. He eventually made out the shape of a large barn in middle of a field and decided to hide out there. However, when he opened the door of the barn, he came upon several German soldiers who had decided to sleep the night away in the very same barn. Because they were supposedly safe, miles behind their own lines, no sentry had been posted, or if there was supposed to be one, he had dozed off, and so David immediately found that he 'had the drop' on the enemy.

Naturally terrified that he would be overwhelmed if he let his guard down, or if these now captive enemy soldiers were to shout out or rush him, David somehow kept the soldiers under control, and furthermore, he managed to stay awake for the next 36 hours. What's more, he actually managed to march his prisoners to -and through- their own lines and then handed them over to his comrades once they had reached the British position. Needless to say he was highly applauded for his heroic deed, given a few days off for R&R and then was returned to the battle. He fulfilled the duties that were required of him until the end of the war, at which time he returned home and took up his life – at least until he began to not want to go out of his home, and eventually through the door of his bedroom.

The two psychiatrists wrote in their ensuing article that they had concluded that David had *repressed*, that is, buried in his **unconscious**, the fear, dread, horror and shock - in fact the entire episode of what he had endured, as described above. At that time he had no opportunity, as we would say nowadays, to 'process' his experience and deal with his post-traumatic stress with a suitably trained mental health worker. He simply had to 'get on with it', as his countrymen might be inclined to say. However, after the war was over and by the time that it *was* safe to 'process' his wartime experience, he had already buried into his **unconscious** mind his collection of thoughts, feelings and images of what he had experienced when he opened that barn door. That experience and its accompanying thoughts, feelings and images, though repressed, nevertheless clearly were responsible for the anxiety that he consciously experienced (without recognizing why) whenever he considered passing through any door, and specifically the door of his bedroom.

Repression of thoughts, images and emotions into the unconscious

It often happens that difficult or traumatic experiences are 'repressed' into the **unconscious**. Childhood sexual abuse is frequently handled in the same way at the time it occurs, as are many instances of various horrific events that were experienced in wartime or due to natural or man-made disasters. Indeed, a few years ago an article appeared in the American Psychological Association's monthly *Monitor* publication, relating the fact that many American soldiers from the Vietnam era, who had seemingly made reasonable adjustments back into civilian life afterwards, were beginning to reach retirement age. With much less to distract them once they ceased working, the unresolved thoughts, emotions and images pertaining to what they had endured during the Vietnam conflict were evidently beginning to 'surface' into **conscious** awareness and many of these men and women began seeking refuge in drugs and alcohol.

I wrote a 'letter to the editor' of the APA *Monitor* in response to that article (that was itself published in a subsequent edition of the Monitor), suggesting that these individuals had likely placed (i.e., *repressed*) many of the thoughts, emotions and/or images associated with the horrors they experienced, into their **unconscious** minds. Their day-to-day activities once they were back stateside after serving in Vietnam, allowed them to distract themselves from confronting and dealing with that wartime material. However, once their children had grown up and gone off to take up their own lives, and once they had 'time on their hands' after they retired, it was much harder for them to avoid the very disturbing material from their Vietnam experiences that was pressing for entry into their **conscious** minds. Drink and drugs were the means often employed in the attempt to keep the previously repressed material at bay (i.e., back into the **unconscious**, or at least the **subconscious** layer of mind).

The human mind as a three-layered pyramid

Diagram # 1: The Levels of the Mind Pyramid

Conscious layer of mind

Subconscious layer of mind

Unconscious layer of mind

A helpful way to think of the human mind is to consider it as consisting of three layers, one placed on top of the other, so that they form a pyramid. Like most pyramids, the *bottom layer* is the largest, and that one could be considered to be our **unconscious** minds – a huge reservoir of past and present thoughts, feelings (or emotions), sensations, experiences and memories of which we are not consciously aware of, and which are usually inaccessible even when we deliberately attempt to access that material. Imagine also that the top part of this layer consists, in effect, of a mostly impenetrable cover. This cover does provide for some 'leakage' however, especially when we are asleep; the leakage is often evidenced by the content of our dreams. While awake we may also experience some leakage that occurs during so-called Freudian slips (as when one 'accidentally' says something out loud that was not consciously intended but which has, for us, some validity, and as also can be evidenced during some 'Eureka!' moments of insight).

The middle layer of the pyramid is also sizeable though not nearly as large as the bottom layer, of course, and represents our **subconscious** mind, that is, that part of our minds that contain the thoughts, emotions, sensations, experiences and memories of which we are not **consciously** aware *at a given moment* but can be relatively easily accessed should we choose to. For example, you, the reader, were likely not thinking of your phone number when you began to read this sentence. However, if I ask for it, as I am now doing, you likely can easily access the number from your **subconscious** storehouse of data.

The top layer of the mind's pyramid is the smallest; it represents our **conscious** mind, i.e., that of which we are knowingly aware at any single moment. As mentioned previously, research shows that most of us are only capable, at best, of holding in conscious awareness a maximum of seven discrete pieces of information in any one instant.

Together the three layers of the pyramid structure described above essentially represent the totality of the layers of a human mind.

Supposedly *simple* everyday decision-making can be anything but, and our education systems often fail to recognise this fact.
Five decades ago I was employed for few years as a high school math and science teacher. From my experiences then, as well as from the more recent data I have acquired about how many school courses are still being taught, I am convinced that our educational systems often provide an incomplete appreciation of the *many factors* that are usually involved in the making of *even* our supposedly *simplest* decisions.

So now, I will shortly offer you, the reader, the same exercise that I invite most of my clients to do and that demonstrates the multilayered elements of our decision-making. This exercise helps us appreciate the likely multiplicity of reasons behind someone doing anything as inherently risky and potentially self-destructive as, say, shoplifting.

Just before you do the exercise described below let me reiterate that I believe it is a great failing of most of school systems in North America and elsewhere, that teachers in most courses insist that students provide a *single* 'correct' answer to each question they are asked, either during class or on written exams. While it is true that some subjects/questions do indeed lend themselves to a single correct answer to a direct question (such as, "What is the sum of the two numbers, 8 and 9?"), other subjects, perhaps including literature and history, and certainly social studies and the psychology of human motivation, might well have several more than merely *one* correct answer to the type of question that teachers usually ask.

For example, there might be *several* answers to the question, "Why did the USA invade Iraq in 2003?" As many of us now know, the reasons we have all heard often included one or more of the following: (1) Iraq had weapons of mass destruction; (2) Iraq was a threat to the USA at the time; (3) to bring democracy to that part of the Middle East; (4) Saddam Hussein was an evil man; (5) to secure and control the oil production in that country; (6) to protect Iraq from the influence of Iran, etc... . Now, some (or even all) of these 'reasons' may be valid, at least in part (or not). The point of the following exercise is to make it entirely clear that, **even when it comes to making 'simple' decisions about some of the most seemingly mundane matters, there may well be *many* reasons for what we choose to do or not do.**

****

Exercise # 1: The Multiple Reasons Behind An Everyday Decision
Please write down at least <u>ten</u> reasons why you are wearing the shirt (or blouse, pants, skirt, or decorative jewellery) that you are now wearing. If you find that you are only able to think of one or two or three reasons, just take the time to come up with six or seven more. Do that now, before you read any further, and once you have carried out the exercise on your own, then go ahead and read the following paragraph.

Most folks, when asked to carry out this exercise, at first usually provide only one or two reasons for wearing, let us say, the shirts they have on. I have found, however, that when pressed to come up with other reasons why an individual is wearing *that* particular shirt at *this* particular time, several other answers are relatively easily forthcoming. For example, an individual might first say something like, "I am wearing it because I really like this shirt." As he or she ponders the question further, other answers such as the following, might well emerge.

1. *I like the color*
2. *It was the first thing I saw when I opened my closet this morning*
3. *It goes well with the pants/skirt I am wearing*
4. *I like the feel of the material*
5. *It was already clean and pressed*
6. *Today was going to be a dreary day, weather-wise, and this shirt cheers me up*
7. *Not too many people have seen me wear this shirt*
8. *I was going to meet a friend after work, and I wanted to wear something appropriate*
9. *I think that I look good in this shirt*
10. *I had a presentation to give at work today and so I wanted to wear something that looked business-casual*
11. *My (Significant Other) bought it for me as a present and I thought he/she would appreciate the fact that I was wearing it, especially as we had had an argument last night*
12. *Since I recently lost weight this shirt now fits me especially well, and*
13. *I know it looks expensive and I suppose I wanted to look my 'successful best' when I saw one of our most important clients.*

It is most *un*likely that at the time you chose your shirt this morning, that you were **consciously** aware of *all* of the reasons why you selected that particular shirt and eventually listed as your responses to the question posed in the exercise. And yet, there is likely a good deal of validity to several of the answers you gave, just as there has been for the many hundreds of my clients who have carried out this very same exercise over the years. Incidentally, experience has shown that it is often the *later* reasons that clients come up with that are often among the most pertinent.

There are also likely *several* reasons why an act of atypical theft behaviour has occurred

Now, if there are somewhere in the order of *ten* reasons or so why we are wearing the shirts or tops we have on, and if there are also several reasons for most of the many other decisions we have made and actions we have taken today, then surely it is reasonable to speculate that when an individual who has more than sufficient funds, *chooses* to steal something and thereby risks jeopardizing so very much in terms of reputation, job, etc..., then there are also likely *many* reasons also for that person having committed the act of theft. And it is usually only by exploring the three layers of the individual's mind for the possible answers to the question of "And *why else* might you have stolen, rather than paid for, that book (pen, hat, underwear, etc...)?" are we likely to arrive at the various likely reasons.

Why it is essential to determine *all* (or at least, *most* of) the likely reasons for an act of atypical theft behaviour.
You may have heard the expression, 'garbage in; garbage out'. That expression usually refers to the fact that if a computer is inputted erroneous information, it will likely spew out faulty 'answers'. So it is with medical, psychological or automotive matters. If we do not give our physicians, psychotherapists or auto mechanics clear and complete descriptions of the problem we are dealing with, then it will likely be that much harder (if not impossible) for the professional involved to arrive at a correct diagnosis and then provide appropriate subsequent treatment.

The same sort of thing happens when dealing with Atypical Theft Offenders. Until and unless we uncover at least *most* of the likely reasons for their theft behaviours, we will be unlikely to be able to help those individuals stop their stealing. And my clinical experience clearly indicates that there are indeed almost invariably *several* reasons for a generally honest person's atypical theft behaviour. Furthermore, Atypical Theft Offenders are seldom able to accurately explain to themselves, never mind to their lawyers or the courts, why they did such a seemingly ridiculous thing as steal an item they could easily have paid for, and for perhaps having done so in front of a person they even suspected of being a loss prevention worker or store clerk (as I have had several clients admit they did). So, now, let's consider the kinds of answers I have encountered again and again to the question, *"And why else might you have stolen?"*

At the **conscious** level, the initial explanations (if any) that most clients offer for their theft behaviour will tend to be rather mundane; e.g., the individual might say, "I wanted it," or, "I didn't want to pay for it," or, "There was a long line-up at the cash register and I was in a hurry," or, "I don't know; I guess I did it for a thrill." Now, these sorts of 'reasons' may have *some* validity in particular instances. However, if the theft offender is, let us say, a popular and easily recognizable public school teacher, and let us add that she has stolen from a store across the street from her school that is often frequented by her students and their parents and where she is a regular customer, (and I have had very many clients who were known and recognized customers of the stores where they stole), it surely does not seem rational for that person to risk stealing the item, being caught and possibly losing her job or teaching license for an item worth perhaps just a few dollars, merely because she "wanted it" or "was in a hurry" or "for a thrill."

[As I have pointed out time and time again to reporters and others who have brought up the "for a thrill" excuse, most of the Atypical Theft Offenders I have dealt with had more than enough financial and/or other resources such that they could easily have done one or other 'thrilling' things (e.g.,, downhill skiing, paragliding, biking on city streets, etc....) that would *not* involve committing a crime and risking loss of reputation, job or even their freedom.. Atypical Theft Offenders, I strongly suggest, do not steal 'for the thrill', although, because they themselves almost invariably do not understand the reasons for their theft behaviour, they may readily accept the superficial excuse of wanting to 'have a thrill' because they truly do not (consciously) know any better reason for their conduct.]

And *why else* **might the individual have chosen to steal** *that* **particular item on** *that* **particular day from** *that* **particular store?**
It is the intensive search for the additional answers to this question that is one of the most fascinating aspects of working with Atypical Theft Offenders. What my decades of clinical work in this area of atypical theft behaviour have shown me, time and again, is that there are almost invariably *several* contributing reasons as to *why* the individual did *what* he did and *when* he did it. *And in order to successfully* <u>*treat*</u> *the theft offender, it is absolutely essential that these reasons be uncovered.* Not surprisingly, most of the reasons for risking so much for (usually) so little in monetary terms will be found at the **subconscious** and **unconscious** levels of the theft offender's mind. And accessing these reasons requires a great deal of skill and training on the part of the professional involved in the case.

****

[It may be opportune at this point to mention that, as the reader may already be aware, different mental health professionals have a very wide variety of markedly diverse models of the human psyche. For example, some few professionals still believe that the unconscious mind and/or emotions do not even exist! I well recall attending a major conference of psychologists during which a panel discussion was devoted to discussing various theories of the human mind. At one point, one of the panellists fervently stated his belief that there was "no observable scientific evidence whatsoever" that emotions, including those of sadness and anger, actually existed. As that panellist was putting forward his argument, his voice rose in volume and ferocity and his face turned beet red – observable characteristics that many might say indicated that he was indeed likely experiencing strong emotions at that point. As the atmosphere in the room became increasingly tense during his protestations that emotions do not exist, someone rather close to me said in a soft stage whisper, "I attend his university classes; we all know he is out of his tree – he doesn't believe emotions exist, yet he sure seems terribly angry almost all of the time and his head looks like it is going to explode!" The muted laughter by those within earshot of that remark seemed to suggest that the comment had been met with considerable agreement.]

In order to illustrate many of the above points regarding the various reasons - **conscious, subconscious** and **unconscious**- that may be involved in cases of atypical theft behaviour, consider if you will:

Case # 7: Margaret: The childless obstetrician who repeatedly stole items from children's specialty stores

Dr Margaret Black (a pseudonym, of course) was a popular and highly skilled obstetrician in her mid forties. Married for over fifteen years to a very successful litigation lawyer, they lived a seemingly enviable life in a prestigious part of a major metropolitan city in the American northwest. With a large city home (totally paid for), two luxury cars, and a magnificent getaway villa in Hawaii, most of their friends and neighbors could be excused for thinking that the Blacks were living large the American dream.

Only two close friends and her immediate family members knew that Margaret had already experienced three miscarriages in the previous five years and she was very reluctantly coming to accept the likelihood that she and her husband would not have any children of their own – a heartfelt desire she had held since her earliest years growing up in a large family. After the last miscarriage her own obstetrician/gynecologist stated that she would be very unlikely to be able to conceive and successfully hold to term, a pregnancy of her own. Upon receiving that prognosis, Margaret became very disconsolate; she slipped into a depression, and months later her physician prescribed an antidepressant to help her cope with her response to the apparently final word on the subject of not being able to give birth. Up to the time she began taking the antidepressant Margaret had never shoplifted; her theft behaviour began within a week of her beginning to take the drug.

Meantime, day after day, Margaret's work involved being the go-to doctor for very many women who were experiencing difficult pregnancies. Indeed, Margaret had developed a well-deserved fine reputation for handling the most difficult cases and helping so many women to successfully conceive entirely healthy children. And unbeknownst to most of her colleagues, nearly every day after she learned that the likelihood of her bringing a child of her own to term was miniscule, Dr Black spent time in the privacy of her own office, quietly sobbing. And nearly every night when she returned home from work, she would slip into a profoundly dark place from which her husband could not easily reach her.

Over a period of months following receiving the 'final word' on the matter of being able to conceive a child, Margaret developed the occasional practice of stopping on her way home after work to do some window-shopping at a nearby upscale mall. After she began taking the antidepressant she had been prescribed, more often than not her mall-time involved some shoplifting. Amazingly, even though she shoplifted literally many dozens of items from high-end children's clothing and toy stores in the mall, she had not been apprehended, let alone charged. The fact that she was always elegantly dressed and carried herself with the authority that befitted an experienced and highly respected medical doctor may have made her an unlikely subject for a loss prevention professional, let alone a retail sales clerk, to scrutinize.

Of course, there was that one time that she had been stopped after she left her favorite children's clothing store, when she had been found to have stuffed into the store's large shopping bag, a beautifully-decorated pink sleeper that would have happily graced a delighted infant child getting ready for bed. Margaret eagerly showed the clerk who stopped her the receipt for over $250 worth of clothes and other items that she had just purchased at the store, items meant for her siblings' and friends' children. She assured the clerk that the sleeper had likely been absentmindedly placed into the bag as she was reaching into her purse for her credit card. Taken aback by this mature professional person's strong assertion, the young clerk had fumbled about for the right words of apology, unsure as to whether the item in question had indeed been deliberately shoplifted. As Margaret recounted this story she smiled nervously, acknowledging that it had been a 'close call' but that she was relieved she had thought of a reasonably plausible excuse.

The main reason Margaret contacted me was that her siblings had become aware of her theft behaviour, with at least one of them having been shopping with Margaret for a mutual friend's son's third birthday present, when the sibling saw 'Maggie' take a child's small toy truck off of the shelf and put it into her large purse. When Margaret was confronted by her siblings, after initially denying the theft she finally confessed to not only that occasion of stealing, but to numerous others as well. The siblings agreed that they would not inform any other family members nor Margaret's husband, but only if she sought and received professional help. After a thorough Internet search using keywords such as *shoplifting, theft, stealing*, and *kleptomania*, Margaret read my previous book, *Why Honest People Shoplift or Commit Other Acts of Theft*, and contacted me to work with her via Skype, using the 20-session Intensive Intervention Program I have been employing over the past several years.

As the reader might surmise, Margaret needed to come to terms with the loss of the possibility of her own childbearing ability, and also had to address the other, in her opinion much less satisfactory options, including adopting one or more children and/or possibly putting her maternal energies into caring for a pet. Also, she needed to open lines of communication with her husband in regard to all of these matters, as well as the growing distance between them that had increased over the previous few years. Thankfully, Margaret's husband proved to be an excellent counseling candidate and together with Margaret and myself in marital therapy sessions, these two individuals' mutual love and affection helped them to confront and work through their feelings in regard to these and other related matters. As they did so, Margaret reported that her desire to shoplift had largely evaporated.

In our work together Margaret had reported that she was **consciously** aware of resenting paying "so much" for children's items (mostly clothes and toys) for her siblings' and friends' children. As we explored her stealing activities further, she came to recognize that, whenever she was shopping for someone else's children, she felt a marked **conscious** discomfort. She was also increasingly **consciously** aware that her feelings of envy, anger and disappointment had likely been residing in her **subconscious** and **unconscious** for the previous few years. It is my clinical opinion that, once she was placed on antidepressant medication, the acknowledged side effects of the drug, which included (as is the case for most, if not all, prescribed antidepressants) a potential for increased *hostility, aggressiveness, disinhibition* and an *inclination to become involved in self-destructive behaviour*, likely helped precipitate Margaret's shoplifting.

In 1983 Dr Atcheson and I formulated the **Loss Substitution by Shoplifting Hypothesis** to help explain the atypical theft behaviour that we had noted in the cases of so many of our clients who had experienced what for them were 'perceived unfair personally meaningful losses'. According to this hypothesis, *"In response to experiencing or anticipating experiencing what are perceived to be 'unfair personally meaningful losses', some individuals are inclined to cause someone or someplace else (for example, a department store) to experience unfair losses, by shoplifting."* The loss of the ability to bear and give birth to a child is one that is very emotionally painful for many women, in particular those who have not had any children of their own but very much wished they had. It is my clinical opinion that such feelings of loss, sadness and disappointment were difficult for Margaret to bear, especially because her life's work was a daily reminder of what she was missing. However, she had not shoplifted even though she was experiencing the negative emotions associated with finally coming to terms with the fact that she was very likely unable to conceive – that is, until she was placed on an antidepressant.

In later sessions Margaret recalled that, while a child, she had often played 'mommy' with her dolls, and as the oldest of seven children, she had occupied the role of 'substitute mother' for her own siblings, especially whenever their own mother would take to her bed (which was very frequently) with one ailment or another. Over the course of our sessions it became clear that Margaret's deepest cravings for children of her own and her sense of loss at the prospect of not fulfilling these desires had largely been *repressed* (i.e., kept out of conscious awareness) and resided in her **unconscious**. And yet, of course, given that her work involved being the physician for so many pregnant women, the feelings she had pushed down were constantly being stirred.

Happily, when I heard from Margaret via a Christmas card a few years later, she reported that she and her husband had adopted twins (a boy and a girl) and her description of her deeply felt love for -and commitment to- her children was genuinely heart warming. She also reported that she was not inclined to 'spoil' her children by smothering them with toys and clothes; rather, she relished in the hours she spent in playing with, looking after, and thoroughly enjoying them. Her desire to steal, she reported, had entirely vanished.

****

Exercise # 2: Examining closely an inanimate object's characteristics and functions.
This is a very interesting and informative exercise and I invite you to do it before continuing to read any further. Simply look around the room or place where you are now (presumably) sitting and reading this book, and select an item -any item- preferably one you can hold in your hands. Examine it as if you were viewing it for the first time; you might select a book, keys, your mobile phone, or any other object. Think about its 'characteristics'. If it is a book you have selected you might consider its cover's colors, its weight, thickness, etc.... Make a list of these characteristics on a piece of paper.

Now consider the item's possible 'functions'; in the case of a book, you might think of some of the following: to hold information in a printed form; to place on top of a number of loose pages to keep them in place; to give you pleasure (if a novel) or facts (if a book such as this one, for example); to use as a shield if attempting to protect yourself from the strong sun's rays, etc.... *This exercise is, at the least, interesting due to the fact that we usually do not give very much **conscious** attention to the 'ordinary' objects in our surroundings.*

The reasons for carrying out this exercise include the following: (1) becoming aware of the fact that every 'thing' has *many* characteristics and (2) also *numerous* possible functions. In other words, even the simplest 'thing' (e.g., a paper clip) can be viewed as a versatile object. **And the 'things' that Atypical Theft Offenders people steal, it turns out, usually have a number of *symbolic*, and well as *literal* (i.e., factual), characteristics and functions, as well.** Indeed, the items that these persons steal are seldom simply things chosen at random that have no meaning or value (although most Atypical Theft Offenders are usually not consciously aware of the deeper reasons of why they stole the particular items in question at the particular times when they did). In fact, the meanings and values of the items taken oftentimes only become apparent when the theft offender explores the matter with a suitably trained and qualified therapist.

****

I offer the next case, that of a young woman I have called Georgina, because, even though she was not an Atypical Theft Offender, what she experienced so profoundly and what all of us who were present witnessed, offers a moving, penetrating and superb example of the presence and dynamic power of the unconscious mind that resides in each of us.

Case # 8: Georgina: A remarkable case of the breakthrough into conscious awareness of maternal feelings that had been 'repressed' in a young professional woman's unconscious.

Many years ago, at a time when the so-called 'women's liberation movement' was experiencing a great deal of momentum and attention, a young, single professional woman (lets call her Georgina) took part in a workshop I was conducting for public and high school teachers in a mid-sized city. At one point I invited each of the twenty or so participants to select an object (we happened to be meeting in a play therapy room at a local children's hospital) and spend a few minutes considering the item's characteristics *and* functions- *in other words, virtually the same exercise I offered you just above.*

83

DR. WILL CUPCHIK

To my surprise, as Georgina held a stuffed Teddy bear she had selected for the exercise, she almost immediately began to cry powerfully but silently. When I asked her if she wanted to share with the group why she was so obviously moved, she simply shook her head and firmly indicated 'no'. When our group took a 'coffee break' I noted that she was still shedding copious tears and so I approached her and asked if she was all right. She tried to speak but immediately choked up to the point she could only nod her head to let me know that she was okay.

Georgina chose to not speak for the rest of the two-hour workshop. However, I noted that she continued to firmly grasp the Teddy bear to her chest and cry. As her tears eventually subsided and she indicated to me that a female friend and colleague was going to be driving her home, I was in no doubt that she would be in safe hands. I thought little more of this young woman's response other than to consider that as she held onto 'Teddy' something profound had very likely been going on.

It was three years later, while I was in a university cafeteria having a light dinner prior to teaching a class in psychotherapy to graduate students, that I was approached by a young woman who introduced herself and said she was visiting Toronto to meet with some university colleagues, and that she was the friend who had driven Georgina home after the workshop I had given and that they had both attended. She told me that Georgina had given her permission, in case she happened to see me, to share with me the answer to the riddle of Georgina's remarkably powerful response to having held the Teddy bear during the workshop I had conducted. What she recounted to me was the following: Georgina was a public school counselor who was a strong supporter of the 'women's liberation' movement. In addition, she had decided that she was <u>absolutely</u> not interested in getting married or having children of her own, and she had intended to continue living the life of an independent, single professional for many, many years to come. However...

*Apparently, as Georgina held onto the plush, soft Teddy bear she was literally overwhelmed by what she recognized as a maternal desire to have, hold and care for a <u>child</u> of her own. This response had emerged from her **unconscious**; up to that point, at the level of her conscious mind, she had been certain that she had no such interest whatsoever. That little exercise had opened the floodgates of her **unconscious** to release into **conscious** awareness the most powerful feelings of maternal longing.*

Furthermore, I was informed that, in the three years since the workshop, she had met, become engaged to, and married a young lawyer, and she was now happily pregnant, excitingly waiting for the arrival of their first child.

I mention Georgina's story for several reasons: (1) it offers a graphic example of the sudden bursting into **conscious** awareness of thoughts, emotions and desires that had, to that point, been resident in her **unconscious**; and (2), it offers all of us a caution that suggests that, while we may think we are disposed one way in regard to any particular aspect of our lives or any subject of interest, we might, in certain instances, find that there are other strong thoughts and/or feelings at a deeper level of our minds, that might be seeking our acknowledgement, if not immediate acceptance.

The dictum, 'Know thyself', is always worthwhile keeping in mind as we move ahead in our lives. Over the decades I have had many clients who have come to some crucial insights or awareness about the state of their marriages, the suitability of their current vocations, and even their sexuality. In an instance regarding the latter issue, about two decades ago a young married man was in my office for a counseling session about his satisfaction –or the lack thereof- in his marriage, when suddenly he stopped speaking and was literally unable to utter an audible sound for over ten minutes. When he had finally found his voice again, he softly said, "I think I am gay. No, I *know* I am gay. I didn't know and was not willing to accept that until a few moments ago. I had always thought my several casual encounters with other men were merely aberrant experiments. Now I am ready to accept that they were much more than that and I realize that I have to talk about how to let my wife know that I need to leave this marriage and find out who is out there for me." In the sessions that followed, this man dealt with his now **conscious** awareness and acceptance of his true sexual orientation and prepared himself to deal with his marital situation.

Why the use of Cognitive Behaviour Therapy [CBT] alone is likely insufficient when assessing and treating Atypical Theft Offenders

I have related the last few cases partly to highlight the point that for most individuals it is vital that they 'get in touch with', i.e., bring into **conscious** awareness, matters that are crucial for them to address in order to get on with their lives in more appropriate ways. Some behaviour therapists take the position that thoughts create feelings (but not vice versa) and therefore one need only change what one *thinks* in order to change how one *feels*. Now, in fact, among the many kinds of therapeutic approaches I typically employ with Atypical Theft Offenders are Behaviour Therapy and its cousin, Dr Albert Ellis' Rational Emotive Therapy. Without a doubt these are very helpful approaches to use with clients – at times and for specific purposes. But unless one also uncovers and addresses the major underlying issues behind most atypical theft behaviour, these therapy approaches may well be insufficient to help stop the individual's stealing.

In addition to the above approaches I also employ, if, when and as I determine that it would be appropriate, a variety of other therapeutic approaches including: (i) Gestalt therapy, (ii) Transactional Analysis, (iii) Redecision Therapy (an integrated Transactional-Gestalt approach), (iv) Relationship-based therapy, (v) making therapeutic use of family and other photographs, (vi) Clinical Imaginative Imagery (my own development that helps examine and act therapeutically in regard to one's relationships with significant others), and (vii) Reintrojection Therapy (another of my own developments, one that allows for altering the attitudes and emotions that we hold towards Significant Others, including parental figures). The latter two therapeutic approaches have shown themselves to be particularly helpful in dealing with Atypical Theft Offenders. In my previous book I referred to the overall psychotherapeutic approach I take with Atypical Theft Offenders as S.T.A.T.O., or *Specialized Treatment for Atypical Theft Offenders*.

The fact that I have been conducting psychotherapy for over 49 years has given me the benefit of having learned which therapeutic approaches may be most helpful at a particular juncture in the treatment process, and I do not cling rigidly or exclusively to any *one* therapy modality.

There are numerous troublesome issues that many, if not most, Atypical Theft Offenders have experienced in their lives, including severe verbal, emotional and/or sexual abuse and/or other traumatic events such as experiencing giving birth to a still-born fetus, losing one's child in an accident caused by a drunk driver, being separated from those who mattered most by being forced to live many miles away, or dealing with the infidelity of one's spouse.

In one case I dealt with, the client reported having been working in a field during WWII while a youth and holding in her arms her father who had been lethally injured and who died while she was cradling his head in her arms. (All these events have indeed been the lot of individual Atypical Theft Offenders with whom I have worked.) In such instances, it is my clinical opinion that it very likely requires therapeutic approaches that more directly confront these difficult or tragic circumstances and events within the clinical sessions, before one is ready to utilize the otherwise valuable approach of say, Cognitive Therapy.

One of my own original therapeutic approaches, Reintrojection Therapy, helps many clients do the necessary, emotionally laden therapeutic work to resolve or in some other ways, come to terms with such issues as the ones referred to above. Indeed, psychologist Christine Courtois, in her excellent book, *Healing The Incest Wound*, specifically recognized the value of Reintrojection Therapy in assisting those who have been victims of childhood sexual abuse.

A remarkable example of when my own unconscious directed my overt behaviour
A highly personal experience of my own **unconscious** influencing my behaviour at a clearly observable level, occurred on the occasion of the death of my closest male friend, Hal, a psychiatrist with whom I had shared many wonderful personal and professional experiences over many years.

During a particularly cold winter a number of years ago, I was awakened early one morning by my telephone's insistent ringing. The caller was the wife of my dear friend, Hal, who at the time was in his early 70s. She told me that Hal had had a massive cerebral haemorrhage in the middle of the night, and was at that moment laying on a gurney in a major downtown hospital. And, she added, the doctors had said that he was already brain dead with no possibility of recovery.

Hal was taken off life support within 48 hours. I had the excruciating privilege of providing one of the eulogies at his funeral service the very next day, an experience I found both very humbling and exceptionally emotionally draining. The police-escorted procession of cars leaving the funeral home to travel through city streets to the cemetery many miles away was very long, slow and sad. Our car, with my wife and I inside, was in the middle of the procession - and I was driving.

While all the other cars traveled straight through a particular intersection on the way to the cemetery, I suddenly turned the wheel of my car to the right and headed down another street altogether. When my wife asked me why I had just made the turn *I said that I was not sure*, but perhaps the way I was going would be quicker. Of course, my response to my wife made little sense since the procession had a police escort to stop opposing traffic whenever required, and within the space of traveling a city block or so, the rational part of my brain kicked in and I began to question my own illogical behaviour of having left that police-escorted funeral procession. I told my wife that I was amazed at what I had just done; that it made no sense to me; I wondered if I should double back and try to rejoin the procession of cars as they made their way to Jack's final resting place. I then almost immediately told her that I didn't want to rejoin the other cars, and that perhaps I had left the procession because I was not at all ready to see Hal's remains lowered into a grave.

As we drove along, my professional training kicked in, and I found myself marveling at what I had just done in leaving the line of cars going to the cemetery. Certainly I had *not* **consciously** thought of leaving the procession before I did so. As we discussed my clearly inappropriate actions, we soon concluded that the totally unexpected death of my dearest friend in town, my visit to the hospital to say goodbye, and then the funeral itself and my eulogizing him, had taken a weighty emotional toll on me.

I soon concluded that my **unconscious** had sent a clear message to my arms to literally steer me away from going to the cemetery, perhaps a not entirely different act than that of a usually honest person, one for whom theft behaviour is definitely not acceptable, who, in response to some severe emotionally evoking event, might suddenly put something into his or her pocket or purse and leave a store without paying. (An example of this conduct might well be Case #1, that of Victor the Holocaust survivor described previously.) In such circumstances, the theft offender might indeed know what he or she is doing, but the action may not be one that had been **consciously** planned. Indeed, I have often expressed the opinion to media interviewers that *some* **instances of** *atypical theft behaviour* **offer among the best examples I know of, where we have indirect but seemingly profoundly clear evidence of** <u>unconscious</u> **feelings**

precipitating remarkable acting out behaviour at an unmistakably observable level.

The indistinct 'line' that often separates the <u>sub</u>conscious mind from full conscious awareness at any moment

Imagine a time recently when *you* were driving a vehicle and you and your passenger were engaged in an engrossing and entertaining discussion. Next, suppose that your passenger had asked you, "Have you been fully **consciously** aware of your hand and foot movements while you have been controlling the vehicle's actions over the last few minutes during which time we have been talking?" The likelihood is that you were *not* fully **consciously** aware (unless you were a novice driver out for a driving lesson or test) of precisely when and whether you had applied the brakes, depressed the accelerator and/or turned the wheel clockwise or counterclockwise during the previous several minutes while you were engaged in conversation. Nevertheless, you did manage to safely drive the vehicle during that period. So how did you manage that feat?

At the very least we can probably say that, while your **conscious** mind was partly and perhaps even *primarily* focused upon the conversation you were having, a part of your **conscious** as well as your **subconscious** mind were assessing the driving conditions and issuing instructions to your hands and feet to make the necessary adjustments so as to safely maneuver the vehicle along the road. The fact that you were *not fully* **consciously** aware of your hand and foot movements does not negate the fact that they were, indeed, maneuvering the vehicle.

Similarly, in the case of an Atypical Theft Offender, his or her act of stealing may be obvious to a careful observer. He had been looking around and his hands have moved as he picked up the item and put it away in a pocket or bag and we might therefore deduce that he 'knew' what he was doing. While he was at least partly **consciously** aware of his actions, he may not have been *fully* **consciously** aware of *all* the thoughts and/or feelings that were *precipitating* his actions. At some level of his mind, he may have been acting out in response to deeper (i.e., **subconscious** or **unconscious**) thoughts and/or emotions.

It is my overwhelming clinical experience that when usually honest persons act out by stealing, they are indeed **consciously** aware of *what* they are doing, although they may not be entirely sure *why*. It is also my clinical experience that most of these individuals will recall, if only they are asked, that they were probably angry or resentful towards someone or about something that had very recently happened or was about to happen. Whether they were fully **consciously** aware of their feelings of anger or resentment at the very moment of stealing, a query in that regard virtually always will prompt the theft offender to recall that, *yes*, he or she was indeed angry with someone or about something, at the time he or she stole. In other words, if not *fully* **consciously** aware of experiencing anger at the precise moment that the act of theft was carried out, a simple inquiry will usually elicit that relevant information.

As an example, one of my clients, when initially asked about her predominant feelings at the time that she stole, claimed to *not* be very angry with *anyone* or about *anything* at the moment she stole a modestly priced bathroom scale, placed it in her large shopping bag and exited the department store without paying for the item. Further questioning, however, soon elicited the fact that her husband of over thirty years had, earlier that very day, ridiculed her for having gained weight over the prior several months and she had been furious with him for insulting her in his typically sarcastic fashion. It surely stretches the imagination to consider the fact that she happened to steal a bathroom scale only a couple of hours after his comment was entirely unrelated to her husband's comment or her anger towards him, especially as she pointed out that she had no need for such an cheap product since they already had a much more expensive -and very accurate- bathroom scale at home. This woman's anger towards her husband had been very pronounced at the time she stole, although she did *not* recall being **consciously** aware of thinking of his demeaning comment at the very instant that she stole. Indeed, she had initially claimed that she had no idea at all why she would steal anything, let alone an entirely unneeded bathroom scale, at that particular time.

Some pharmaceutically oriented clinicians appear to ignore inquiring about possible psychological reasons for their clients' atypical theft behaviour

Ignoring gaining a psychological (as opposed to a pharmaceutical) understanding that might help to explain atypical theft behaviour appears to be a relatively recent and most curious activity amongst some clinicians. Imagine a physician restricting her questions of an individual who shows up in the emergency room of a hospital with a severe stomach ache, to queries such as, "How do you feel right now?", but not bothering to also ask what the patient had eaten previously or what else had been going on in the patient's life that day. It is surely a hallmark of physical medicine to make inquiries into what may have been happening in the patient's life during the previous few minutes, hours or days, and not simply restrict the medical inquiry to only or primarily to what the patient is experiencing at the moment. It might take only a very few questions to determine, for example, that the turkey soup that had been ingested earlier that day had tasted markedly 'off' (as actually happened to a close friend a few years ago, resulting in a severe case of food poisoning).

The key questions for the clinician (who genuinely wishes to understand what psychological issues, events and/or circumstances in the person's life may have triggered atypical theft behaviour) to ask of the usually honest person who has stolen, are the following:

(i) **"What was happening in your life in the minutes, hours and days just prior to your stealing?**

and

(ii) **Was anything upsetting you at the time that you stole?"**

Persistently ask these questions and you will likely be told what you need to know.

PART IV

The Main Findings

Of My Three Major

Clinical Studies

(Conducted In 1983, 1997 And 2013)

Into

Atypical Theft Behaviour

Chapter 8

WHY ATYPICAL THEFT OFFENDERS STEAL: SUMMARIZING FINDINGS OF MY 1983 & 1997 STUDIES

The findings of my three main clinical studies completed over the span of three decades (1983, 1996 and 2013 respectively) have been highly congruent with one another, i.e., there have been no inconsistencies whatsoever among the three studies. At the same time, each study has added considerably to the collection of relevant information that enhances our understanding atypical theft behaviour. Given that the initial study carried out in 1983 involved some 34 cases, that the 1996 study drew upon 36 cases, and that the most recent 2013 study involved 30 cases, <u>these three studies together have involved data collected from 100 cases</u> out of my entire cache of well over 700 cases in all. In all three studies, the client samples were chosen at random from among at-the-time recent clinical assessments and treatments that I had personally carried out.

For the 1983 and 1996 studies, over eight hours of direct, one-on-one clinical contact with each individual case was involved.

For my most recent 2013 study, an *average* of over 20 one-on-one direct-contact clinical hours per case were involved, with a range of 10 to 31 clinical hours having been spent in direct client contact. This much time spent in direct, one-on-one client contact likely greatly exceeds the amount of 'direct one-on-one clinician-client assessment and treatment time' that has been spent in any other study conducted by other clinical investigators of atypical theft behaviour, or as some clinicians continue to erroneously refer to, as cases of 'kleptomania'.

In order to give you a full accounting of my clinical findings over these past more than thirty years, let me review the findings of my clinical studies in chronological order, beginning with the first one conducted by me and psychiatrist Dr Don J Atcheson, and whose data were originally presented in our article titled <u>Shoplifting: An Occasional Crime of the</u>

Moral Majority, published in peer-reviewed journal, the *Bulletin of the American Academy of Psychiatry and the Law*, in 1983.

****

The most important findings of my earlier studies

I - Atypical theft behaviour often occurs in response to 'perceived (actual or anticipated) unfair personally meaningful losses'
The most prominent finding of our first study pertained to what we deduced to be a causal relationship between shoplifting and what the individual perceived to have been either actual or anticipated personally meaningful loss(es). In fact, most of the persons in this first study (28 of 34 cases, or **83%**) committed acts of shoplifting in 'close' or 'very close' proximity, time-wise, to what, for them, were perceived to be actual or anticipated 'unfair personally meaningful losses'.

Actually, this unexpected finding was so prevalent that Dr Don Atcheson and I articulated what we termed the **Loss-Substitution-by-Shoplifting Hypothesis**, in which we stated that, *"In response to experiencing - or anticipating- experiencing, what were perceived to be 'unfair personally meaningful losses', some persons are inclined to cause other persons or places (e.g., relatives or friends, workplaces, department stores, etc...) to experience unfair losses, by committing acts of shoplifting. These 'perceived unfair personally meaningful losses' might include the loss of a relationship, spouse, child, job, home, country, etc...."*

The loss-substitution phenomenon may well be hard-wired into a number of species, not only in human beings. For example, I was both surprised and amused when my own mother-in-law's almost year old Maltese puppy, Scooter, was visiting our home and arrived downstairs in the living room with one of my socks in his mouth. As soon as I extracted the sock, however, he turned around, went back upstairs to our bedroom, and promptly returned downstairs with the first sock's mate tightly held in his mouth. It is likely that he was carrying out what we might refer to as innate 'compensation-by-substitution' behaviour, *compensating* himself for the 'unfair' loss of the first sock by *substituting* for its loss with the second one.

The reader is asked to consider whether parents and other adults 'program' children to expect that, when they lose something, they will get or gain something else to compensate them for the losses they have experienced. How many of us have assisted this programming by telling children that after they lose any 'baby teeth', the tooth fairy will leave a quarter or some other gift under their pillow. And if a child's pet dies, how many parents will immediately run out and purchase a substitute. Also, how many of us, after a particularly painful loss (of a promotion, a relationship, *something*) will compensate *our*selves with a little extra 'treat', be it an extra slice of cake, new pair of shoes, or some other desired item.

(At least a couple of decades ago a divorced acquaintance of mine was excitedly speaking with me and referring enthusiastically to having been spending her weekends with "Thomas." As she went on at length, joyously describing their rides together through the woods, resting by a bucolic pond, etc..., surely I might be excused for having thought that she was sharing the good news that she had a new man in her life, a little more than a year after receiving her divorce from her husband of twelve years. Later, as she spoke of how much she enjoyed "brushing him down", "feeding him", and "walking him", I became (*how shall I put this?*) both a little uncomfortable yet increasingly curious. Noticing my growing quizzical expression, she stopped recounting her tales of her and "Tommy", and burst out laughing! "Oh, dear!" she said. "I can see that you are confused, Will. Actually, Thomas is the name of the horse I bought soon after my husband moved out." It was not only the fact that she had bought the animal shortly after her husband left, or just the fact of her having given the horse what most would consider to be a male human's name, but also, the gushing descriptions of their times together, suggested to me that -perhaps- this was, *at least in part*, a case of compensation-by-substitution, carried out after experiencing the loss of her marital relationship!)

Many of the Atypical Theft Offenders whom I have dealt with, have likely stolen in order to compensate themselves for what they perceived to be 'unfair personally meaningful losses' - by taking and 'substituting' something else for the loss – via shoplifting.

II - *Why else do some Atypical Theft Offenders steal?* Noteworthy occurrences of loss-substitution in response to the anticipated or actual occurrence of <u>cancer</u> in self or a 'Significant Other'
In fully 8 (or **22%**) of the 34 cases in the original 1983 study, the identified 'unfair personally meaningful loss' was the occurrence (or anticipation) of *cancer* in either the theft offenders or someone close to them (who we clinicians usually refer to as a 'Significant Other' or S.O.). In nearly every instance the shoplifting had occurred very close to a diagnosis, surgery or loss of life related to cancer. Another way of viewing this statistic is to consider that these 8 cases were among the 28 cases where 'personally meaningful losses' were involved. <u>Therefore we can say that cancer *may* have been a motivating or triggering issue in 8 of 28, or 29% of the cases where losses were possibly a key trigger for atypical theft behaviour.</u> As one example, recall if you will, the case of the lawyer whose child was undergoing chemotherapy for cancer at the very time he stole a tube of toothpaste from a nearby drugstore.

III - More about the possible causal connection between the occurrence -or anticipation of- cancer in self or S.O. *and* atypical theft behaviour
Is it really possible that the occurrence, or the anticipation of the occurrence, of cancer might help precipitate atypical theft behaviour? Having assessed and treated many hundreds of Atypical Theft Offenders over nearly four decades, I have been repeatedly struck by the co-occurrence of cancer and atypical theft behaviour. As a result of this very frequent at least 'co-incidence', I have had ample time to formulate what I believe to be a highly plausible hypothesis in this regard.

As we are all only too well aware, cancer is one of the most prevalent diseases in North America, second only to heart disease in terms of causing fatalities. Furthermore, cancer cells usually start out as ordinary cells that then mutate in some fashion. Indeed, <u>cancer may be considered to be an invasion of a host body's ordinary cells and 'stealing them away'</u>, so that they cease to be ordinary cells and are transformed into cancerous cells.

In an analogous fashion, <u>shoplifting, for its part, may be considered an invasion of a host body (such as a department store) by the theft offender, and the stealing away of what belongs to the host body.</u>

As you may be aware from reading about the 'symbolic meaningfulness' of dreams, our **unconscious** minds are able to produce in our night dreams, images and scenarios that symbolically represent issues of current concern in our daily waking lives. To take a simple example, if a woman dreams that she and her family are in a boat that is quickly sinking into the ocean, we might readily appreciate the symbolic significance of the dream if we also were to learn that she is facing imminent foreclosure on her home. Likewise, if a man dreamt of the Leaning Tower of Pisa collapsing, it might not be terribly surprising if we were to learn that this person recently had sexual encounters during which his penis had become prematurely flaccid.

How does the **unconscious** mind know how to generate dreams that symbolically represent or replicate what is happening in the individual's waking life? The short, fairest answer is to say, 'we just don't know' for certain. But we *do* know that night dreams are very capable of fashioning symbolically meaningful 'movies' that do, sometimes startlingly, mirror that which is happening in the dreamer's waking life.

Most people have heard of the term, 'Freudian slip'. In these instances, a person who **consciously** intends to say one particular word, instead utters another actual or pseudo-word, that may or may not sound similar, but that in fact more truly represents what he may or may not be **consciously** thinking, but would not have **consciously** deliberately chosen to vocalize. For example, suppose one **consciously** intended to say to a friend who had obviously gained at least 40 pounds since their last meeting, "You look fabulous," but instead said, "You look flab-ulous." *Oops!*

In this book are cases in which the theft offender appears to have acted out in response to an anticipation - or the actual occurrence - of cancer in self or other. Perhaps no other case is more illustrative of this phenomenon than that of Alice, below. Because of its clear and classic Atypical Theft Offender features, I previously included a partial transcript of our one and only clinical session, in my earlier book, *Why Honest People Shoplift or Commit Other Acts of Theft*.

****

DR. WILL CUPCHIK

Case #9: Alice: the woman who stole whenever her husband had another bout of cancer
Alice telephoned my office at the Clarke Institute of Psychiatry in the early 1980s. She was very tearful and seemed highly anxious. She told me that she had kept in her purse a local newspaper report published the previous year about our investigations into shoplifting. She said that this article had provided her with some relief as it seemed to offer the first plausible explanation of why she had occasionally shoplifted over the previous <u>eleven</u> years! She was now highly distressed because, <u>even though she had never been caught</u>, she said; "I'm doing it again! Ever since my husband's cancer came back last month. This time I didn't even know what I was taking. I think you call the things I stole 'wrenches', or something like that. Why did I do that? I don't need anything; <u>I never keep what I steal! I just throw the stuff out into the Goodwill box right away.</u>"

When Alice came in for an interview a few days later, I asked if I could record the interview. She agreed, and a remarkable (for its blatantly psychodynamic and clearly symbolic elements) session followed.

It is noteworthy that Alice and her husband were deeply religious persons who attended church almost every Sunday. She stated emphatically that she believed in the Ten Commandments, had never, <u>ever</u> stolen in her life before her husband's first bout with cancer, and was extremely distressed by her theft behaviour. She said that she had only recently realized that each new recurrence of her husband's cancer was followed, within a day or two, by another one of her stealing episodes. This desire to steal had first come upon Alice very soon after her husband's initial diagnosis and treatment for prostate cancer some eleven years earlier.

Without any understanding on her part as to <u>why</u> she stole, and why she stole <u>what</u> she stole, she first stole some lingerie. Interestingly, she said that she never wore anything in bed and so she could make no sense of why she would choose to steal lingerie. In our interview, however, she revealed that her husband's treatment for cancer of the prostate had left him impotent, and she noted that her sexual frustration had increased even as her sense of herself as an attractive woman had diminished. It seemed highly likely to me that the choice of lingerie was related to these factors.

100

It is probable that Alice's resentment, frustration and depression in response to being 'robbed' of a normal sex life by the start of the cancer and its treatment's side effects had led to her acting out in a symbolically significant way. But neither at the time of her offence, nor afterwards, had the cause-effect connection been recognized by Alice. For her, the theft behaviour had remained a nonsensical, upsetting aberration, until we fully addressed the matter in our interview.

****

Other Reasons Why Atypical Theft Offenders Steal

IV- Shoplifting as a Symbolic Act

In very many cases that I have assessed we have been able to determine that *what* had been stolen likely held some symbolic meaning related to the issue that was distressing the theft offender at the time of the theft, as was rather obvious in the case of Alice above. Consider another of my clients, Dr Margeret Black (Case # 7), who was mentioned earlier on in this book; a wealthy, childless physician who stole children's clothing and toys. At the time she stole, she was in great distress about having been told that it was virtually certain that she was incapable, for physiological reasons, of giving birth.

And consider, as well, the first case presented in this book, that of Victor, the Holocaust survivor who had survived a death march along railroad ties that led to his feet being bruised and bloodied, and who in 1995, on the exact 50th anniversary of that horrific march, had stolen from a drug store a covering for bruised feet, even though he always made sure, ever since he arrived in the USA, that his shoes fitted him perfectly and in 1995 he had absolutely no need for the item he had stolen.

Why else do some Atypical Theft Offenders steal?
V - Shoplifting as Unconscious Manipulation

On many occasions, I have dealt with theft offenders whose acts of theft were most likely meant to hurt, or at least influence, a close relative. In almost no instance, when *first* asked to consider the possibility of such a motivation, has any Atypical Theft Offender acknowledged that he or she had been *consciously* thinking of such an action being aimed at injuring or affecting someone close to them. For instance, the woman who stole from a nearby mall in the wealthy California enclave to which she and her husband had retired, said most emphatically that she did not think her actions were aimed at convincing her husband to move back east, where all of their grandchildren lived. Over the course of a few sessions, however, her intense anger towards her husband for having badgered and berated her until she finally acquiesced to his desire to live in the warm Southwest (but away from all of her own relatives, friends, and – most importantly – her seven grandchildren) became abundantly clear. She was likely, at least **unconsciously**, hoping that by her theft behaviour, she would sufficiently embarrass her husband among the friends and neighbors in their upscale gated community to the point that he would consider moving away and hopefully closer to their relatives, her friends and especially their grandchildren.

Why else do some Atypical Theft Offenders steal?

VI - The relationship of theft behaviour to much earlier, traumatic events in the offender's life

In the majority of Atypical Theft Offender cases that I have dealt with over the years, the individuals involved had, while children, experienced considerable verbal *and/or* emotional *and/or* physical *and/or* sexual abuse, and it became clear in the course of their assessment and treatment, that they still had major unresolved thoughts and feelings in regard to these earlier highly distressing experiences. As a result of these early events and their long-lasting effects, most of them had acquired considerable resentment towards authority figures, and when stressed in their personal lives as adults, they often regressed in the direction of entirely inappropriate, essentially rebellious, acting out, atypical theft behaviour.

****

In my second major study, published in 1997, in fully 30 (i.e., **83.3%**) of the 36 cases investigated, earlier life events were very likely related the clients' atypical theft behaviour. The case of Robert, poignantly makes the point!

Case # 10: Robert, the physician who was brought up in a home with a violent, alcoholic father who also happened to be a senior circuit court judge

Robert was a 52 year old cardiologist at the time he presented for assessment. He had been arrested for stealing three memory sticks for his digital camera from a major electronics store close to his home. He readily acknowledged that he had carried out four separate incidents of theft over the previous two decades but he was unable to articulate any plausible reason for such behaviour.

In relating his personal history going back to early childhood, Robert became very emotional as he described his father's drunken and violent outbursts towards his mother, his siblings and himself. His tone became angrier and his words more derogatory as he sarcastically recalled his father's very different, highly positive standing in their community. After all, his father was a circuit court judge who reviewed some of the most famous trials in the state over a period of many years. Seemingly scrupulously upright, fair and firm, his reputation was unblemished as far as the community at large was concerned.

Robert's father's conduct at home, however, was quite another matter. Robert told me that throughout his childhood, his father would begin to drink from the moment he entered the family home at the end of the day. As he did so, he became increasingly loud and short-tempered. With only the slightest provocation, as far as Robert was concerned -say, the soup was not hot enough; Robert's baseball glove was on the floor in the entry way, etc...,- his drunken father would fly into a rage and begin screaming, swearing and hitting the person he was apparently, at the moment, upset with the most. Robert remembered that he paid great attention to his father's 'heavy, black, lawyer's shoes', as they were the objects that were usually involved in inflicting the most damage, through brutal kicks.

On a few occasions Robert's mother managed to call the police while his father was in one of his 'states'. Invariably, however, once the officers arrived and realized who the 'man of the house' was, they showed great deference to his father who invariably somehow managed to appear very reasoned, sober and polite. The officers would soon leave, and within minutes his father would once more resume his alcohol-fueled tirade. Robert left the family home at age eighteen when he entered university on scholarship, and seldom communicated with his parents from that point on until his father died of complications of cirrhosis of the liver when Robert was 23 years old. After that event, Robert would occasionally visit with his mother, but found such encounters to be very troubling, as her own alcohol consumption had increased markedly following her husband's death.

Once Robert was established in his professional life as a physician in the county hospital, he progressed rapidly in position and salary, until, at age 48, he became the youngest-ever head of the cardiology department. An exemplary physician, Robert married, became a father, and was heavily involved in his church's social activities. While most of his life seemed to be going well, he acknowledged to me that, when dealing with an alcoholic, authoritarian-minded individual (such as the director of his hospital or his church's pastor) he found that he had an exceedingly short fuse. Sometimes he was known to storm out of business and professional meetings and not return. On those occasions he frequently headed to a mall and shoplifted, mostly low-value, non-essential items that he could well afford to purchase. He said that as he wandered the mall's stores, he found that he would replay the actual or imagined verbal exchanges he had just had with the individual who had upset him, and soon he would become angrier and angrier. That is when, he acknowledged, he was most likely to shoplift.

The last occasion of stealing had occurred just two weeks before our first appointment. He related the events of the day, and in particular, the upsetting encounter he had had with the "alcohol-fuelled chief of staff of the hospital" just before Robert stormed out of a 'heads of departments' meeting. A careful review of this encounter revealed that, like Robert's father, the chief of staff was a very tall, overweight and foul-mouthed individual, who would grow increasingly impatient with Robert over what appeared to the latter to be nitpicky items, such as an employee-review report being inadequately filled out. An examination of Robert's prior incidents of shoplifting indicated that each was preceded by an angry encounter with either his strong-willed, demeaning wife or another person in a position of some authority.

In order to reduce the likelihood of recidivism on Robert's part, it became essential to work on the still-lingering strong feelings of resentment and anger towards authority figures that Robert had carried with him from his childhood. He also had to learn to recognize his state of escalating negative emotional arousal when he was inclined to become incensed by a perceived current authority's inappropriate conduct. In addition, Robert recognized that he had to deal with his resentment towards his mother for having not protected him and his siblings from their father, and for having indulged in alcohol when "things became too much" for her.

It turned out that Robert's wife bore a very strong resemblance to his mother in size, shape, voice quality and mannerisms, especially when she became distressed or angry – although, he said, "at least she doesn't drink to the point of getting totally drunk!" At times of strong disagreement, Robert's lingering resentment towards his mother tended to surface and he would even shout, "Stop acting like my mother!" in his wife's direction. Perhaps not surprisingly, Robert had married a woman who also had some of his mother's other personality traits as well. When matters became very heated between them Robert would sometimes leave the house and drive over to the nearby shopping mall to 'cool off'. Unfortunately, as he acknowledged in one of our later interviews, after such encounters with his wife, he was aware that he "just felt like taking something" from the stores at the mall. On three separate recent occasions, he said, he had actually taken items from various stores but had only been apprehended one time.

****

It is my firm contention that Atypical Theft Offenders must deal with the underlying issues that have helped to precipitate their acting out.

Simply placing a pharmaceutical band-aid (antidepressant or tranquilizer) over the psychological abscess of hurt and/or anger and/or sadness and/or depression will do little to arrest atypical theft behaviour. Most Atypical Theft Offenders carry with them a good deal of anger pertaining to un-dealt with issues that they have to resolve, usually in treatment, in order to lessen the likelihood that they will re-offend.

Depression and atypical theft behaviour: Initial comments

As well, and in large part as a result of traumatic experiences in childhood, most Atypical Theft Offenders will acknowledge that they have been markedly depressed for a good deal of their adulthood. As will be discussed in greater detail later on, the idea that these Atypical Theft Offenders should be given antidepressants to 'combat' their inclinations to shoplift, is a very common error, one that often does little to alleviate their underlying anger and pain in regard to their childhood experiences. **Furthermore, according to my clinical findings, the use of antidepressants may well *increase* the likelihood that they will commit acts of theft behaviour in the future.**

The results of my most recent study of some 30 additional cases, concluded in 2013, are presented in the next chapter. They corroborate the findings of my two earlier studies already referred to in this book (consult my earlier book for more details of these earlier studies). In addition, the most recent study provides considerable additional significant information that will be of great interest to Atypical Theft Offenders, their relatives and friends, their lawyers, the judges involved in their cases, and their therapists.

Chapter 9

FINDINGS OF MY 2013 STUDY OF ATYPICAL THEFT OFFENDERS

In this chapter I present the key findings of my recently completed clinical study into the atypical theft behaviour of usually honest persons. As you will learn below, the findings are consistent with, and elaborate upon, those of my earlier 1983 and 1996 studies. This most recent study also offers important information regarding the likely inappropriate prescribing of major antidepressants, by far too many clinicians, for clients who present with atypical theft behaviour.

The 2013 study's 30 cases or 'Subjects' [Ss]

In this study 21 women and 9 men were selected randomly from among the hundreds of individuals who have sought assessment and treatment with me over the last sixteen years. Fourteen of the individuals (**46.7%**) were from the USA; sixteen (**53.3%**) lived in Canada. All American residents (except one) took part in either 3- or 4-day Intensives in my office that involved between 16 and 22 sessions. The exception was an individual who took part in a 20-session Skype-based Intensive Intervention Program (in my clinical opinion, the optimal - and now the *only* - Program that I offer).

****

Below are some of the key findings of my 2013 clinical study.

These findings were arrived at as a result of reviewing over 15,000 individual pieces of information (data points) derived from a thorough assessment of the materials gathered via an average of more than twenty one-on-one clinical sessions with individual Ss.

Table One (Part A): Basic Demographic Data Of the 2013 Sample (N=30)

Gender	# of cases	Findings
# of women (70% of sample)	21	Average age: 45.5
# of men (30% of sample)	9	Average age: 48.4
Marital Status		
Currently married	20	66.7%
In Second Marriage	5	16.7%
Divorced or Separated	4	13.3%
Common-law, heterosexual	1	3.3%
Homosexual, lived with partner	1	3.3%
Never married and living alone	4	13.3%
Gross Household Annual Income		
Less than $50,000	4	13.3%
Between $50,001 & $100,000	9	30%
Between $100,001 & $500,000	14	46.7%
Between $500,001 & $1,000,000	2	6.7%
More than $1,000,000	1	3.3%

****

From Table One (Part A) above you will note that 21 (70%) of the 30 clients in this study were women and 9 (30%) were men. Most were married (20, or 66.7%); for 5 (16.7%) this was their second marriage. A minority (4 or 13.3%) were either separated or divorced, and four (13.3%) of the 30 clients were single and living alone.

It is particularly noteworthy that the great majority of the 30 clients were financially well off: 17 (56%) had a gross annual household income of more than $100,000. Two individuals (6.7%) had gross annual incomes of between $500,001 and $1,000,000, and one of the clients in this sample of 30 earned over $1,000,000 a year as the sole owner of his highly successful business. Clearly, these persons hardly needed to steal the items they took, especially as most of the items stolen were worth less than $50. These thefts, therefore, constituted what can most definitely be considered bizarre and/or nonsensical acts.

The fact that the majority of the clients in this study, some seventeen (56.7%) in total, lived in households *where the total gross annual income was at least $100,000,* strongly indicates that stealing items usually worth a relatively few dollars were, to say the least, hardly necessary acts. You will also agree, I am sure, that the client who earned over $1,000,000 annually, most assuredly did not likely shoplift for financial gain. In fact, his stealing items of clothing and accessories from department stores had gone on infrequently but for years; he had actually never been caught but sought my help for fear that his 'luck' would run out, and destroy both his reputation and successful business.

> It should be noted that all the cases of theft included in this study occurred *prior* to the recent so-called 'Great Recession' of 2008 *or,* at the least, the perpetrators were not significantly affected by it. In several of the cases that comprise this study, the theft offenders did not contact me for some time following their theft behaviour.

It has been true, throughout the more than 39 years of my clinical investigations of atypical theft behaviour, that the proportion of male to female theft offender clients in my practice has been close to 1:1.

In this study, however, as chance determined the selection of the cases to be reviewed, the females were 21; the males, 9.

There exists, I believe, a still commonly held -and erroneous- belief that many more women than men are shoplifters. This may have a great deal to do with the fact that, as one loss prevention officer told me a number of years ago, "If I have the choice between apprehending a 130 pound, 5' 3" woman or a 210 pound, 6' 2" man, who do *you* think I am going to choose to apprehend?" *And this loss prevention officer was a powerfully built amateur bodybuilder!*

****

Table One (Part B): More Basic Demographic Data Of the 2013 Sample (N=30)

Attendance of a 'Significant Other' [S.O.] for at least one clinical session	26	86.7%
S.O. in attendance was the spouse or common law partner	17	56.7%
One or both parents of the adult client took part in at least one session	7	23.3%
Client lived in USA	14	46.7%
Client lived in Canada	16	53.3%

In Table One (Part B) above, the reader will observe that in 26 (86.7%) out of the 30 cases, a so-called 'Significant Other' (S.O.) attended for at least one clinical session (usually alone; otherwise, with my client) in order to help me gain some (invariably) valuable perspective of -and information about- my client and, of course, to provide me with an opportunity to arrive at my own impressions of the S.O. with whom the client had to deal in his or her personal life. In most cases the Significant Other who chose to attend (if invited) for one or more sessions, was also the 'intimate partner'. **I have usually found that the willingness of the S.O. to attend and actively participate in one or more clinical sessions has been a reasonably accurate predictor of eventual success regarding the client's finally stopping to steal.**

In a minority of instances, my theft offender clients have not wanted to have their partners attend for *any* sessions, or even to know that they had been stealing at all, let alone the *extent* of the stealing. [The attendance of the S.O. is virtually always helpful, except, of course, in cases where there may be the possibility of physical violence or other dire consequences for the theft offender.] I always respect the choice of clients who do not wish to have a S.O. attend *any* sessions.

As is also noted in the Table above, nearly half of the clients in this study lived in the USA. One of the participants in this study lived in California and all our clinical work was done using Skype. [As I mentioned previously, now, after more than five years using this remarkable Internet-enabled technology, it has become entirely clear to me that the 20-session Skype-enabled Intensive Intervention Program I have developed is as at least as efficient and effective as having the client physically present in my office. Indeed, as of June 2011, having determined that working in this manner is entirely satisfactory (and so much more convenient and less expensive for my clients), I now *only* work with theft offender clients in this fashion.]

****

Learning to model stealing and/or lying behaviour that was witnessed as a child.

In 6 (20%) of the cases, the clients reported having learned about lying/deceit from their own parents. In some instances, the clients' parent(s) had shoplifted when the client was a young child, sometimes in the child's presence. In one case, in order to survive wartime conflict, the client (who was a child at the time), was acutely aware that her father, a usually scrupulously honest, highly ethical church elder, arranged to hide his family in the attic of a compassionate neighbour's home for over a year, and repeatedly bribed, lied, deceived and stole from the occupying forces until he was able, together with his wife and children, to escape to another country. Most unfortunately, this client copied these wartime ways (by stealing) that her father had used in order to save his family, in entirely different, peacetime situations and for no good purposes.

It appears very likely that in some cases, clients learned to model their stealing behaviour from their parents' conduct, as a way of being (in an entirely inappropriate way, of course), *'just like dear old mom (or dad)'*. In virtually all such cases, the desire to duplicate the parent(s) behaviour appeared to have been driven from the unconscious, and in response to inappropriately dealing with an extremely low sense of self-esteem, as discussed below.

****

The low self-esteem of most Atypical Theft Offenders
The great majority of Atypical Theft Offenders, both male and female - even those who, objectively speaking, have achieved much in terms of formal education, professional success, and/or monetary remuneration - often possess remarkably low self-esteem. This poor sense of one's own personal worth was usually a result of being subjected to considerable sexual, physical, emotional and/or verbal mistreatment as a child.

Three of the clients in the 2013 sample were physicians. All three (two men and one woman) were highly trained, experienced specialists in their fields, earning well over $300,000 per annum each. Nevertheless, their self-esteem was very low indeed, and their professional and other accomplishments seemed to hardly keep their severe self-deprecating attitudes at bay.

****

Case # 11: Charlene: A senior accountant with very low self-esteem, repeatedly - and in obvious ways - stole over $380,000 from three successive employers in the same (highly visible) type of business, in a city of less than 300,000 citizens.
Charlene, a woman in her sixties who possessed an advanced accounting degree, held a well-paying, secure position with a privately held company in the U.S. Southwest. She matter-of-factly informed me that she always insisted in holding what she considered to be a particularly prestigious brand of credit card, and invariably offered to pay for everyone with whom she dined, whether it was for business purposes or not - and whether or not she actually had the funds with which to subsequently pay her credit card bill. In fact, she was frequently unable to pay her monthly bill using her own available funds, and told me that she sometimes stole from her employer in order to pay off her credit card balance. When I suggested that she seemed to be somewhat overly attached to what she considered to be _the_ most prestigious credit card, and that, as a worthwhile exercise, she should consider obtaining and using another kind of credit card, she became profoundly offended and actually nearly bolted

112

out of my office. She was her credit card company's 'perfect' customer (at least in one sense), someone who repeatedly relied upon the card to vouch for her own 'OK-ness'.

To make matters worse, this individual used her position with her employer to frequently 'gift' relatives, friends, and acquaintances with some of the expensive products that the company sold. When apprehended she was charged with stealing over $150,000 from the company where she was then employed. In total she said she had stolen over $380,000 from her last three employers.

In a later session Charlene sheepishly told me that, over the previous two years, she had also repeatedly forged her husband's signature to several of his checks, for over $55,000 in total, in order to pay off her credit card debts.

A thorough review of her theft behaviour clearly suggested that her thefts were carried out in such ways as to virtually guarantee that she would be apprehended sooner than later. Yet, her sense of self-esteem was so low that she found it virtually impossible to stop 'giving away' things that were not her's to give, or buying other people things that she knew full well she could simply not afford.

It was of considerable clinical interest to me that, when she was 14 years old, Charlene's father died of a rare kidney disease, leaving Charlene's mother, her four siblings and herself in considerable financial distress. Soon after her father's death Charlene obtained part-time work after school at a small supermarket where she would frequently 'neglect' to ring up the full costs of the food and supplies that her mother brought to her checkout counter. She said that she saw herself as a sort of juvenile 'Robin Hood' who took from the relatively wealthy (in this case, the store-owner) and gave to the poor and needy (herself and her family members). Even after she was married for more than 30 years, and was actually very well off financially, she compulsively carried on with her apparent 'largesse', to her own, her employers', and her husband's detriment and in entirely inappropriate ways, in order to gain the approval of others by 'paying' for it. In my opinion Charlene had never fully dealt with her early childhood's devastating loss of her father and the matter of her life-long low self-esteem.

DR. WILL CUPCHIK

*Thankfully, Charlene had found her way to an experienced and
excellent psychologist whom she trusted and who diligently worked with on
her non-theft related issues. This psychologist, recognizing that dealing
with the theft behaviour problem itself was beyond his expertise, had
sought me out and referred his client to me in order for us to directly focus
upon her theft behaviour. After our work together, and after she had served
a brief prison term for her very sizable thefts, Charlene again worked with
her psychologist on the numerous issues we had identified as likely having
helped to trigger her theft behaviour.*

It is worthwhile noting that Charlene was what I have termed a
'mixed-type' theft offender, i.e., someone who displayed ample amounts of
both Atypical Theft Offender *and* Typical Theft Offender qualities.
Keeping in mind that she purposefully planned and carried out her illegal
activities and stole *what* she wanted *when* she wanted, she certainly
demonstrated Typical Theft Offender features; at the same time and on the
other hand, her stealing was carried out in remarkably unintelligent ways,
thereby virtually guaranteeing that she would be apprehended much sooner
than later. For such a highly intelligent person her conduct was therefore
decidedly bizarre – thereby demonstrating Atypical Theft Offender
features.

Furthermore, her attachment to a particular brand of credit card was
beyond that which could be considered as reasonable. As I mentioned
above, when I suggested that she might be better off with what might be
considered a somewhat less prestigious credit card, she made it clear that
she was genuinely insulted, and threatened that if I were to attempt to
somehow enforce such a change she would cease our relationship.

****

Table Two: Lying And Deceit Amongst Atypical Theft Offenders

What the Ss lied about to their Significant Others:	# of Ss	Percent of 30 Ss
Had not *fully* informed their S.O.s of the extent (and in a few cases, even the *fact*) of their stealing	27	90%
'Purchases': either not paid for or hidden from S.O.	25	83.3%
Extramarital involvements	11	36.7%
The extent of his/her abuse of alcohol	7	23.3%
The extent of his/her abuse of drugs	7	23.3%
Having had an eating disorder	7	23.3%
His/her financial situation	3	10%
* Having learned a good deal about lying/deceit from parent(s)	6	20%

*In these cases, for various reasons, the Ss' own parents were particularly duplicitous and the theft offenders could be said, at least in part, to have learned to model their own misdeeds after those of their parents.

My clinical work has shown that Atypical Theft Offenders frequently lie to their spouses/partners about the fact -and/or the extent- of their stealing. Of the thirty cases in this study, the great majority (27 or 90%) had *not* fully informed their S.O.s of the extent (and in a few cases, even the *fact*) of their stealing. A full 25 of the subjects (83.3%) said that they often lied about their 'purchases' and whether they had actually paid for them.

In my earlier book, *Why Honest People Shoplift Or Commit Other Acts Of Theft*, I included a so-called *'Letter to the Significant Other'* in which I aimed to make clear that my decades of work with Atypical Theft Offenders had definitely indicated that the active (if and as requested) involvement of the S.O. in one or more clinical sessions could be of great assistance during both the assessment and psychotherapy part of the Intervention process. Essentially I suggested that the Significant Other could either be part of the solution or part of the problem, when it comes to helping my client stop his or her atypical theft behaviour. At the least, it is most helpful to have the Significant Other read my earlier and/or this book so as to better understand my client's seemingly nonsensical theft behaviour.

****

Table Three: Extramarital Involvements Of The 20 Married Ss

Extramarital involvements acknowledged by married Ss	11 of 20 married Ss	55% of married Ss
Extramarital involvements acknowledged by married female Ss	8 of 15 married female Ss	53.3% of married female Ss
Extramarital involvements acknowledged by married male Ss	3 of 5 married male Ss	60% of married male Ss

More than one-half (55%) of the married Ss admitted that they had had extramarital involvements. Eight or 53.3% of the married female Ss in the study acknowledged such involvement. A slightly greater proportion, 60%, of married males Ss admitted to such activities. While reliable statistics of infidelity in the general North American married population seem somewhat elusive, it is probably safe to say that many Atypical Theft Offenders who have offended against their own ethical code by stealing might also be inclined to act out in other ways as well.

Atypical Theft Offenders spend an inordinate amount of time in an essentially rebellious state of mind. [In 'Transactional Analysis' terminology, *to be discussed in detail in Chapter 11*, these Atypical Theft Offenders are considered to be in the so-called 'Rebellious Child' [Cr] ego state much of the time.] **As we will discuss further in Chapter 11, stealing by Atypical Theft Offenders is almost always carried out from within a Rebellious Child [Cr] ego state and this fact is vitally important for their therapists to appreciate and take into account in**

attempting to help their clients stop their atypical theft behaviour. Their drug/alcohol/food abuse and/or extramarital involvement are likely also carried out, at least in part, from the Rebellious Child [Cr] ego state. Recognition of this fact can assist clients to become sensitive to the likelihood that, if they are in the Cr state, they may be inclined to act out by stealing or in one or other of the other ways mentioned here; therefore they may be well advised to avoid going shopping or placing themselves in other tempting situations at those times, or at least move out of the Cr ego state and into their Adult [A] ego state. [The Adult ego state will also be discussed in more detail in Chapter 11.]

As mentioned above, somewhat over 1/2 of the female and nearly 2/3 of the male, married Ss acknowledged having had extramarital involvements. In many cases the timing of these affairs coincided with marked animosity that the theft offenders were experiencing towards their spouses. However, since, according to Atwood and Schwartz (2002 - Journal of Couple & Relationship Therapy), some 45% - 55% of married women and 50% - 60% of married men in the USA engage in extramarital sex at some time or another during their relationship, the statistics arrived at in this study cannot be considered exceptional vis-a-vis the general population. In other words, we *cannot* state that Atypical Theft Offenders are markedly different from their *non-theft offender* fellow citizens in this regard. However, on the basis of the extensive clinical interview materials gathered in these cases, we *can* definitely state, that in the case of Atypical Theft Offenders, their extramarital involvements appeared to reflect, at least partly, the strong resentments that they had towards their partners and likely influenced their inclination to act out via having extramarital affairs and/or stealing.

In several cases, the Atypical Theft Offenders viewed their marital partners as very authoritarian, and they were aware that they were likely acting out of the Rebellious Child ego state when having extramarital involvements. A number of the theft offender clients had spouses who were police officers, lawyers and, in one case, a loss prevention worker – persons whose 'authority/legal' professions may tend to 'invite' atypical theft behaviour by their rebellious and angry partners.

****

Table Four: Professions Represented In The 2013 Study (N=30)

Profession or Occupation	# of Ss	% of Ss
Homemaker	6	20%
Teacher (public/high school)	4	13.3%
Physician	3	10%
Nurse*	3	10%
Business owner	2	6.7%
Office Manager	2	6.7%
Pharmacist	1	3.3%
Chartered Accountant	1	3.3%
Bookkeeper	1	3.3%
Administrative Assistant	1	3.3%
Other work-related activities**	3	10%
----------------------------------	------------	---------------
Married to a physician	3	10%

*Actually, *four* of the 30 Ss had worked as registered nurses; however one came from another country and was not able to work in her profession; she worked as a caretaker/cleaning person.
** One of these 3 Ss was the *former* nurse: another was a highly successful artist whose works sold for many hundreds of dollars each. The third person was unemployed.

Some of the most fascinating data to emerge from the 2013 study pertains to the occupations to which the individuals in this study belonged. The 30 participants included three physicians and three nurses currently working in their fields. There was also one pharmacist in the study; he worked in a major hospital and was assigned to its large cardiac intensive care unit. In total, therefore, there were fully 7 (23.3%) of the subjects who, on a nearly daily basis, dealt with patients who might well be confronting life-and-death circumstances.

An Important Note: The fact that nearly one quarter of the Ss in this study had to deal with the prospect and/or occurrence of death on a nearly daily basis, in my clinical opinion, had a direct psychodynamic bearing upon their theft behaviour.

Most employed members of our societies work in the retail, manufacturing, education, service and IT sectors. A minority of adults work in fields that repeatedly bring them face to face with the possibility of the loss of human life, perhaps on a daily basis. These doctors, nurses, soldiers, firefighters, police officers, military personnel, clergy and paramedics have professions that demand that they deal with serious injury, illness, or death. *And I have had many members of each of these professions as theft offender clients!*

In order to carry on with their work-related responsibilities, the professionals mentioned in the previous paragraph have to develop a certain 'emotional distancing' ability. But maintaining a 'professional distance', it is clear, often comes at a substantial price. Many of the persons who practice these professions have learned to suppress or even repress into their **unconscious** minds their fear, anger, sadness and the other emotions that laypersons might more naturally allow themselves to actually **consciously** experience when confronted with similar dreadful circumstances. After all, we rely upon the professionals involved in these intense, life-threatening or life-taking situations, to 'keep it together' at such times. As a result, many of these professionals suppress or repress these human reactions and emotions in order to properly fulfill their professional mandates.

Now, there may be a 'chicken or egg' issue here: Is a person contemplating working in one of the above or similar professions more likely to be an individual who is inclined to suppress or repress strong emotions related to life-and-death situations *or* does working in these professions 'teach' the individual to suppress or repress these emotions? Or might a combination of both alternatives be at work here? [As a sixteen year old requiring a summer job, I myself once briefly worked in a large cemetery, covering the caskets with earth after the funeral parties had left, and I still remember, now more than 55 years later, having to 'get over' my squeamishness working among the graves. I became aware that emotions of sadness and compassion were to be quickly suppressed, if not entirely repressed, just so that my fellow workers and I could do our jobs day after day.] Yet if one fails to deal with (or *process'*, as we in the helping professions might say nowadays) one's emotions regarding, say, the tragic death of a child, in order to maintain a 'professional approach' to the work, what happens to the very human feelings of sadness, loss, perhaps guilt, compassion, etc... that one might otherwise consciously experience? And at what price?

Imagine, if you will, having the child you are trying to help, in your capacity as a physician, paramedic or police officer, literally die in front of you. As a 'professional', you are not supposed to overtly express feelings of profound sadness or unhappiness and, certainly, your colleagues do not expect you to actually cry. So what do you do with these emotions and their search for expression? And how *should* you deal with being present at times when such losses occur?

I once asked a relative who had done his medical specialty residency at one of the most prestigious medical clinics in the USA, how he and the other doctors dealt with losing a patient on the operating table. I inquired whether they ever talked about such occurrences (which happened on a nearly daily basis at that institution, hardly surprising since it generally took on primarily the most serious cases) when they met in the doctors' lounge or with their close colleagues. He responded by saying simply and with conviction, *"We never, ever talk about those things!"* The same is usually true, I have been told, for police officers, paramedics and others. No wonder, then, that some of the members of these life-and-death-situation-encountering professions are no strangers to divorce, alcoholism, drug abuse, depression, suicide – and shoplifting.

As mentioned previously, as early as in our 1983 article that was published in the *Bulletin of the American Academy of Psychiatry and the Law*, my co-investigator, psychiatrist Dr J. Don Atcheson and I identified the prevalence of *'(perceived) unfair personally meaningful loss'* as a likely major trigger of atypical theft behaviour. Persons who work in professions where they may almost daily experience the prospect of 'unfair' fatalities, should therefore be considered especially vulnerable to acting out, including by stealing.

[By sheer coincidence, perhaps, on the day that I wrote the previous paragraph, an article appeared in a major Canadian newspaper (the Toronto Star, May 31, 2012) titled "When doctors grieve the loss." This piece cited an article that had appeared in the *Archives of Internal Medicine*, referring to a study done using 20 oncologists at major hospitals in Ontario. The newspaper's writer wrote that, *"Many of those surveyed said they felt not just grief when a patient died, but also a sense of powerlessness, self-doubt and failure- and those feelings often go untreated, as they remain taboo within the profession."* This study's findings obviously mirror those of my own most recent study, and therefore, I would contend, at least a minority of those in the physical medical helping professions may be prone to act out, perhaps by atypical theft behaviour, in response to being exposed to what they consider "unfair personally meaningful losses."]

Incidentally, as is well known, being married leaves one potentially vulnerable (and certainly exposed) to one's spouse's mental, emotional and/or physical state of being. It may be of interest to note that three (10%) of the Ss in the 2013 study were *married* to physicians. One of the three was also a physician. Therefore, fully eight (26.7%) of the members of the study were either in a health care profession and/or married to someone who was.

****

Table Five: Number Of Sessions Held With Clients In The 2013 Study (N=30)

Average # of clinical sessions per client	20.9 sessions
Total # of sessions for all 30 Ss	628 sessions

It is worthwhile noting that the clients in this study were seen for over twenty sessions, on average, a large number of one-on-one direct clinician-client sessions, especially perhaps, when compared to other studies of atypical theft behaviour. My decades of clinical experience in the area of atypical theft behaviour have convinced me that most Atypical Theft Offenders, possibly because of the fact that they *do* tend to be generally honest, hardworking and ethical individuals, usually find their seemingly irrational and bizarre theft behaviour to be so shameful and embarrassing that they are initially very reluctant to open up fully and divulge the true extent of what might be called (in Jungian terms) their very active, thieving 'shadow side'.

In order to ascertain a reasonable breadth and depth of familiarity with the goings on in the lives of these Atypical Theft Offenders, one must take the time necessary for the clinician-client relationship to develop and for a corresponding level of trust to deepen. For this to happen, this therapist of over five decades knows of no shortcut to taking the time required to allow the professional relationship to strengthen and deepen.

I well recall the church-going business owner who told me on the *first* occasion that I saw him, that he had stolen about ten times in his life, in total. During the *second* session he confessed that he had probably stolen about two hundred times in all. Then, during the *sixth* session, he announced that he had actually stolen *thousands* of times, on nearly a weekly basis during the previous more than forty years. It was then only during the *eighth* clinical session, that he spoke, very hesitantly at first, of the particularly violent and terrifying, repeated sexual abuse he had experienced at the hands of a pastor when he was less than eight years old. (I was the first person to whom he had ever divulged what to him were such shameful experiences.) He also told me that soon after the abuse began, he started stealing clothes from his siblings, cousins, and the children's sections of stores that he frequented with his mother. The stealing had continued throughout his adolescence and into his adulthood, even though he had been a very wealthy person for decades.

Clinicians and researchers <u>must</u> be willing to provide sufficient time and opportunity for a strong, positive therapeutic alliance to develop if they truly want to learn about the often troubled and embarrassing early experiences of these clients.
Simply doing the more usual sort of psychological assessment, comprised, typically, of a very few (1 to 6) hours, most of which time is often taken up with formal psychological testing or other pencil-and-paper tasks, is not likely to afford much opportunity to gain meaningful insight into the true motivations behind Atypical Theft Offenders' stealing. After all, these individuals are frequently relatively highly functioning members of society, persons whom their relatives, friends and working colleagues would likely describe as relatively 'normal' individuals, virtually indistinguishable in any marked psychological sense, from those persons most of us likely come in contact with on a daily basis.

In the earlier years of my own professional experience dealing with theft offenders, I carried out daylong formal psychological testing with Atypical Theft Offenders who presented at the Clarke Institute of Psychiatry outpatient service for psychiatric and psychological assessment. Test results indicated that these Atypical Theft Offenders were, for the most part, psychologically 'normal' and the usual 'psyc-testing' proved to be of very little value in most of these cases. Once every approximately100 cases, however, and if I have not been able to establish what I believe to be a psychologically robust understanding of an individual's atypical theft behaviour, I may conclude that formal and exhaustive psychological and/or neuropsychological testing might be worthwhile having done in order to perhaps offer additional relevant insights into the theft offender's psyche and theft behaviour. In such instances I would refer that client to an experienced forensic psychologist to carry out a (sometimes three-day long) full battery of psychological and neuropsychological testing. In most cases where this has been done, the results have <u>not</u> been definitive insofar as deepening our understanding of the reasons for the individual's atypical theft behaviour.

The reasons why an individual Atypical Theft Offender would risk so much for (usually) so little in terms of monetary gain, will likely only be uncovered by an experienced and knowledgeable clinician who is practiced in this area of criminal behaviour, and who is willing to put in the 'face' time necessary to uncover the answers. Unfortunately, a great many clinicians still remain misinformed about the reasons for atypical theft behavior. Part of the reason for this may well be related to the continued *mis*information that remains in much of the professional literature, even a full three decades years after our 1983 article titled *Shoplifting: An Occasional Crime Of The Moral Majority* provided, in detail, the first important findings of our original study in this area. Incidentally, that 1983 article was still available, as least as of December 22, 2012, on the website of the American Academy of Psychiatry and the Law, at the link: *http://www.jaapl.org/content/11/4/343.full.pdf+html?sid=331bd4e2-bd09-431c-858b-38bd3e11cb9d* .

[Possible reasons behind the continuing flow of misinformation and lack of understanding of atypical theft behaviour will perhaps become clearer in the next chapter.]

****

**Table Six: Levels Of Stress Reported By The Ss During
Their Periods Of Stealing**

Levels of Stress experienced during their periods of stealing, as reported by Ss	# of Ss	% of 30 Ss
Low level of stress	0	0%
Medium level of stress	0	0%
High level of stress	15	50%
Very high level of stress	15	50%

From the above Table it is clear that *all* of the 30 Ss reported experiencing at least 'High' levels of stress; indeed, for 50% of them, the reported level of stress was 'Very High'. This finding is characteristic, in my clinical experience, of virtually <u>all</u> Atypical Theft Offenders. Can one really imagine that if a usually responsible, genuinely ethical, reasonably well educated, and at least moderately financially secure individual were *not* experiencing a marked level of stress, that he would be likely to jeopardize his personal and working life and offend against his own moral code, by stealing?

Among the many hundreds of cases I have assessed I have virtually never encountered any person who could be considered an Atypical Theft Offender who was *not* experiencing a relatively high level of stress at about the time that the act of stealing occurred.

Now, if we can accept that an honest person would probably not steal unless he or she was under a marked level of stress, what *emotions* might such a person be experiencing around the time that the stealing occurred? One of the crucial answers to this question, according to the theft offenders' self-reports and as noted previously, is the emotion of <u>anger</u>!

****

The Prevalence of Consciously Experienced Anger Amongst ATOs

In my clinical experience, the emotion that is nearly always consciously present at the time that atypical theft behaviour is carried out by a usually law-abiding person, is *anger*! It is vital to understand that I am referring here to <u>consciously experienced anger</u>.

In other words, the clinician has only to inquire of the possible Atypical Theft Offender whether there was any*one* (or any*thing*, circumstance, situation, etc...) towards whom or about which the individual was *consciously* aware of experiencing anger just prior to, or at about the time of the theft, for that person to almost invariably acknowledge that he or she was indeed experiencing *pronounced anger* towards a specific person or in regard to a particular situation or circumstance at that time.

For example, one of my clients, a highly religious and ethical CEO with no prior involvement with stealing whatsoever, shoplifted a rib steak from a supermarket (by putting it in his overcoat pocket and attempting to walk out of the store) within an hour of being informed by his wife during a telephone call that she wanted a divorce, and that she was planning to move in with her long-time boss from work. (Psychoanalytically-oriented clinicians are hereby invited to enjoy speculating on the fact that the theft offender stole a <u>rib</u> steak on this occasion.)

Another client, after having been informed that an expected promotion was going instead to another co-worker, stole $200 from the purse of a colleague before leaving work for the day.

A third client, a well-to-do woman whose marriage was a sham and who felt pronounced and ongoing anger towards her husband, would, whenever they had yet another upsetting argument, feel compelled to leave the house and drive to a large upscale mall near their home. While she walked through the mall she would suddenly feel inclined to shoplift and would often act on that inclination.

DR. WILL CUPCHIK

Another very important note: In nearly every single case of **atypical theft behaviour that I have ever assessed, the theft offender had *not*, prior to our clinical sessions, been aware of the likely psychological (*psychodynamic*) *causal connection* between the pronounced feeling of anger that was being experienced and the subsequent act of stealing.** This has been true, regardless of how well educated or intelligent that person has been. Indeed, it was only after having assessed a great many cases of atypical theft behaviour that psychiatrist Dr Don J Atcheson and I first became aware of this connection, once we realized that this association had presented itself over and over and over again in these cases.

The Intensive Intervention Program client who doubted that her anger was related in any way to her stealing
One individual who came to my office in Toronto from her home in California to participate in the 4-day Intensive Intervention Program that I offered at the time, told me on several occasions during the first two days of the four days we were to work together, that she just didn't see how there could be any connection at all between her acknowledged occasional strong feelings of anger and her inclination to steal. However, on the morning of the third day of her Intensive, in response to my efforts encouraging her to address clearly unresolved issues that kept on presenting themselves during our work together, she became quite incensed with me. As she left for lunch a half-hour later, slamming the office door behind her, she was obviously still very agitated.

When this same client appeared some two hours later for the afternoon session, she entered my office smiling broadly and happily excited. As soon as she sat down she told me that she had experienced an *Eureka!* moment as she sat in her car after having left my office to go for lunch. She described having been very consciously aware of wanting to immediately drive to a local mall and steal *something!*

To her credit this client did *not* start her car's engine but instead tolerated experiencing her strong feelings and attempted to think through *why* she wanted to go somewhere and steal. Her conclusion was that she was very angry with me and she had a clear sense that if she proceeded to steal something her anger would somehow diminish. Furthermore, she also recognized that this was a very familiar pattern; i.e., responding to experiencing pronounced anger by wanting to steal something. Having

126

now identified this *felt connection* between marked anger and a desire to commit an act of theft, she was ecstatic! She said she believed that she would easily recognize this connection in the future and was therefore in a position to protect herself against acting out by stealing. As well, she recounted several other occasions during the previous few months when she had been angry with her parents, her husband and/or her children, and when she (unfortunately) did, in fact, go shoplifting.

One of my aims in writing this book is to bring to the attention of more and more persons, this most likely causal connection between consciously experienced anger *and* acting out by stealing behaviour. The previous example was merely one of the most illuminating examples of this oft-occurring phenomenon.

Note: Atypical Theft Offenders do *not* steal for the 'thrill of it'!

Another not uncommon misconception is that Atypical Theft Offenders steal because it is so 'thrilling' to do so. In fact, a reporter for a major U.S. weekly magazine once left me a voicemail, requesting my comments about this supposed phenomenon. She added that she had an editorial deadline fast approaching; unfortunately, I did not get her voicemail until after the deadline or I would have attempted to disavow her of this fallacy.

The fact is, of course, that many of the usually honest persons who do steal *can easily afford* to take part in exciting, 'thrilling' activities such as mountain biking, skateboarding, snowboarding, etc... or even so-called extreme sports/activities/hobbies such as bungee jumping, motocross, flying, or skydiving, if their primary desire is to experience 'thrills'. These activities can usually be done relatively safely, however, *without breaking the law and thereby jeopardizing the individuals' personal and/or professional reputations, and perhaps even their very freedom*. I suggest that because almost all Atypical Theft Offenders are at a loss to explain why they would do something so apparently 'stupid' as to risk so very much for (often) so very little in material gain by shoplifting, and because they are aware of the adrenalin 'rush' that may have accompanied the act of theft, that they make up the 'thrill' explanation to themselves for lack of a more apparently obvious understanding of their behaviour. **In my clinical opinion, however, the 'adrenalin rush' is the *result* of their carrying out the theft behaviour, rather than a precipitating *'cause'* of it.**

Now, of course, the act of stealing may well elicit an adrenalin 'rush', which is not surprising since so much is often being risked in order to do something that is illegal, and for which the gain is usually so relatively little in monetary terms. But having a 'thrill' is hardly why an Atypical Theft Offender is likely to put in jeopardy a long and distinguished personal reputation and/or career. Any clinician who wants to uncover *the more likely reasons* for atypical theft behaviour must be willing to assist the client to search for deeper levels of motivation than the notion of a 'thrill', which is likely merely a byproduct of the theft behaviour, not its cause or primary motivation.

It is important to remind the reader that in this book we are primarily dealing with adults, not teenagers or little children. For teens and younger persons, stealing *is* often a testing of limits and an acting out behaviour that can be accurately considered to be genuinely 'juvenile'. But, when an intelligent and usually responsible and honest <u>adult</u> acts out by atypical theft behaviour, that person is surely very much past the 'testing limits by stealing' phase of their chronological development.

I have had a few teenaged clients whose psychological motivations were indeed very much like those of the adults who are the main focus of this book, and when I have assessed and treated such young people our clinical work together has been very similar to that I describe in both this and my earlier book for adult Atypical Theft Offenders. However, most children's theft behaviour involves testing limits, expressing anger and aggression in an immature manner, and yes, even getting a 'thrill' (i.e., trying to get away with a rebellious, illegal act against authorities).

[Coincidentally, the day after I wrote the above paragraph I happened to be in a supermarket in a very upscale part of Toronto where the average price of a detached, single family, four-bedroom house is well over two million dollars. On that occasion my attention was drawn to the forceful voice of the store's manager informing a group of four teenaged boys that she was 'onto them' and that they should not dare to carry off the bottles of carbonated water that were stacked up near the front door. The boys scurried off and I inquired of the manager what the commotion was about; she informed me that some of the students who attended the (costly) private school in the vicinity had been making a practice of "trying out" such risky theft behaviour, most likely, she hypothesized, to satisfy a dare. She said she had previously caught a number of such groups of boys who had attempted the same thing. This rebellious, testing limits sort of adolescent behaviour is obviously not the main subject of this book.]

****

Table Seven: Intense Feelings Of Anger By Ss Consciously Experienced At The Time Of Their Stealing (N=30)

Anger and Stealing, as reported by Ss	# of Ss	% of Ss
Intense feelings of anger were consciously experienced by Ss at the time of their theft behaviour	27	90%
Experienced intense anger towards one or both parents at the time of the theft behaviour	26	86.7%
Experienced intense anger towards another person (other than a spouse/partner or parent) at the time of the theft behaviour	25	83.3%
Experienced intense anger towards spouse/partner at the time of the theft behaviour	24	80%
Has had a longstanding history of consciously experiencing intense anger	30	100%

From the above Table the most striking finding, of course, is that *all* **the subjects in the 2013 study**, which included 9 males ranging in age from 34 to 63 years (average age, 48.4 years), and 21 females ranging in age from 33 to 59 years (average age, 45.5 years) and *all* essentially bright, competent, successful and financially reasonably well off, individuals, **had a long-standing history of experiencing pronounced anger.**

Furthermore, 27 (90%) of the 30 Ss reported that *they were* *consciously* *aware of experiencing pronounced feelings of anger* *at the* *very time* *of carrying out their theft behaviour.*

DR. WILL CUPCHIK

An Important Note: The vast majority of the hundreds of atypical theft offenders whom I have assessed have stated that they had a longstanding history of experiencing intense anger on virtually a daily basis. Since these persons were, (i) *consciously* aware of being very angry with some person or circumstance or situation *at the time* of their stealing, and since, (ii) one of the defining criteria of labelling someone as suffering from 'kleptomania' (according to the diagnostic and statistical manual of the American Psychiatric Association – DSM-IV-Revised still current at the time of the publication of this book) is that "the stealing is not committed to express anger or vengeance," therefore (iii) it is very highly probable that it is a most serious error to label most usually honest persons who have shoplifted as suffering from 'kleptomania'.

Another Important Note: As of the time that this book was published (February 2013), there may have been a move afoot to remove the above exclusionary criterion for a diagnosis of **kleptomania** that "the stealing is not committed to express anger or vengeance." Removing a psychological, and indeed, a psycho*dynamic* motivation, i.e., *not* taking into account a possible *psychological* motivation for atypical theft behaviour for which there is such abundant evidence, might be considered a however innocently ignorant, inadvertent attempt to ignore the influence of any psychodynamics that may be involved in atypical theft behaviour. Doing so may then lead to inappropriate diagnoses and thus generate erroneous and ineffective treatments.

As possibly the most experienced clinician (at 39 years) in investigating cases of atypical theft behaviour, it is my firm clinical opinion that, since *consciously experienced anger and/or a desire for vengeance* is such a clearly prevalent theme in virtually all cases of atypical theft behaviour, ignoring the *existence*, to say nothing of the *importance* of this factor, is decidedly a great error.

Most of the subjects in this study readily described having pronounced feelings of anger directed towards their spouses and/or other significant persons and/or situations in the their personal and/or working lives. For example, in more than one case the theft offender was clear that she knew that her husband intensely resented dishonesty, and therefore by stealing and getting caught she was able to irritate him mightily. As previously mentioned, another subject resented her husband insisting that they move to an exclusive gated retirement community in the southern

USA, thousands of miles away from their grandchildren. She was consciously aware that her husband would be so ashamed of their new friends knowing that his wife was a 'thief' that there was a distinct possibility that he might agree to move back east. A third subject, a financially secure businessman, was very angry that his thirty-something stepdaughter was still living with him and his wife, and that she frequently would eat certain 'specialty' foods that, as far as he was concerned and had stated more than a few times, were intended exclusively for him. On several occasions he stole the identical products from a nearby upscale supermarket, usually on the days following the ones when he found that his step-daughter had consumed the foods in question.

Of course, not all persons who carry feelings of intense and frequent anger necessarily commit acts of shoplifting or other kinds of theft. So why is it that *some* persons who have long-standing anger *do* act out in this way? An at least partial answer can be found in the results presented in the next Tables -- **the very common difficulty Atypical Theft Offenders share - specifically, difficulties with appropriately asserting themselves.**

****

Table Eight: Number Of Ss Of The 2013 Study Who Had Difficulty Asserting Themselves At Home And/Or At Work (N=30)

Ss who have marked difficulty asserting themselves with...	# of Ss	% of Ss
parent(s)	21	70%
partner/spouse	20	66.7%
his or her own child(ren)	14	46.7%
at work with bosses and/or employees	14	46.7%

It should now be clear that some highly competent and accomplished individuals, <u>because they tend to have problems asserting themselves</u> in ways that might resolve whatever issues they are upset about, could be inclined to act out. When an adult person has difficulty asserting him or herself in problematic situations, frustration and anger are almost bound to result. Of course, most of us become angry from time to time, but to the extent that we have learned appropriate ways of asserting ourselves and use coping mechanisms that provide us with the means of dealing with our anger in productive ways (e.g., by 'talking things out' with the offending party, a friend or acquaintance, or by 'getting our anger out' through exercise or creative activities), our anger usually dissipates in reasonably short order.

But what happens if an individual has serious difficulties with self-assertion and consequently does not deal with his anger in ways that move him and the issue at hand towards resolution? Then the anger may continue to fester until 'something gives'. In some instances the individual may act out in physical ways *(for example, by fighting, throwing things, drinking, taking drugs, etc...)* in an attempt to relieve some of his frustration and anger. For others, more surreptitious ways of acting out may occur; stealing is one such way.

****

Table Nine: The Levels Of Self-Esteem Reported By Ss Of The 2013 Study (N=30)

Ss' self-reported levels of self-esteem	# of Ss	% of Ss
Very low self-esteem	19	63.3%
Low self-esteem	8	26.6%
Medium self-esteem	1	3.3%
High self-esteem	2	6.7%
Very high self-esteem	0	0%

In this study, 27 (90%) of the Ss reported having either 'low' or 'very low' levels of self-esteem. This finding accurately reflects my years of experience of dealing with Atypical Theft Offenders, who, time and again, and in spite of the fact that they were often highly intelligent, well educated and professionally and/or financially successful, have presented with painfully low levels of self-esteem. How can this be so? For the most part, the answer appears to lie in the long-lasting effects of their upbringing.

A most interesting manifestation of the remarkably low self-esteem that so many Atypical Theft Offenders have, is that they are sometimes very reluctant to spend money on themselves; indeed, they may incessantly look for sales and even then may shoplift as a means of 'spending' even less [specifically, ZERO dollars!] on themselves.

This *dis*inclination to spend money on themselves sometimes also extends to even not investing in their own health and wellbeing. A large minority of these persons (interestingly, many of whom were among the *wealthier* Atypical Theft Offenders I have dealt with), after being caught and charged, would spend many thousands of dollars in lawyers' fees and supplementary purposes (which, of course, did nothing to help them uncover why they stole in the first place and what matters they needed to address in order to not re-offend). At the same time, however, some Atypical Theft Offenders will express considerable reluctance at the prospect of spending considerably less than what they are paying their lawyers, in order to get the psychological help they need. They may not think that they *deserve* to spend money on improving their own mental and emotional wellbeing, even though by so doing they might be less inclined to steal in the future.

Problems with self-assertion are often tied to very low self-esteem

And what might be the reason that these individuals have difficulties asserting themselves? The answer to this question emerges from other findings of the 2013 study of these thirty primarily honest, ethical, intelligent and at least reasonably financially successful persons. **The problem is almost invariably one of *poor self-esteem*,** usually incubated in the individual's childhood, and hardly altered for these now adult individuals by their academic, professional and/or financial successes.

The 30 Ss in this study included:
(a) A **cardiologist** who taught part-time at a university's renowned medical school, yet whose mother, throughout his childhood, had continually berated him for being "stupid", "lazy", a "know nothing", and for being, as he was repeatedly told, "a constant disappointment." In later years, when the mother developed a serious heart problem that was within the purview of her physician-son, she refused to seek his advice, saying, "You don't know anything anyway; I don't know how you got your degree."

Apparently the mother had treated all five of her now highly educated children similarly, and most of them had developed major emotional problems that continued into their adulthoods and that kept them from reaching their full personal and professional potential. My client repeatedly risked losing his medical license as time after time he stole from the same major department store known for its state-of-the-art 'loss prevention' division. At the time that I saw him, this doctor had yet to be caught but was understandably terrified by the prospect. He also carried considerable anger towards his wife that he did not deal with directly; she was an ivy league-trained lawyer, in comparison with whom he felt very inadequate. Whenever she put him down in arguments, he felt like he had when his mother had belittled him, and then unbeknownst to his wife, he was at increased risk to go shoplifting. Interestingly, the fact that their joint income of nearly one million dollars annually did not deter him from stealing items usually worth less than $50. [Incidentally, I have often told clients that, no matter how intelligent they may be, if they are married to *lawyers*, they may well lose over 95% of all the arguments they will have with their spouses since most lawyers' are very highly practiced in constructing seemingly convincing arguments, no matter how fallacious their points might actually be.]

(b) A female **event planner** whose own father had belittled *his* wife and all of his female children. Having had a terrible marriage to an emotional bully of a husband, followed by a particularly nasty divorce, this highly financially successful but low self-esteem client had great difficulty asserting herself in any situation, and would even react to issues that arose between her and her own young children, by shoplifting.

(c) A **daily church-going mechanical engineer** was brought up in a household as the only son of a brilliant and high profile father who had founded a hugely successful high-tech company. The father frequently, and virtually always unfavourably, compared my client to his more financially and academically successful siblings. Both parents also let him know early on that he was not considered sufficiently good material to succeed his father as the head of the family business, the position that was indeed passed on to his younger sister. Moving from job to job, this man managed to steal increasingly large amounts of money from a series of employers in progressively more blatant ways that virtually guaranteed he would be caught - and sooner than later. His resentment towards his parents and his siblings motivated him to compensate for his poor sense of self-esteem and relatively low level of success, by stealing money to support an ostentatious lifestyle. When he first contacted me he had been charged with stealing over $500,000 from his most recent employer. [For several reasons, this man was a good example of the Mixed-Type of theft offender; i.e., he displayed numerous Atypical Theft Offender *and* Typical Theft Offender aspects.]

Most of the Ss in the 2013 study came from middle class homes. A few came from clearly upper socio-economic level families. The issues of having difficulty asserting oneself, holding onto anger and experiencing distinctly low self-esteem, are obviously matters that may be exhibited by individuals who emerge from all strata of society, and the great majority of the subjects in this study demonstrated these qualities in full measure.

So, the findings of the 2013 study clearly demonstrate that generally honest, ethical and hardworking individuals who display seemingly nonsensical and bizarre atypical theft behaviour, are usually acting out in ways that reflect their problems with self-assertion, poor ways of coping with anger and markedly low self-esteem. In effect, they learned to *not* openly express their ideas and tended to hold onto their anger, partly because they didn't think they deserved to be treated any better. Their low self-esteem made it unlikely they would assert themselves, and therefore their anger was not likely to be dealt with in healthful ways. Their subsequent stealing was usually: (i) a way of releasing (however temporarily and poorly) some of their pent-up frustration and anger; (ii) a way of compensating themselves for perceived mistreatment by their parents, spouses, children, etc...; (iii) a means of acquiring things that they didn't believe they deserved to *purchase*; (iv) an unconscious way of seeking negative attention, and/or (v) potentially self-destructive ways through which to call out to receive the help that they, at a deeper level within their psyches, likely knew they needed.

Atypical Theft Offenders need the help of professionals who will recognize, for example, that when an award-winning public school teacher who loves her vocation, steals a bunch of flowers from a supermarket across the street from the school where she taught, or a senior physician earning more than $500,000 a year shoplifts a small package of cookies from a local convenience store where she frequently shops and could be readily recognized, that *surely* there are likely some serious psychological issues that need to be addressed in such cases. Furthermore, how the theft offender deals with uncomfortable feelings and how he or she views his or her own self-worth, are relevant issues to deal with in these cases.

A fine illustration of the fact that many Atypical Theft Offenders truly are compassionate, contributing members of society, and that involvement of the client's Significant Other can be most helpful

One of the Atypical Theft Offenders I assessed a few years ago was a nurse who had had several convictions for theft. Over a period of days I became increasingly impressed by this individual's intelligence, depth of emotional insight and empathy. Also evident, however, was the very low level of self-esteem in which she held herself. It was only when her husband participated in a session, however, that I learned of his wife's extraordinary bravery and the depth of her humanity. Evidently, one day my client was driving to work during wintertime when she came upon a traffic accident that had obviously happened only minutes before. Pinned underneath one of the vehicles was a young girl who was grievously injured. My client had pulled over, exited her car, and without hesitation, crawled on her stomach under the vehicle that was precariously positioned on top of the injured girl. My client comforted this person as best she could until, unfortunately, the girl died. My client's low self-esteem undoubtedly kept her from informing me of this incident and the commendation that she received from the police chief and mayor of the city where this occurred. (Her husband later sent me a photocopy of the citation she received.) Of course, she was a theft offender, yet her actions on that winter's day spoke volumes about the quality of person that she was – and I certainly made mention of this in the Report that I wrote for the court in this case.

Chapter 10

SUMMARIZING THE FACTORS THAT CAN CONTRIBUTE TO ATYPICAL THEFT BEHAVIOUR

In this book I have described in some detail the results of my years of clinical investigation into atypical theft behaviour. I have also provided the reader with the major findings of three major studies that I have conducted over the years, using sample cases from the over 700 clients whom I have assessed, and in most cases, treated. Together these three studies involved some 100 cases.

I also mentioned previously that the findings of the three studies were very simpatico with one another. The findings of the three studies have been very congruent with one another and each successive study has allowed me to deepen and broaden my understanding of the atypical theft behaviour of usually honest adults.

The various contributing factors that can precipitate atypical theft behaviour

Without delving too deeply into the injunctions against stealing among most religions, it is nevertheless interesting to ponder the fact that this injunction is explicitly included in the ten commandments of both the Jewish and Christian religions. Islam and most other religions also consider stealing wrong and/or a 'sin'. As you have already learned by reading to this point, among the many possible but not-mutually-exclusive contributing factors that can precipitate atypical theft behaviour, are the following:

- stealing in response to earlier and/or more recent unresolved personal issues and/or inappropriately dealt-with anger, usually associated with problems in self-assertion and having low self-esteem;

- stealing as loss-substitution, in response to actual or anticipated (as perceived) unfair personally meaningful losses, including that of one's health, job, spouse or partner, child, parent; in other words, stealing as compensation-by-substitution;

- stealing as acting out in response to experiencing extreme stress;

- stealing to satisfy a desire to get caught and thereby be punished for that which the offender feels guilty about, including in the most extreme cases, so-called 'suicide by cop';

- stealing in response to having experienced verbal, emotional, physical and/or sexual abuse;

- stealing in response to having perceived oneself as having been wronged; *and*

- stealing related to post traumatic stress disorder.

Case # 12: Louisa, a prominent medical researcher who stole from her teaching-hospital employer after she had become permanently partially disabled due to the inadequate safety measures provided by the administration

Louisa was a world-renowned researcher who, once the Berlin wall came down, moved from East Germany to a research position at a major hospital that promised to provide her with a state-of-the-art, secure and safe laboratory where she could continue her groundbreaking medical research. Unfortunately the institution where she obtained employment was simultaneously carrying out investigations into the effects of certain lethal viruses upon civilians inside the same building and most unfortunately, directly on the floor above her. As unlikely as it might seem to a reasonable and prudent adult, the physical plant of the research facility did not adequately ensure that there was proper venting and capturing of the albeit miniscule amounts or residue gases that were produced on the upper floor. On numerous occasions, after Louisa began having profoundly disturbing symptoms of lung and other bodily systems' failures, she quickly deduced the likely source of the problem and wrote memos to the CEO and other senior executives of the institution, first requesting -and then, when no action was forthcoming- demanding, that the hospital fix the venting system that was leaking toxic gases into her own laboratory, or at least move her to a separate building in the hospital complex.

Having reviewed the reams of exchanges of correspondence provided by my client attesting to the leakage of specific toxic and potentially lethal gases into Louisa's lab from the facility located directly about her, and after examining the exchanges of letters and emails between Louisa and the hospital administration produced over a four year long period in her attempts to get appropriate action taken, and having corroborated the truly bizarre stonewalling and punitive responses with which senior management reacted to her requests, it was entirely clear that Louisa was getting no satisfaction whatsoever in her dealings with the hospital's executives and that she had become extremely frustrated and angry.

Increasingly frightened as her own health deteriorated, Louisa requested that the state governmental agency responsible for workplace safety in hospitals in her state do its own investigations. This agency, after carrying out a number of sophisticated scientific readings, concluded that Louisa was indeed being exposed to an almost certainly eventually lethal quantity of toxic gases that originated in the suspect laboratory on the floor above. As astounding as it might seem to the reader and to myself, even after having been presented with the governmental agency's report, the hospital's executives took only minimal measures that hardly dealt with the source of the problem.

Filled with rage, Louisa acted out by stealing some $1000.—of office equipment and supplies over a period of six months for her own personal use at home. Her theft behaviour was uncovered when an inventory of office materials was done and the hospital subsequently charged her with theft. Louisa then sued her employer for having already caused a major and irreversible deterioration in her health.

In the Psychological Report that I wrote about this case, I mentioned that, given the real and extreme danger to which the hospital had subjected her over such an extended period of time, and the absolute refusal of the administration to take suitable corrective action, I was impressed that Louisa had actually exercised relatively great restraint and I was genuinely surprised that she had not acted out against senior management and/or the hospital in a much more potentially devastating fashion than by 'merely' absconding with $1000.—worth of office supplies. In an attempt to avoid litigation, the hospital eventually withdrew the charges against Louisa, moved her laboratory to another building and compensated her *financially for the "extreme distress and permanent physical and physiological damage" that they had been responsible of subjecting her to over a number of years.*

You will appreciate from a review of this case, that Louisa was possibly acting out via atypical theft behaviour *in response to* several of the factors mentioned at the beginning of this chapter, including:

- loss-substitution, specifically of her good health;

- extreme stress;

- having experienced verbal, emotional, and physical abuse;

  and

- unresolved anger towards a management that almost entirely ignored her pleas to have her health safeguarded.

One of the major reasons that I continue working with Atypical Theft Offenders after nearly four decades of clinical investigations in the area, is that each case provides a rare opportunity to uncover the particular psychodynamics invariably involved in precipitating the albeit entirely inappropriate acting out by usually upstanding, highly responsible and generally honest individuals. Each case is unique, even as it also shares a number of features in common with many other cases of atypical theft behaviour. The challenge is always to be alert to clues as to what issues and dynamics may be operating in each instance of atypical theft behaviour.

In the next chapter I provide an overview of how I approach psychological treatment with Atypical Theft Offenders.

Chapter 11

APPLYING TRANSACTIONAL ANALYSIS AND THE 'DRAMA TRIANGLE' TO UNDERSTANDING AND TREATING ATYPICAL THEFT OFFENDERS

As I have indicated previously, rarely do *so many* risk *so much* for relatively *so little* as occurs *so frequently* among those shoplifting individuals who can accurately be termed Atypical Theft Offenders. So, what psychological theory might best explain why do they do it?

Using the Transactional Analysis (TA) model of personality to understand and treat Atypical Theft Offenders

From my years of academic studies in psychology and after teaching graduate students the theories and practices of various types of psychotherapy, the model of personality and interpersonal interaction that I have found to be the most useful and at the same time, most easily taught to my own theft offender (and other) clients, has been that of *Transactional Analysis*. The TA model was originally developed by psychiatrist Dr Eric Berne. Dr Berne summarized his initial ideas in a book he titled *Games People Play* that was primarily meant to be read by other clinicians. To his (and undoubtedly his publisher's surprise) the book became an immediate best seller.

[In fact, as of May 2012, an Internet search indicated that *Games People Play* actually ranks 19th on the New York Times All-time Bestseller list, having been on the non-fiction bestseller list for 109 weeks, the last time on 9/10/1967. Contrast that accomplishment with that of the extraordinary novel *To Kill A Mockingbird* that ranks further down the list, in the 24th position, and one gains some perspective of just how popular and successful Dr Berne's book has been and just how wide an audience it has reached.]

I first learned of the Transactional Analysis model of personality and interpersonal interaction in 1972, just prior to the time that I attended a month-long workshop at the *Western Institute for Group and Family Therapy* in Watsonville, California. The co-directors were psychiatrist Dr Bob Goulding and his wife, social worker Mary Goulding, and they led most of the training. Bob and Mary had blended Transactional Analysis with Gestalt Therapy in a most unique and powerful manner; they called their approach 'Redecision Therapy', and I use much of what I have learned from them to this day. Indeed, when assessing and treating Atypical Theft Offenders, I find this model to be invaluable, in part because it allows me to transmit important information and teachings to my clients in ways that assist them to gain virtually immediate insight into their own personalities and atypical theft behaviour, as well as their interpersonal interactions with their family members, friends and those with whom they need to interact with at work.

Most importantly for our purposes, the seemingly simple theoretical formulation of Transactional Analysis is especially useful in helping all of us to understand and treat atypical theft behaviour!

Summarizing the Transactional Analysis (TA) model of personality

Most clinicians would concur that, at any moment in time, it may be said that an individual is in one of three so-called 'ego states'; - the **Parent, Adult** and **Child** ego states. These are states that are easily identifed by the individual and any observers by carefully paying attention to the words, tone and posturing being displayed.

According to the Transactional Analysis model there are two versions of Parent ego state – the **Nurturing Parent (Pn)** and the **Critical Parent (Pc)**, as well as three variations of the **Child** ego state – the **Free Child (Cf), Adapted Child (Ca)** and **Rebellious Child (Cr)**.

The Parent Ego State:

One is usually in the **Parent** ego state when being either judgmental or caretaking. The language of the person who is in the **Parent** ego state often consists of implicitly or explicitly stated 'shoulds'; e.g., "You *should* do your homework", or "You *should* take a break from working."

To be more specific, the so-called *Nurturing* **Parent [Pn]** is the ego state one is usually in when lovingly looking after another or oneself. Often the **Pn** will be heard saying things like, "You should go lay down now; you are clearly so tired (or sick)", or "Let me make you some tea or chicken soup," or "You did such a wonderful job: I am so proud of you."

The *Critical* **Parent [Pc]** ego state is the state one is in when being highly critical or demeaning. The **Pc** will be heard saying things like, "You are so stupid!" or "That is just plain wrong!" or "I have heard quite enough of you for now, young man. Go to your room right now!" The **Pc** will sometimes use an accusatory *pointed finger* aimed in the direction of the one whom he is addressing.

Incidentally, when clients are asked, "Which of your parents spent most of their time in which ego Parent state (i.e., **Nurturing Parent** *or* **Critical Parent**) when interacting with you and/or your siblings or one another?" they usually can rapidly identify whether it was their mother or father who tended to be more nurturing or more critical much of the time. They can also (if they have children of their own) usually quickly declare whether they or their spouse/partner tends to be more nurturing or critical when it comes to dealing with their own children or even with one another! This is important information to consider when examining interpersonal relationships. You, the reader, are invited to answer the same questions in regard to you and your own first and current family constellations.

The **Adult [A]** ego state is the state one is in when being rational and thinking or speaking in a logical manner. The **A** is basically devoid of feelings. It neither deals with 'shoulds', 'should nots' or emotions.

The **Free Child [Cf]** is the ego state one is in when 'in touch with' one's body and/or genuine emotions. At the time of writing this sentence the best example I can give is of my third oldest grandchild who, at age three, is so obviously filled with wonder and joy most of the time. His laughter and beaming smile attest to his being happily in touch with his emotions and body as he *runs* from one end of the hallway to the other, for no apparent reason other than the pure pleasure he experiences when so doing. Of course, the **Cf** is not necessarily only or always happy but can experience and display all sorts of emotions – positive and negative. Indeed, my wife and I recently met another three-year old boy, one whose mother had tragically died only three months earlier. He seldom smiled and his sadness and deep sense of loss were clearly etched on his too young face and in the way he tightly held his body. When, at various times, our lovely daughter-in-law and my wife took turns holding and hugging this child, his face 'lit up' and he appeared to be clearly relishing and absorbing the caring and compassion that their Nurturing Parent **[Pn]** states were attempting to provide.

Whenever we as adult persons are in touch with our deepest/truest emotions and/or our bodies, we often are in **Cf**. Sexual activity and exercise workouts are other occasions when we may be in the **Cf** ego state, and that may be one of the principal reasons that these activities are so often pursued by so many persons.

The **Adapted Child [Ca]** is the state that we are often in when we are feeling and/or behaving in the ways we have *been taught* or *learned* to feel and behave as children. And we carry on into adulthood using our **Ca** ego state a good portion of the time. A way to distinguish between **Cf** and **Ca** is that the latter is the version of the Child ego state that we *learned* was acceptable to our parents or other caregivers while we were very young while the former, **(Cf)** ego state, is the one we are in when we are just being our truest self. So, for example, to use a very basic example, a one year old child might still be used to having a bowel movement or urinating at the very first moment that he or she feels the urge. This is **Free Child (Cf)** behaviour. But virtually all caregivers will 'toilet train' their children by suggesting (either from **Nurturing Parent** or **Critical Parent** and/or perhaps even from **Adult** ego state) that *"Now that we are visiting granny, please let me know if you have to 'go' and I will take you to the 'potty'."* This is one of the many ways that the child is introduced to what psychologists refer to as 'delayed gratification', i.e., holding off doing something we want to do until a more appropriate time or when we are in a more suitable place.

There are not many of us, on an especially beautiful summer's day, who would *not* prefer to be in **Free Child**, perhaps being outside participating in our favorite activities (walking, biking, playing golf or tennis, sailing, etc...), rather than having to stay in the classroom or at our work station until the end of a designated work period. Most of us are very good at delaying gratification, or to put it another way, the majority of us have a very effective **Adapted Child**. Of course, some of us may overdo it, that is, we may have difficulty moving into **Free Child** when we *are* in a position to and/or when it is appropriate to do so. As a result, a good many adults will choose to have a drink or some other 'relaxant' when they arrive home after a day at work, in part to help them shift into a more **Free Child** state – although interestingly, when they do partake of alcohol or drugs they may go into a different, less satisfying ego state than the one they had desired.

Now we finally come to the so-called **Rebellious Child [Cr]** ego state. Most of us will be at least somewhat familiar with the so-called 'terrible twos', the time in a young child's life when *"No!"* becomes standard fare. When a child is in the **Cr** ego state, her oppositional position becomes very clear. *"No, I <u>don't</u> want to eat my vegetables!"* or *"I <u>don't</u> want to go to sleep!"* Of course, this rebelliousness is actually a very important phase to experience; it is a way of differentiating ourselves from any 'others' and gaining some degree of self-confidence and self-assertiveness. Again, though, some persons may have difficulty letting go of the **Cr** ego state for a variety of reasons. Thus we know, or know of, adults who are known to be 'rebels', with or without a cause. As a former high school teacher, lo those many decades ago, I well remember a few students whose rebelliousness was perhaps overdone. Indeed, they seemed to have difficulty getting out of the **Cr** ego state and 'settle down' in the classroom, which may have required that they shift into a more appropriate **Ca** ego state.

In my clinical experience, when usually rational, intelligent and successful individuals nevertheless risk so very much for so very little by committing acts of relatively minor theft, they are at those moments behaving in a clearly *non*-rational, *non-Adult* manner, especially when they could easily have afforded to pay for the items stolen, and/or in some cases, didn't even want the items.

Indeed, it is almost certain that when such usually law-abiding persons commit an act of what is, for them, *atypical* theft behaviour, they are not in their rational **Adult** ego state. <u>On the contrary, they are virtually always in the **Rebellious Child [Cr]** ego state at that time</u> and this fact makes it vitally important to assist Atypical Theft Offenders to become more attuned to the ego states that they are in from moment to moment, so that if they recognize that they are in the **Cr** ego state when they are distressed, they will hopefully stay away from stores or other temptations until they have moved into a more **Adult** ego state (or, 'frame of mind').

In fact, once clients become familiar with the Transactional Analysis model, they usually rapidly become aware of when they are even *likely* to move into the **Rebellious Child** ego state, and will take the preemptive measure of *not* going to places where they might be tempted to steal something. As an Atypical Theft Offender client recently told me, *"I was very angry and frustrated with my husband earlier this week, I could feel*

145

*myself wanting to just go to the mall and walk around. I knew that that was the last place I should be going. So instead, I just took my **Rebellious Child** for a long walk and then came home in a more **Adult** state."*

Diagram # 2: The Six 'Ego States' Of The Transactional Analysis Model

Nurturing Parent [Pn] *ego state*	Critical Parent [Pc] *ego state*
The **Pn** is the nurturing, gentle, supportive part of the Parent ego state.	The **Pc** is the more offensive, harsher, less clearly supportive Parent ego state.

Adult [A] *ego state*
The Adult [A] ego state is the state the individual is usually in when being rational, logical and realistically thoughtful. Keep in mind that some intelligent persons, including especially highly experienced lawyers, are able to *sound* reasonable and rational even when presenting arguments that they themselves realize are very flawed.

Free Child [Cf] *ego state*	Rebellious Child [Cr] *ego state*	Adapted Child [Ca] *ego state* The
The ego state when one is 'in touch with' his genuine emotions and/or his body. Very little children often spend a great deal of their time in the Cf ego state.	This ego state is also a natural part of a person's psyche. **Atypical Theft Offenders, when they act out by stealing, are almost invariably in this state.**	state that an individual has usually *learned* to be in when emotional. Some children have learned to not show anger or sadness or, in cases, even joy.

One further note about ego states: It is even possible to say something as presumably bland as "Pass the butter" from *any* of the ego states mentioned above. For example, one can say "Pass the butter" in a warm, kind voice [Pn]; in a cold, demanding voice [Pc]; in a matter-of-fact, non-emotional way [A]; with some excitement or enthusiasm [Cf]; in a 'I'm a very good boy,' manner, [Ca]; or in a 'tough guy' or sulking voice [Cr]. Try it!

And that is why, when person X says to person Y, "Why are you upset with me? All I said was, 'Pass the butter!'", X's words alone may not have been the whole message that was conveyed. X's tone of voice (perhaps harsh), <u>facial expression</u> (possibly demeaning) and/or <u>body position</u> (e.g., think of the pointed finger) may have simultaneously been conveying negative [**Pc**] communication elements while making the seemingly straightforward request to "Pass the butter."

One of the most valuable hallmarks of successful treatment with Atypical Theft Offenders is to have helped them to recognize *which* ego state they are in at *which* times, and to assist them to <u>change</u> to a more suitable/appropriate ego state, at will. Learning to do so can do wonders for one's personal relationships in general.

****

THE DRAMA TRIANGLE AND ITS RELEVANCE TO ATYPICAL THEFT BEHAVIOUR

One of the most clinically important conceptualizations that I have learned in the past forty years, and one that continues to be of considerable help with very many of my clients, is that of the Drama Triangle, as first articulated by psychiatrist Dr Stephen Karpman. As a psychotherapist I have always been very grateful for this exceptionally easy to follow and useful conceptualization. [The reader will find a much more detailed exposition of the Drama Triangle on the website www.KarpmanDramaTriangle.com .]

The Drama Triangle is present and operating at times in virtually all persons who have, at least in part, a small neurotic component: keep in mind that a good layperson's definition of a **neurotic** is "one who is an *intelligent* individual who <u>thinks</u>, <u>feels</u> and/or <u>behaves</u> *unintelligently* – or to put it plainly, *grossly inappropriately!*" Of course, most of us, if we are honest with ourselves, can lay claim to having had at least some moments when we thought, felt and/or behaved in ways that can hardly be defined as 'intelligent'. Atypical theft behaviour by usually honest persons virtually invariably represent not their finest hours!

According to the Drama Triangle formulation espoused by Karpman is the idea that **in every drama there are always three characters or 'positions' – that of Persecutor, Rescuer and Victim.** (Think of the last dramatic movie, television news item, book or magazine or newspaper article you heard, saw or read and you will very likely be able to identify the three roles in regard to the dramatic event or circumstance being described.)

Now, of course, there are many instances when someone (or some animal) *is*, in fact, a genuinely innocent **Victim**; this individual may have been the victim of an act perpetrated by someone, or some animal we can refer to as the **Persecutor**. What makes such situations not only dramatic but especially satisfying is when there appears on the scene some *one* (say a firefighter or good Samaritan) or some *animal* (think of Lassie) who comes to the rescue of the **Victim**; the term **Rescuer** can be used to describe this person or animal.

To repeat, there are indeed many situations or circumstances in which there are genuine, *non-neurotic* Victims, Persecutors and Rescuers. Some professions, including those of firefighter, paramedic and animal control officers, have as part of their official or unofficial job descriptions, an imperative to act to save persons and/or animals who may have become victims through no fault of their own.

It is also evident from my clinical investigations that nearly all Atypical Theft Offenders have experienced events, circumstances and/or situations in which it is accurate and fair to say that they were genuine Victims. Usually their Victim-ness came about during childhood, when they may have been subjected to serious family disruptions (many come from homes where one or other parent left or died) and/or as a result of their having experienced verbal, emotional, physical and/or sexual abuse. In other words, they originally became Victims through no fault of their own. They were genuinely Victims. In later years, however, even in instances where they were personally, interpersonally, vocationally and/or financially successful, they may be inclined when stressed or distressed, to once again invoke - or in some cases of atypical theft behaviour, *invite* – the Victim position.

Atypical Theft Offenders almost invariably invite - or even create - situations in which they view themselves as, and may indeed become, Victims. For example, some individuals may put themselves in dangerous situations wherein they are put upon by others in not entirely unexpected circumstances. A recent case of a man who evidently chose to jump into a tigers' enclosure at a zoo may be considered to have placed himself into a situation where he would likely soon become a Victim. If then attacked by one of the tigers in that enclosure (as actually happened) he was certainly a **Victim** of the attack, and the tiger could be easily labeled a **Persecutor**. Now imagine an animal handler that works in that part of the zoo comes to the man's assistance. The handler would, of course, be seen as a **Rescuer**.

Many years ago the Toronto papers reported a situation in which a large, powerfully built man was physically assaulting a much smaller and seemingly helpless woman on a subway platform. Within moments a so-called 'good Samaritan' came to the woman's rescue. Unfortunately for him, as the Rescuer was pulling the Persecutor away from the Victim, the latter turned on him and joined the man who turned out to be her 'intimate other' in beating up the good Samaritan. In other words, the Rescuer soon became the Victim, even as the supposed Victim became one of his Persecutors.

I can report without hesitation that nearly all Atypical Theft Offenders, at the time that they are stealing (say, from a department or grocery store), see themselves as Victims. Perhaps the Atypical Theft Offender had just been fired or has had an argument with his or her spouse, and is feeling very hard done by (in other words, a 'Victim'). That person's theft behaviour at a retail store may be a case of acting out in response to having perceiving himself or herself as being hard done by – in other words, Victimized. Of course, from the store's perspective, it is the store that is the Victim and the theft offender who is the Persecutor.

And indeed, that is the hallmark of atypical theft behaviour; the theft offender sees himself or herself as a Victim, acts out by stealing, and in effect -and in fact- becomes the Persecutor of the store; the latter is now the Victim of the theft. When a loss prevention person is called, he or she becomes, from the theft offender's perspective, the Persecutor, and the theft offender now sees himself or herself, once again, as a Victim.

<u>**It is these switches of positions from within the Drama Triangle conceptualization that helps denote neurotic behaviour.**</u> I have had innumerable theft offender clients who have told me that they thought the stores were charging too much for their wares (i.e., the stores were the Persecutors, from the theft offenders' viewpoints). In many cases, the theft offenders reported that they had already spent a lot of money at those

stores and were just 'taking a little bit, for 'free'' for themselves. In other words, they saw themselves as having been taken advantage of by the stores (the latter being viewed as, in a sense, Persecutors) and they believed that they had already spent too much money for the items they had bought and paid for (they therefore viewed themselves as 'Victims' of the stores' supposedly unreasonably high markups). When they stole, of course, they had acted as Persecutors and the stores became *their* Victims. And if they were caught and charged, then the stores were viewed by the perpetrators of the theft behaviour as once again, Persecutors, while the theft offenders considered themselves to once again be the stores' Victims.

It is understandable if, after having read the above, the reader has just now experienced the equivalent of 'mental whiplash'. After all, the switches of Drama Triangle positions described above have been many and rapid. So let me now present the above in a point-type sequence.

1. the Atypical Theft Offender has had a very upsetting experience within minutes or hours of his or her theft behaviour taking place. He or she feels angry towards the person or situation that has very recently transpired; i.e., he or she feels hard done by – in other words, Victimized. **(V-1)**. The perpetrator of the action or comment (perhaps the spouse, a relative or boss) is viewed as having been a Persecutor **(P-1)**
2. the Atypical Theft Offender goes to a shopping mall or store and perhaps buys a number of items (this is a straightforward, i.e., not a neurotic, action). Of course, in many cases the theft offender does not buy *anything* before stealing.
3. the same customer may now view himself or herself as the Victim **(V-2)** of what he or she considers to be the unfair high prices that have just been paid for the items that were bought. The store, in other words, at least from the customer's viewpoint, is a Persecutor **(P-2)**
4. the customer decides to steal one or more items, thereby becoming a Persecutor **(P-3)** of the store, and
5. the store is now the Victim **(V-3)** of the theft offender
6. a store employee catches the customer in the act of stealing. At that moment the employee, from the customer's point of view, is the new Persecutor **(P-4)**
7. when caught the theft offender-customer views himself or herself as the now Victim **(V-4)**.

Of course, the customer could be said to have initiated the entire sequence of events described above. In most instances, he or she had the choice of not shopping at that store if the prices were considered too high. And note that the theft offender views himself or herself as, firstly, taken advantage of and then seeks some sort of revenge by stealing, and finally feels hard done by when apprehended and possibly charged with theft.

As I indicated above, many, and probably most, Atypical Theft Offenders run through some variation of the above scenario. They act out by stealing, justifying their actions to themselves, if they are aware of having had any conscious thoughts at all to *why* they just did what they did. It is intellectually breathtaking that intelligent Atypical Theft Offenders are able to justify their stealing by the convoluted sequence of neurotic thinking as outline above – and yet many of them do exactly that.

One of the most astounding illustrations of the above neurotic sequence of neurotic, Drama Triangle thinking and behaviour, was described to me many years ago by a distinguished, retired professor emeritus of a major university. (I included this case in more detail my previous book.) His wife had just left the hospital after receiving treatment for her cancer and was shortly afterwards found by a mutual acquaintance wandering the aisles of a supermarket in a dazed condition, a seemingly endless stream of tears running down her cheeks. The friend called my client and told him the state in which she had found his wife. Of course he immediately rushed to get his wife, recalling that he was furious that no employee of the supermarket had approached his obviously very upset wife to inquire if she needed some assistance.

Two weeks later the retired professor was arrested in a different supermarket after he stole a bottle of Paul Newman's salad dressing. (He later told me that never in his life had he ever stolen anything, and I believe him.) In my office for the first time several days after his theft behaviour this gentleman said, *"Dr Cupchik, I want to tell you about the ridiculous thinking I was indulging in at the time of my theft. I had asked a clerk if the store had Paul Newman salad dressing. He said that the store did not carry that brand. A few minutes later I saw the exact product I was looking for and said to myself, 'Well, if you say you don't have Paul Newman salad dressing, but I've now found it, then I shouldn't have to pay you for it.' I completely realize, Dr Cupchik, that what I said to myself was totally illogical, but that was indeed what I remember saying to myself!"*

This professor was a prime example, I would suggest, of a highly intelligent person whose thinking, at that moment, was very 'unintelligent', indeed; in other words, an example of Drama Triangle-type neurotic thinking.

In order to help determine the very start of a Drama Triangle sequence it is always vital to inquire of the theft offender exactly what distressing event or circumstance had been going on in his/her life just prior to the atypical theft behaviour. In fact, the two most important questions that I have learned to ask a usually honest person who has committed one or more acts of theft are the following:

(1) *"Would you kindly tell me what was going on in your life in the hours and days just prior to your stealing behaviour?"*

and

(2) *"Had you experienced any important loss(es), marked frustration, resentment and/or anger towards anyone or about anything just prior to your act of theft?"*

In virtually every case of atypical theft behaviour, the answers provided by the client to these two questions will offer important clues as to *why* that individual stole *what* and *when* he or she stole.

An important caveat: Over the decades I have learned to ask the above questions *much more than once* and *in different ways* of the same client. I do so because usually honest clients who have stolen often do not, initially, associate what has been going on in their lives with their aberrant theft behaviour.

I well recall, for example, a client who, after she had initially replied in the negative to the two questions presented above, returned for her next session and immediately informed me that, when she had told her husband of the two questions I had asked and her answers, he had been shocked at her responses and reminded her that in the two months prior to her stealing spree, two of her closest relatives and her best friend had *died* (the latter, just the day before she stole) and she had clearly been very greatly affected by these deeply personal losses.

I have indicated in both this and my earlier book that when usually honest and ethical individuals offend against their own moral code through their atypical theft behaviour, they invariably do so in response to some upsetting events, situations or circumstances. It is therefore astounding, in my opinion, that some clinicians appear to take a surprisingly seemingly superficial, **non-psychological** approach to dealing with the problem of atypical theft behaviour by usually honest persons, and it is relevant to inquire why this may be so. To examine this matter further, we need to consider the kinds of questions that some investigators *do* ask persons who present with what is for them definitely *atypical* theft behaviour, and consider whether these clinicians' inquiries are sufficiently robust to yield any more than the most superficial -and therefore very possibly inadequate- responses and conclusions in such cases.

Chapter 12

OTHER KINDS OF THEFT COMMITTED BY THE ATYPICAL THEFT OFFENDERS OF THE 2013 STUDY

In our original **1983** article, *Shoplifting: An Occasional Crime Of The Moral Majority*, we examined a sample of some 34 theft offenders, all of whom had shoplifted. My second (**1996**) study, described in the original (1997) edition of my first book, *Why Honest People Shoplift or Commit Other Acts of Theft*, included 36 new cases. In this second study, of the 36 theft offenders, 25 cases involved only acts of shoplifting; 6 cases involved acts of fraud; 3 cases had committed acts of B&E (break *and* enter); and 3 of the cases involved acts of employee theft. In my latest, 2013 study of some 30 additional cases, as you can see in Table 10 below, acts of shoplifting, employee theft, fraud, stealing from relatives, friends, coworkers, strangers (other than via shoplifting), as well as 'reselling' occurred.

From considering Table Ten below it will be clear that, while slightly more than ¾ of the 30 Ss in this study committed acts of shoplifting, nearly ¼ committed acts of employee theft. Also, nearly ¼ committed acts of fraud. Stealing from relatives, friends, co-workers and/or strangers occurred in 3 cases, and acts of forgery and reselling occurred in one case each. The reason that these numbers add up to more than 30 is, of course, because in 7 cases, more than one kind of the theft behaviour had been involved.

Indeed, atypical theft behaviour may appear in many different forms and it takes a suitably trained and experienced professional to distinguish the individuals who commit such acts from the more garden variety –and psychodynamically different –Typical Theft Offenders.

At first it may be difficult for some readers (and professionals, for that matter) to accept that someone who repeatedly committed various blatant acts of theft behaviour over an extended period of time could actually be an *A*typical Theft Offender. However, recall the cases of James, Case # 5, who stole over $500,000 and of Charlene, Case # 11, who stole from three successive employers in the same kind of business in the same relatively small city. I would contend that, when the particulars of each case is taken into account, it is difficult to come to any conclusion other than they belonged closer to the Atypical Theft Offender end of the **Theft Offender Spectrum.**

Table Ten: Kinds Of Theft Committed By The 30 Ss of The 2013 Study

Kinds of theft behaviour committed by the 30 Ss	# of Ss who committed this kind of theft	% Ss who committed this kind of theft
Shoplifting	23	76.7%
Employee theft	7	23.3%
Fraud	5	16.7%
Stealing from relatives, friends, coworkers, and/or strangers (but not via shoplifting or fraud)	3	10%
Forgery	1	3.3%
Reselling	1	3.3%
Cases where more than one kind of theft-related behaviour was involved	7	23.3%

Over the years I have come to recognize the various kinds of *atypical theft behaviour* that are committed by Atypical Theft Offenders. Through carrying out comprehensive and thorough assessments I have also come to appreciate how important it is to do the hard work of distinguishing Atypical Theft Offenders from Typical Theft Offenders. If sufficient time and effort is *not* put in to make this determination, we risk making erroneous judgments that will then almost certainly lead to ineffective treatments, perhaps followed by further theft behaviours, and the cycle may be repeated again and again.

Chapter 13

A SUMMARY OF FINDINGS OF THE 2013 STUDY

In this chapter many of the findings of my most recent study that have already been presented above will be grouped together in ways that now allow you to consider them all 'at once'. And if *you* are the theft offender about whom you are concerned, you can choose to place a check mark (√) in either the "Me too!" or "Not me!" columns, and then compare your responses with those of the Atypical Theft Offenders I have assessed. Do keep in mind that these tables are provided for your consideration only; no conclusions should *necessarily* be drawn from the results. At the same time, if you find that you have checked off a relatively large number of items that are representative of most Atypical Theft Offenders, then it may be worthwhile considering the distinct possibility that you do indeed belong to that category of theft offenders *and* it may be appropriate to take appropriate actions to help stop your self-destructive theft behaviour.

Table Eleven: Commonly Shared Clinical Findings Of The 2013 Study, With Columns Provided For Your Own Personal Responses*

Most of the 30 Ss of the 2013 study shared the following:	Me too!	Not me!
Had very difficult issues stemming from childhood		
One or both parents were very verbally abusive		
One or both parents were very physically abusive		
One or both parents were very emotionally abusive		
One or both parents were sexually abusive		
Another older person was sexually abusive		
Have *low* or *very low* self-esteem, regardless of how intelligent, attractive, educated, or financially or professionally successful		

Table Eleven: continued

Most of the 30 Ss of the 2013 study also shared the following:	Me too!	Not me!
Were taking prescribed antidepressants at the time(s) they have been stealing		
Lived in homes where the gross annual income was greater than $100,000		
Reported feeling very depressed at the times they stole		
Were married at the times they stole		
Admitted lying to their intimate other about having stolen the items they did, or did not admit to stealing the items at all		
Acknowledged that their basic relationship to their spouse/partner was grounded in a <u>Rebellious Child</u> to <u>Critical Parent</u> dynamic		
Total number of the 13 items to which you responded, `Me Too` →		

* Not to be copied without the explicit permission of Dr Will Cupchik

In the next table, Table Twelve, an even more extensive list of shared matters amongst at least some of the 30 Ss, including <u>personal qualities, early histories</u> and <u>life experiences</u> is offered. Each of the items indicates the percentage of the 30 Ss who shared these factors. The last two columns offer the reader the opportunity to check off each of the items as ones to which he or she does or does not relate. It is hoped that an honest evaluation of one's own responses to these items will give the reader some better sense of the issues that he or she may share with the cases included in the 2013 study, and very possibly point the way to matters that might be best dealt with via the route of psychotherapy with a suitably trained and highly experienced clinician.

Table Twelve: A _Rank-Ordered_ Summary Of Shared Personal History, Qualities and Experiences of Atypical Theft Offenders (as drawn from the 2013 study), with columns provided for your own self-evaluation

	The following items indicate the *percentage* of the 30 cases in the 2013 study for which the statements were true:	Me too	Not me
1	All of the sample reported that the levels of stress they were experiencing during their periods of stealing was high (50%) or very high (50%); in other words, *all* of the 30 persons in the study reported experiencing at least 'high' levels of stress during their periods of stealing. Therefore total was 100%		
2	All declared that they had a longstanding history of anger (100%)		
3	All declared that they had a longstanding history of resentment (100%)		
4	Acknowledged feeling angry at the time they last stole (90%)		
5	Having learned the Drama Triangle formulation, they stated that they identified themselves most closely with the Victim (as opposed to Persecutor or Rescuer) position. (90%)		
6	Acknowledged feeling angry towards a person and/or situation at the time they last stole (87%)		
7	Declared that they had a longstanding history of sadness (83%)		
8	Acknowledged feeling angry towards their spouse/partner at the time they last stole (80%)		
9	Were facing charges at the start of their work with Dr Cupchik (77%)		
10	Acknowledged having stolen at least 40 times in all (77%)		
11	Having learned Transactional Analysis theory, they acknowledged that they probably stole while in a Cr (Rebellious Child) ego state (77%)		

Table Twelve (continued, Part 2)

12	**Acknowledged stealing from retail and food stores (77%)**		
13	Estimated that the total value of all the items they had ever stolen ranged between $1,000 and $10,000 (67%)		
14	Acknowledged stealing as a child (60%)		
15	Reported that feelings of guilt were a large factor in their lives (50%)		
16	Stole from relatives (40%)		
17	Estimated that the total value of all the items they had ever stolen ranged between $10,000 and $100,000 (20%)		
18	Acknowledged stealing from close friends (10%)		

Other Issues That Emerged From The Study's Findings

	Other illegal behaviours	Me Too	Not Me
19	Committed acts of fraud (40%)		
20	Used illegal drugs (30%)		
21	Sold items they stole (17%)		
22	Significant speeding or other traffic violations (13%)		
	Other inappropriate or excessive (but not illegal) behaviours		
23	Lied a great deal (77%)		
24	Carried out shopping compulsively (57%)		
25	Shopped excessively (50%)		
26	Other OCD (Obsessive-Compulsive disorders) (30%)		
		Me Too	Not Me
27	Abused alcohol (30%)		
28	Past and/or present eating disorders (27%)		

Table Twelve (continued, Part 3)

		Me T o o	Not M e
29	Gambles excessively (3%)		
	Other important findings		
30	Feeling depressed at the time of their theft behaviour; for men (89%); for women; (95%)		
31	Acts of theft were at least somewhat symbolically meaningful (87%)		
32	Acknowledged sexual problems in the primary relationship (73%)		
	Socioeconomic level		
33	Socioeconomic level: Were of at least medium socioeconomic level (90%)		
34	**Were of at least medium-high to high socioeconomic level (70%)**		
	Actual or anticipated losses in close proximity to theft behaviour		
35	Actual or anticipated (as perceived) unfair meaningful losses in close proximity to act of theft (67%)		
36	Occurrence or threat of occurrence of cancer in close proximity to act of theft (17%)		
	The nature of the perceived unfair personally meaningful losses:	**Me T o o**	**Not M e**
37	Of a relationship (57%)		
38	Of closeness to spouse/partner (40%)		
39	Job (30%)		
40	Standard of living (30%)		
41	One's own health (23%)		
42	Of child, by separation (23%)		
43	Due to cancer in self/spouse/relative/another Significant Other (20%)		
44	Occurrence or threat of occurrence of cancer in close proximity to act of theft (17%)		

Table Twelve: (continued, Part 4)

45	Of locale (by moving) (13%)		
46	Of a child, by death (7%)		
47	Of contact with grandchild (3%)		
	Recommendations that additional therapy be sought		
48	Recommendation of additional therapy was made (90%)		
49	Recommendation of couples therapy was made (73%)		
	Extramarital Involvement by client and/or Significant Other	**Me too**	**Not Me**
50	*Either* the theft offender *and/or* the partner had extramarital involvement in close temporal proximity to theft (33%)		
51	Atypical Theft Offender had extramarital involvement in temporal proximity to theft (23%)		
52	Spouse/partner had extramarital involvement in proximity to theft (10%)		
	Disturbing or traumatic events in childhood		
53	Father and/or mother was alcoholic and/or drank a lot (53%)		
54	Father was alcoholic and/or drank a lot (33%)		
55	Physically abused client (33%)		
56	Sexually molested client (20%)		
57	Mother was alcoholic and/or drank a lot (20%)		
58	Lost parent before the age of 15; (13%)		
59	Parents separated before the age of 15; (7%)		
60	Adopted (3%)		
	Religion		
61	Christian (77%)		
62	Jewish (13%)		
63	Muslim (3%)		

Table Twelve: (continued, Part 5)

	Highest level of schooling achieved		
64	Finished bachelors degree or college course (40%)		
65	Completed Post Graduate degree (37%)		
66	High school only (6%)		
67	Public school only (3%)		
	Parent and/or sibling stole		
68	Client knows that a parent and/or sibling stole when client was a child (10%)		
	Occupations/Professions		
69	Homemaker (20%)		
70	Nurse (13%)		
71	Teacher: Public or high school (13%)		
72	Physician (10%)		
73	Married to a physician (10%)		
74	Managers (7%)		
75	Admin Assistant (6%)		
76	Pharmacist (3%)		

If you are a theft offender and have checked off a relatively large number of the above items in the "Me Too" column, then it appears that you may have a good deal in common with the 30 individuals of the 2013 study. Consider that, in a real sense, this may be considered a *good* sign, in that it may well mean that by identifying and appropriately dealing with the pertinent past and/or present distressing and/or unresolved issues in your life, you may be able to significantly reduce the likelihood of further acting out theft behaviour.

PART V

The Questionable Use

Of Antidepressants

With

Atypical Theft Offenders

Chapter 14

SOME CLINICIANS' PHARMACEUTICAL APPROACH TO THE STUDY OF ATYPICAL THEFT BEHAVIOUR

The peril of focusing primarily or solely upon relatively superficial levels of observations and inquiry when deciding upon a psychiatric diagnosis.

Stephen Covey Ph.D., in his deservedly best-selling book, *The Seven Habits of Highly Effective People*, recounted a moving incident that produced, for him, what he termed a "mini-paradigm shift." Evidently, one Sunday morning when he was on a New York City subway, he and the other few people in the car he was in, were sitting quietly minding their own business when a man accompanied by some children, entered the same subway car. The children were so very loud and seemingly uncontrolled that Covey noted that the atmosphere in the car changed almost instantly.

Covey described himself as being quite irritated when the adult accompanying the children sat down near him but did nothing whatsoever to attempt to control the youngsters, who were now yelling, tossing papers around, and even interfering with some of the other passengers. Covey reported that his inner conversation was not very kind towards the man who was seemingly entirely unwilling to curb the children's highly disturbing behaviour. Indeed, Covey became perturbed to the point that he decided to cautiously confront the man about possibly doing something to restrain the children.

Covey poignantly described what happened next. In response to his gentle comments to the man, the latter softly responded that Covey certainly had a point; he explained matter-of-factly that he and the children had just come from the hospital where their mother had died an hour earlier. He added that he felt at a loss as neither he nor the children knew how to cope with this horrific situation.

Covey described the instantaneous paradigm shift that he experienced when he learned of the children's mother's death; his

165

perceptions, thoughts, feelings and actions changed immediately. His irritation with the man and the children evaporated straight away, and he was left feeling only compassion and concern towards these suffering human beings - father and children - and the exceptionally painful emotions that they were experiencing.

Now, **imagine for a moment, if Covey had *not* been open to gaining some deeper insight into the conduct of this adult and the children who had entered the car in which he was riding and if he had not acquired some information about what had happened in these children's lives just prior to their acting out** in the subway car. Indeed, imagine instead, if perhaps another mental health professional, say a psychiatrist whose practice focused almost exclusively on the use of prescribed medication to treat aggressivity, had been on that same subway car at that time. It is conceivable that the psychiatrist, noting what appeared to be the adolescents' seemingly hyperactive, aggressive, possibly hostility-fuelled behaviour, might have reached a conclusion that the children were perhaps suffering from an *impulse control disorder* or possibly some genetically shared *organic mental disorder*, or perhaps even some sort of *adjustment* and/or *personality disorder* and that, therefore, the administration of some heavy-duty prescribed medication was in order. The same clinician might also have hypothesized that the adult who had accompanied them onto the car but who had done nothing to modify the children's misbehaving, could himself have a physiologically based vision or hearing problem, and/or some sort of personality or other psychiatric disorder of his own. Meanwhile, at least some laypersons in the subway car might simply have concluded that the children were undisciplined, spoiled brats!

By staying focused only on the virtually immediate and seemingly obvious behavioural-observational level and by *not* attempting to determine whether there might possibly be some deeper, psychological or situationally driven motivation for such behaviour, a serious misdiagnosis and judgemental injustice could have been committed, even if only in the psychiatrist's or laypersons' minds.

As I have mentioned at numerous points throughout this book, the still current (at the time of publication of this book) American Psychiatric Association's DSM-IV-R diagnostic criteria for Kleptomania specifically states that *the stealing must not have been committed to express anger or vengeance.* In fact, in over 39 years of clinical assessment and treatment involvement with the atypical theft behaviour of hundreds of usually honest persons I can recall only a single instance of atypical theft behaviour (assessed nearly thirty years ago) when the individual did not appear to have acted out in anger and/or with a desire to seek vengeance. In other words, having investigated this clinical area for decades, and having assessed over 700 individuals, it is my firm clinical opinion that cases of 'kleptomania' as defined in DSM-IV-R likely hardly exist in the real world. Therefore, I have been astounded when I have encountered articles in professional journals that purport to report upon dozens or even hundreds of cases of kleptomania having been located and dealt with during a single clinical investigation. How is this possible?

Are we dealing with entirely different populations? Given that nearly half of the cases I have assessed since 1986 were Americans living in the USA, that is not very likely. Rather, I would suggest that the assessment tools and criteria of some other investigators might not have employed the full time, depth and directions of investigation required to make a sufficiently robust assessment. In some cases, the screening interviews that have been used to make a determination as to whether to diagnose an individual as suffering from kleptomania have focused primarily, if not exclusively, upon whether the individual had urges to steal, thought about stealing, what emotions he or she had just before, during and immediately after the theft behaviour, and whether that individual was distressed by the theft behaviour as well as whether such behaviour interfered with the person's life. Not a single question may have been addressed to what events or circumstances (arguments, loss of a job, illness of a loved one or oneself, separation or divorce, etc...) might have occurred in the individual's life prior to the stealing or having had an urge to steal.

The fact is that the DSM IV-R specifically states that if the stealing has been committed to express anger or vengeance, that would be a disqualification as far as diagnosing someone as suffering from kleptomania is concerned. It would therefore surely make it vitally important to include *at least some questions* in these regards in any genuinely reliable and valid questionnaire or assessment that would claim to aim at making such a diagnosis.

Might industry-funded clinical studies influence the structure and/or findings of psychiatric and/or pharmaceutical studies? **Important Note: Of course, nothing in this book is intended to impugn the motivations or professionalism of any particular clinicians in any areas of clinical investigation.** At the same time, it is only fair and prudent to note the clear findings of many academic and clinical investigators regarding the possible influence of pharmaceutical companies' payments to clinicians and/or funding of clinicians' investigations upon the design, execution and/or the reporting of results of their studies.

Indeed, a substantial number of articles have appeared in peer-reviewed professional journals over the past several years that have addressed important questions related to the matter of the possible corporate influence upon professional researchers, the nature of their studies and their subsequent findings.

In his article titled, *How Pharmaceutical Industry Funding Affects Trial Outcomes: Causal Structures And Responses,* by Sergio Sismondo (a 2011-2012 Network Fellow of Harvard University's Edmond J Safra Center for Ethics), published in the journal, *Social Science & Medicine,* 66 (2008) 1909-1914, Dr Sismondo points out that *"Three recent systematic reviews have shown that pharmaceutical industry funding of clinical trials is strongly associated with pro-industry results."* His article *"builds on those analyses... and the creation of social ties between those companies and researchers. These are all rooted in (the) close contact between pharmaceutical companies and much clinical research...* **Pharmaceutical company funding of clinical trials is strongly associated with published results favoring those companies' interests.** *This is an important issue, as biases created by funding sources influence the medical literature, its representation in medical journalism (van Trigt et al., 1995) and its condensation in evidence-based medicine (De Bries & Lemmens, 2006). ...* **Twenty studies published between 2003 and 2006 found an association between industry support and published pro-industry results,** *typically a strong association; only two studies in those years failed to find such an association. The findings are similar whether one is looking at presentations at professional meetings or the most prestigious journals in the field."*

FYI: My own clinical studies are not, and have never been, funded by any for-profit corporation or organization

My own clinical investigations began while I was in the employ of the forensic service of the Clarke Institute of Psychiatry (which was at the time affiliated with the University of Toronto) and for the dozen years I was working at the Clarke (1974-86), at no time were my clinical studies of atypical theft behaviour funded by any corporation – pharmaceutical or otherwise.

Our initial article on this subject, titled *Shoplifting: An Occasional Crime of the Moral Majority*, was published in the 1983, Volume 11, No. 4, edition of the <u>Bulletin of the American Academy of Psychiatry and the Law</u>, a journal that, incidentally, did not at the time and does not currently accept advertisements from any pharmaceutical or other companies. [At least as of November 1, 2012 this article was available for reading, in its entirety and for free, at http://www.jaapl.org/content/11/4/343.full.pdf+html?sid=331bd4e2-bd09-431c-858b-38bd3e11cb9d]. Readers of this book may well find that original article to be very interesting and its findings are still valid.

Since leaving the employ of the Clarke Institute of Psychiatry in 1986, I have carried on my clinical studies of atypical theft behaviour from within my own private practice, without either requesting or receiving any funding from any corporate source whatsoever.

The reader might be well advised, when considering the worth of the methodology and findings of published clinical studies in regard to any medical clinical studies in general, and of any behavioural, psychiatric or psychological problem in particular, to determine whether any of the named researchers have received funding for their studies or any other remuneration or support (e.g., receiving drugs for use in their studies, for free or at minimal cost; having been paid by the same companies to give talks or other presentations; or having any financial investment in the drug they are investigating) from the pharmaceutical companies whose drugs they are employing. Thankfully, a few determined Internet searches may divulge this information, but usually only to a limited extent (e.g., whether the clinician has received less or more than $5000 from a pharmaceutical company).

DR. WILL CUPCHIK

Of course, the fact that a clinical investigator has received any kind of financial support or compensation (e.g., for presentations at drug company sponsored or supported events) does not *necessarily* mean that the clinician's studies have been unduly influenced in any particular direction. At the same time, however, the reader might wish to take into account the findings of Sergio Sismondo and others.

A possible effort by some investigators to designate atypical theft behaviour as an 'addiction'; What does the term *'behavioural addiction'* mean and could the stealing committed by Atypical Theft Offenders be considered a 'behavioural addiction'?

According to Wikipedia, the concept referred to by the term *behavioural addiction* [as retrieved January 2, 2013] has been neither sharply or accurately deliniated and/or universally accepted. Nevertheless, it has been proposed that the term may include or "involve <u>a compulsion to repeatedly engage in an action</u> until said action causes serious negative consequences to the person's physical, mental, social, and/or financial well-being. One sign that a behaviour has become addictive is if it persists despite these consequences."

A major question to pose in regard to the application of term *behavioural addiction* is as follows; What if the particular behaviour of a specific individual being considered occurs only occasionally, say once or only a very few times over a period of one or several days, and then perhaps, not again for years or even decades? Can an activity that occurs so seldom and with very long intervals between occurances, really be considered an 'addiction'?

During my decades of clinical investigation of atypical theft behaviour I have encountered many Atypical Theft Offenders whose theft behaviour occurred very infrequently indeed, <u>and virually always in response to one or more external situations or circumstances</u> such as (i) the loss of a marriage, job, or child; (ii) extremely high stress at work or at home (the latter perhaps in response to, say illness or death of a loved one); (iii) a desire for retribution or (iv) acting out in anger and/or with a desire for vengance. I would strongly suggest that in such cases of infrequent acts of theft behaviour -especially when possibly precipitated as a response to external events- the use of the term *'addiction'* is not appropriate, any more than it would be appropriate to to label someone as suffering from a 'sexual addiction' is he or she had been involved in only one or a very few short-lived extramarital encounters over a period of, say, more than twenty or thirty years of marriage. Of course, the intent here is not to excuse such behaviour; rather, simply to point out that refering to such actions as indicative of a 'behavioural addiction' would, in my clinical opinion, be entirely inappropriate.

Prior to the time of the publication of this book, in March of 2013, various articles have appeared in print and online publications suggesting that in the forthcoming DSM-V (expected to be published in May of 2013) the term 'behavioural addiction' might be applied to a variety of behaviours, perhaps including compulsive gambling and overeating. Now, these behaviours are often acted upon on a *very* frequent basis (perhaps almost daily and for many years, or as long as money or food is available) and the application of the term 'behavioural addiction' in these instances *may* perhaps be justified. However, the use of the word 'addiction' when refering to very infrequent atypical theft behaviour is likely to be an example of casting much too wide -and inappropriate- a net.

In the next chapter I shall report upon the findings of my 2013 study in regard to atypical theft behaviour and the use of major antidepressants.
The findings of my **2013** study of some thirty Atypical Theft Offenders have direct implications regarding the possible misuse of antidepressants when it comes to the matter of atypical theft behaviour, and these results are in marked disagreement with the findings of some other clinicians, in particular some of those whose studies have been supported financially by the pharmaceutical companies whose drugs (and their efficacies) they were investigating.

One other note regarding the upcoming publication of DSM 5 and its perhaps casting a net too far: The possible mislabelling and misdiagnosis of normal grieving as a serious psychiatric condition
In an article titled *"Last Plea to DSM 5: Save Grief From the Drug Companies"* written by psychiatrist Allen J Frances, formerly the chair of the DSM-IV Task Force and Professor Emeritus of the department of psychiatry at Duke University School of Medicine (and posted on the *Psychology Today* website January 3, 2013 (retrieved on January 28, 2013 http://m.psychologytoday.com/blog/dsm5-in-distress/201301/last-plea-dsm-5-save-grief-the-drug-companies), Dr Frances referred to what he called "this dreadful mistake that flies in the face of clinical common

sense…" when he was referring to what he termed the DSM 5 "medicalization of grief", a position which he stated had been opposed by many other mental health professionals as well. He stated that "making grief a mental disorder will be a bonanza for drug companies, but a disaster for grievers." On the Huffington Post Canada website (retrieved on January 28 2013) from http://www.huffingtonpost.com/allen-frances/saving-grief-from-dsm-5-a_b_2325108.html Dr Frances also stated that it is essential that persons who are grieving a major loss of a significant other should not be unnecessarily and inappropriately impacted "by a spurious medical diagnosis that is not supported by the scientific evidence."

I share the same concern as expressed by Dr Frances in regard to grieving. In addition, I also am concerned that the prescribing of antidepressants and other medications as a 'treatment' for atypical theft behaviour may be 'a bonanza for drug companies, but a disaster' for Atypical Theft Offenders.

Chapter 15

MY MOST RECENT (2013) STUDY RESULTS REVEAL *CONTRA*INDICATIONS FOR USING ANTIDEPRESSANTS WITH 'ATYPICAL THEFT OFFENDERS'

It has long been evident to me that among the many hundreds of Atypical Theft Offender clients who I have assessed and/or treated these past nearly four decades, very many have reported during intake interviews that they had been prescribed and were taking prescribed antidepressants. **During interviews they invariably reported that their theft behaviour had *not* decreased after having started taking these medications, although many said that they understood that they had been prescribed such drugs, at least in part, specifically to reduce or eliminate their inclination to steal.**

Indeed, a substantial number of clients reported that when their shoplifting did not initially decrease, the *dosages of antidepressants were increased*, again to no avail insofar as reducing their theft behaviour was concerned.

Furthermore, in some cases clients reported that *their theft behaviours had increased* after having been prescribed higher dosages of antidepressants! Furthermore, this cycle of increased dosages was sometimes followed by an increase in the frequency of shoplifting, leading to further increase(s) in the dosages of antidepressants that again did not reduce the shoplifting behaviour.

Moreover, in *some* cases that I have assessed, clients reported that they had *never* stolen until *after* they began taking an antidepressant medication.

Among my Atypical Theft Offender clients have been a relatively large number of <u>physicians</u> and <u>nurses</u>. In fact, these two medical professions, taken together, represent the largest proportion of all professions amongst the Atypical Theft Offenders that I have seen over the years. The fact that these clients were medical professionals suggests strongly, I believe, that they were particularly well suited to relatively objectively recognize the influence and side effects of prescribed medications upon themselves. Consequently, their self-reports of the *absence* of a reduction in theft behaviour while taking antidepressants, or an actual increase in their theft behavior, are most noteworthy.

****

Table Thirteen: Reported Experiencing of Depression Among Subjects in the 2013 Study (N=30)

Level of Depression Self-reported by Ss	# of Ss	% 0f Ss
Not feeling at all depressed	0	0%
Feeling mildly depressed	1	3.3%
Feeling moderately depressed	6	20%
Feeling very depressed	21	70%
No clear information regarding severity of feelings of depression.	2	6.7%

After noting the very frequent occurrence of the taking of antidepressants among my theft offender clients, for many years I have asked my clients about their use, and the timing and effects of the use of these drugs, in relation to their stealing activities. From the 30 cases randomly selected for the **2013** study, the findings in regard to these issues are very illuminating, and should be taken into consideration by the reader who takes such medications, or is considering taking them, and has problems with stopping to steal.

From viewing the above table it is obvious that the great majority of Ss were experiencing depression at the time they first presented for assessment. A full 21 (70%) of them reported being *very depressed*. Now, the fact that these usually honest, ethical, and successful persons had been committing seemingly bizarre and/or nonsensical acts of theft that they themselves recognized threatened their personal and/or working lives in many ways and were feeling 'very depressed', is hardly surprising. On the contrary, it would be astonishing if they were *not* feeling very depressed, when they were aware that their theft behaviours potentially -or already were- jeopardizing important aspects of their lives.

Interestingly, most of the thirty cases in the 2013 study reported having been experiencing depression for significant amounts of time – often many months, years or longer before they sought my help. This is a very common feature of Atypical Theft Offenders upon initial presentation. In fact, of the many hundreds of cases I have personally dealt with, the vast majority were personally very familiar with marked feelings of depression.

One of the most prominent and consistent findings of my work with Atypical Theft Offenders relates to the highly questionable use of antidepressants with probable Atypical Theft Offenders.

As was noted above, of all the categories of professions represented in the 2013 study, experienced medical professionals were the among the most prevalent (with the exception of teachers) in this study; among the 30 Ss were three physicians, three nurses and a pharmacist (the latter worked in a critical care unit at a major hospital). It is reasonable to hypothesize that these professionals were relatively reliable reporters of their theft behaviours while taking these medications. <u>In all seven cases of these medical professionals, they reported that the frequency of their stealing behaviours neither stopped entirely nor was even reduced while taking antidepressants.</u> **In fact, one physician reported that he had *never* shoplifted until *after* he began using antidepressants.** Such self-reports were consistent amongst the cases in the 2013 study, as they have been throughout my years of investigation of atypical theft behaviour. **In fact, to reiterate what I stated above, of the many hundreds of cases I have dealt with, not a single theft offender has ever reported that his or her theft behaviour ceased or even was reduced while taking prescribed antidepressants.**

Why theft offenders might frequently be prescribed antidepressants: *Part I*
It is certainly true that most Atypical Theft Offenders report being depressed. This should not be very surprising; common sense would suggest that a basically *happy* person would not be inclined to risk potentially destroying his life(style) by breaking the law through stealing. Indeed, my clinical investigations have found that when usually honest, often hard working, generally ethical -and sometimes even genuinely

religious- persons steal, their theft behaviour is directly related to their feelings of anger, frustration, loss, depression and/or sadness. Often these persons also tend to partially suppress or repress dealing with the issues related to these difficult emotions, with the result that what they experience *at a conscious level* is not only anger but also a feeling of depression. The depressive and angry feelings could be said to function as an emotional blanket, keeping at bay (in their subconscious or unconscious) the full brunt of the feelings and issues with which they are having such trouble dealing.

As a result of the individuals being *consciously* aware of feelings of depression when they speak with their family doctor or psychiatrist, their medical professionals will often prescribe a so-called *anti*depressant to counter the feelings of depression. **The problem is that, as a result of employing an antidepressant, the emotions underlying the (blanketing) depression too often do not then get dealt with effectively, if at all.** As a result, the hidden and undealt-with emotions and the underlying situational and/or intrapsychic (i.e., psychological) reasons for them, press for expression or release. Too often, the individuals may then act out inappropriately, perhaps by overworking, overeating, excessive alcohol and/or drug use, overly aggressive driving, extramarital involvement, excessive sleeping, obsessive television viewing, compulsive housekeeping, too much shopping and/or even shoplifting or other kinds of theft or illegal behaviour; all such behaviours have been exhibited by various Atypical Theft Offenders whom I have assessed. **In other words, an antidepressant *may* (or may not) alleviate the *conscious* experience of depression, but it will likely do very little to assist the individual to resolve the underlying issues that are related to the original distress.**

Why theft offenders might frequently be prescribed antidepressants: Part II
An early, very small, clinical study of the supposed efficacy of antidepressants to treat supposed cases of 'kleptomania' was reported upon in the January/February 1999 issue of the professional journal, Clinical Neuropharmacology, titled *The Treatment of Kleptomania with Serotonin Reuptake Inhibitors,* authored by Elie Lepkifker and colleagues of the Chaim Sheba Medical Center, in Israel. These investigators reported upon the effects of treating this disorder using SSRIs with a sample of only **five** patients. They suggested that the use of serotonin reuptake inhibitors had *"successfully treated... five cases of kleptomania patients... in combination*

with a psychotherapeutic intervention." They also reported that, "*In one case, the discontinuation of the medication repeatedly led to the resurgence of the kleptomanic behaviour.*" The authors went on to state, "*our case series illustrated the effectiveness of SSRIs in kleptomania. It thus supports the assumption that this syndrome involves a dysfunctional serotoninergic mechanism.*" These authors also stated that kleptomania might result from a fall in the brain's level of the neurotransmitter serotonin, which may be corrected by the drug treatment in question. <u>The authors indicated that additional studies might be required to confirm the benefits of SSRIs for patients with kleptomania.</u>

Several other studies aimed at curbing supposed 'kleptomania' have been conducted over the past fourteen years, frequently <u>conducted by psychiatrists and other clinicians whose research was partly or wholly funded by the pharmaceutical manufacturers of the antidepressants they were studying</u>. Of course, the mere fact that these researchers' studies were funded by pharmaceutical companies should not be interpreted to *necessarily* mean that their studies and/or findings were skewed in any particular direction. However, at the same time, investigations of the possible effects of the influence of pharmaceutical companies' funding upon the findings of the studies, as noted previously, is one that has indeed, in my clinical opinion, led to some disturbing findings.

One study that investigated the use of escitalopram (Lexapro) to curb what were labelled cases of kleptomania involved 19 participants and was conducted by lead investigator Lorrin M. Koran of Stanford University. According to the Psychiatric Times, (retrieved on January 28, 2013 from http://www.psychiatrictimes.com/print/article/10168/53546?printable=true) "the (clinically relevant reduction in stealing) disappeared during the double-blind discontinuation phase when compared with placebo", as originally reported in the March 2007 issue of the Journal of Clinical Psychiatry. The results of that study, the Psychiatric Times reported, <u>"do not support benefit from the SSRI class of antidepressants"</u> insofar as 'kleptomania' is concerned.

DR. WILL CUPCHIK

Why theft offenders might frequently be prescribed antidepressants: Part III

As mentioned above, The American Psychiatric Association's *Diagnostic and Statistical Manual (DSM IV-R)* specifically states that one of the criteria for kleptomania is that the stealing has *not been committed to express anger or vengeance.*

The fact is, however, as I have also stated previously, in very nearly all of the many hundreds of cases of atypical theft behaviour that I have assessed these past 39 years, the acts of stealing by these usually honest individuals indeed appear to *have* been committed, at least in part, to express anger or vengeance. One has only to make a concerted effort to inquire into the goings on in the theft offender's life to quickly determine whether the individual was feeling angry or vengeful at the time he or she stole. Such a vigorous investigation, in each and every case, is surely required, if only to eliminate anger or vengeance as a triggering motivation).

But what if the clinician or researcher does not bother to inquire into the goings-on in the theft offender's life at around the time of the theft behaviour? For example, suppose the person has shoplifted after having just lost his or her job, home, spouse, parent or, heaven forbid, a child. Is not intense emotion, very possibly including anger, likely to be experienced in response to such an event? Of course it is: think of the case described by Stephen Covey that was mentioned in the previous chapter. But by remaining ignorant, i.e., by not carrying on a vigorous inquiry of the recent events and circumstances of a client's life, one might then reach a premature - and erroneous – conclusion that the person may qualify as a 'kleptomaniac'. Surely it is incumbent upon every responsible clinician to make such an in-depth inquiry. Indeed, to vigorously inquire into the circumstances of the person's life, in part to ascertain whether the person is indeed angry and whether his stealing might be an expression of such anger and/or a desire for vengeance, *should be an absolute necessity!*

What will the American Psychiatric Association's definition of - and criteria for- 'kleptomania' be like in its next edition (evidentally expected to be published in May 2013)?

The American Psychiatric Association's Diagnostic and Statistical Manual has undergone numerous revisions over the years and DSM-V is, at least at the time of writing this book, supposedly due out in May of

2013. As mentioned earlier, I understand that there may be a move afoot to remove the exclusionary note vis-à-vis anger or vengeance when it comes to defining 'kleptomania', thereby essentially eliminating from consideration in any individual case, possible *psychodynamic* motivations for the individual's atypical theft behaviour. As of the date of this book going to press (March 2013), the still current DSM-IV-Revised states that in order to designate someone as suffering from 'kleptomania', it must be true that "the stealing is <u>not</u> committed to express anger or vengeance..." It is my clinical opinion, as very possibly the most senior and experienced investigator of atypical theft behaviour by usually honest persons over the past more than 39 years, that the removal of this exclusionary qualifier from the forthcoming edition of the DSM would be entirely inappropriate and open to serious question, since in virtually every single of the more than 700 cases that I have assessed and (in most instances) treated, anger and/or a desire for vengeance have *indeed* been likely psychodynamic factors!

Two proposals for the American Psychiatric Association to consider in regard to a more useful and realistic future definition of the term 'kleptomania' follow:
Since it is abundantly clear from my own decades of clinical investigation that anger and/or a desire for vengeance are present in most, or perhaps *all* cases of atypical theft behaviour, I would suggest that the American Psychiatric Association consider either:

1. restating the diagnostic criteria for Kleptomania to specifically include that "the stealing <u>is</u> committed to express anger and/or vengeance" (which would, of course, suggest that talk therapy is desirable), *or*

2. the concept of 'kleptomania' (which, as it is defined now, and in my clinical experience, virtually does not exist in the real world) be dropped entirely, and replaced by that of the 'Atypical Theft Offender', defined as "a generally honest and ethical individual whose theft behaviour is essentially an aberration from, and at odds with, the way he or she usually conducts him or herself in the world." The atypical theft behaviour manifested by the offender is a manifestation of one or more of the reasons already provided in this book (including experiencing, or anticipating experiencing, (perceived) unfair personally meaningful losses, compensation-by-substitution, an expression or anger and/or a desire for vengeance, etc...). The *Cupchik Theft Offender*

Spectrum presented earlier in this book affords a means of helping to determine whether and to what extent the theft offender should be considered an Atypical Theft Offender, a Typical Theft Offender, or of the Mixed-type theft offender.

*Dis*inhibition and acting out as possible side effects of antidepressants

In the required disclosure information provided by the manufacturers of antidepressants, reference is made to various side effects of their medications, including a possible *disinhibitory* effect.

To use an analogy, imagine that a female middle-level executive is at an off-site, company sponsored social function, when she is approached and engaged in conversation by a male senior executive who considers her to be very attractive. A male person in his position who is also in full possession and control of his faculties should be expected to temper his behaviour towards the female in question, and *not* make what could be considered a crude physical 'pass' towards her. But what if he had had a number of alcoholic drinks prior to engaging the woman in question in conversation?

As it happens, this was the exact situation that was reported to me by a (non-Atypical Theft Offender) client of mine a few years ago. An up-and-coming very senior executive of a large corporation, a man who was widely believed to possibly have the inside track to replace the current CEO when he retired within a couple of years, while at a management off-site seminar, and in front of several other executives (a few of whom were even senior to him), and after having had a number of alcoholic drinks, physically drew an attractive female manager up against his body and began (as she later described the incident to me) to grope her.

It is not entirely clear whether, in his distinctly inebriated and *disinhibited* state, the executive in question either never realized or remembered that (a) such behaviour was grossly inappropriate, (b) the woman he was literally man-handling had recently received her black belt in karate, and/or that (c) her own sexual orientation was not towards males. In any case, within seconds of making his entirely unwelcome, sexually explicit physical overture, he became airborne and then landed flat on his back, with both his dignity and future promotion possibilities within the company having suffered irreparable damage. Incidentally, a sexual harassment charge was actually laid in this case, and an out of court settlement was reached in due course.

Now, an excessive intake of alcohol is widely known to have a potentially disinhibiting effect upon many persons. Likewise, antidepressants are often listed by their manufacturers as having potentially disinhibiting side effects, as well. Many manufacturers of antidepressants specially warn, in their Compendium of Pharmaceuticals and Specialties, 2011 edition (or as it is called in the USA, *The Physicians Desk Reference*), in their detailed listing of possible side effects, of a *"potential association with behavioural and emotional changes, including self-harm… severe agitation-type adverse events coupled with self-harm or harm to others, including agitation, disinhibition, emotional lability, hostility, aggression… Rigorous clinical monitoring for suicidal ideation… including monitoring for agitation-type emotional and behavioural changes is warranted."* **It appears possible, therefore, that the use of these antidepressant medications *may* actually be a contributing factor in precipitating atypical theft behaviour.**

Other Clinical Investigators Also Question the Side Effects of Antidepressants

It should also be noted that questions have been raised by numerous clinical investigators about the various possible side effects of the use of antidepressants.

[**A personal note:** Like most of us I am sure, I am exceedingly grateful for the development of remarkable prescription drugs such as antibiotics and a whole host of other proven health-saving and life-prolonging medications. The issue that merits further examination and is focused upon in this book, however, is the questionable use of prescribing antidepressants to usually honest persons who present with less than extremely severe depression and have been stealing.]

Some clinical investigators suggest that the use of prescribed antidepressants for *mild* to *moderate* depression may be inappropriate.

A review of high-quality antidepressant clinical trials from January 1980 through March 2009 was published in 2010 in the Journal of the American Medical Association. The authors of the article, *Antidepressant Drug Effects and Depression Severity*, concluded that the use of such drugs for those persons who presented with mild to moderate depression was not particularly helpful. The authors stated that, **"true drug effects of antidepressant medication over placebo were nonexistent to negligible with mild, moderate, and even severe baseline symptoms."**

It is instructive to also note some of the statements contained in an article titled *Recent U.S., Canadian and British regulatory agency actions concerning antidepressant-induced harm to self and others: A review and analysis,* published in the <u>International Journal of Risk & Safety in Medicine</u> in 2004, and authored by Peter R. Breggin. In this important article Breggin states that *"Emphasis needs to be placed upon U.S. and Canadian warnings about the potential production of <u>stimulation</u> and <u>mania</u> with <u>hostility</u> and <u>aggression</u> (when antidepressants are used)....*

"With some exceptions in regard to the severity or frequency of adverse reactions, the SSRIs can be treated as one group in regard to their profile of adverse drug reactions ... The SSRIs include fluoxetine (Prozac), fluvoxamine (Luvox), paroxetine (Paxil), sertraline (Zoloft), citalopram (Celexa), and escilalopran (Lexapro)." He also mentions that the FDA (Food and Drug Administration) issued reports that stated that four other antidepressants *"were found to produce similar adverse behavioural and mental effects and were included in the group: venlafaxine (Effexor), mirtazapine (Remeron), Wellbutrin or Zyban (Buproion) and nefazodone (Serzone)."*

Lastly, Breggin points out that *"Patients and their families should be encouraged <u>to be alert for the emergence of anxiety, agitation...,</u> <u>irritability, hostility, impulsivity,... mania, and other unusual changes in</u> <u>behaviour."</u>*

My own clinical investigations of Atypical Theft Offenders clearly indicates that their theft behaviours certainly constitute 'acting on dangerous impulses', i.e., carrying out theft behaviours that are contrary to their more usual ways of behaving and that risk their personal and/or working situations. My conclusion in this regard is that, for persons who never stole before they were prescribed antidepressants, <u>their subsequent</u> <u>stealing may have been partly precipitated by their increased state of</u> <u>disinhibition and inclination to act on what could be described as</u> 'dangerous impulses'.

I have also hypothesized that in cases where the individuals have been prescribed antidepressants *after* they had already begun stealing, their subsequent inclinations to act out by stealing may not only have *not* been diminished by taking prescribed antidepressants, but may have actually been *increased* due to the potentially dangerous side effects of these drugs, as mentioned above. A case in point: a likely Atypical Theft Offender who recently contacted me from Australia, in response to my specific question, "Since you have been using a prescribed antidepressant, has your stealing markedly increased, lessened or stayed about the same?, stated, *"Definitely increased. The higher the dose, the worse the stealing."*

Incidentally, I have had Atypical Theft Offender clients who have used one or other of most of the antidepressants specifically mentioned in Breggin's article.

Some investigators seriously question the causes of - and solutions for - depression itself (including the use of antidepressants).
According to psychologist Irving Kirsch, the Associate Director of the Program in Placebo Studies at Harvard Medical School, and the author of *The Emperor's New Drugs: Exploding the Antidepressant Myth,* *"Depression is not caused by a chemical imbalance in the brain, and it is not cured by medication. Depression may not even be an illness at all. Often, it can be a normal reaction to abnormal situations ... the loss of loved ones can make people depressed, and these social and situational causes of depression cannot be changed by drugs."* His studies seriously question whether antidepressants are even significantly more effective than placebo pills provided to individuals to counter mild to moderate depression.

Acts of theft in response to the *stimulation* of suppressed or repressed feelings of hostility and aggression
The above information makes it clear that the use of antidepressants may actually have some distinctly unwelcome behavioural effects, including those that might lead to very negative consequences. As has been noted previously, virtually all Atypical Theft Offenders in the 2013 study (and virtually all the many hundreds of theft offenders I have assessed over the years) have reported being angry at the time of their theft behaviour. According to the manufacturers' own published data, many (perhaps even most) antidepressants have the potential to produce or release hostility and aggression. For a person who possibly is already bearing a good deal of

anger, any added hostility and aggression could have very unfortunate results, including triggering possible atypical theft behaviour.

My years of clinical studies have led me to conclude that Atypical Theft Offenders, if they are to reduce or eliminate their atypical theft behaviour, must address the personal issues underlying their actions, including those that are perhaps temporarily being kept at bay by the use of antidepressants.

For instance, if an individual is in a highly destructive marital relationship, and perhaps has low self-esteem and/or very limited independent financial resources or ways of earning a decent living on his or her own, then that person may well feel *trapped* in the unsatisfactory marriage. Frequently, the individual in this sort of situation may have marked feelings of frustration, anger, sadness and/or hopelessness. Thankfully, in modern societies, a variety of potential resources can be called upon to assist such individuals (though, granted, not as many or as helpful resources as are likely needed by everyone.) But until and unless that person reaches the point of being fully willing to address such an issue, he or she might well experience marked depression. If this person receives no psychotherapeutic (i.e., talk therapy) efforts aimed at dealing with whatever issues the individual is avoiding, it is surely clear that issues such as the individual's marital situation, financial stress, poor relationships, etc..., are not likely to be somehow magically improved by the use of an antidepressant, and so the underlying reasons for feeling sadness, frustration, anger, etc..., will not disappear, although the medication may (or may not) help keep them in the individual's subconscious. However, given the potential *side effects* of the antidepressant the person has been taking, the possible disinhibitory effect of the drug might lead to inappropriate acting out that may include stealing.

Case #13: Alba: An Atypical Theft Offender in her 50s who had been taking prescribed tranquilizers, and then antidepressants, for many years.

Her lawyer referred Alba after she had been convicted of her fifteenth shoplifting offence in the previous twenty years. In our first session she confessed that she had actually shoplifted hundreds of times over that time period.

A person with very little formal education, it was nevertheless clear from the start that Alba had a very high intelligence and, in spite of her rather poorly spoken English, was more than capable of articulating her thoughts and feelings using simple yet profound visual metaphors. As she discussed her background it also became apparent that she had lived a very difficult life made all the more so by her familial situation.

Alba had been married to her husband, Fritz, who was eighteen years older, for over thirty years. Immigrants from southern Europe who came to the USA when she was still a teenager, she and her husband had worked hard and saved judiciously while he worked at his own appliances repair business, and had managed over the years to buy a modest house and even help put their two children through university. While Fritz's siblings and parents had moved to America shortly after they arrived, and lived just a few houses away from them, Alba's first family's members – including her four siblings and both her parents - remained in Europe. As a result, she felt extremely isolated and lonely throughout their marriage, especially given that Fritz's siblings and parents looked down upon her and treated her more like a maid than a relative.

Alba informed me that she had been prescribed tranquilizers for several years after she first came to America. Then, as antidepressants became more widely used, her family doctor switched her to this form of medication, and she had been on a relatively heavy dosage for the previous fifteen years. As we discussed her personal history Alba was able to describe how, even though she loved and respected her husband, she deeply resented the fact that he almost never stood up for her when she was dealing with her sisters-in-law and his mother. In fact, even when she and Fritz and their children went on summer holidays, Fritz had insisted that they had to vacation with his sisters and their families. Furthermore, while the rest of them relaxed at the beach for most of the day, Alba was expected to make everyone's meals, their beds, do the cleaning and so on.

In our one-on-one session Fritz confirmed to me that his wife's rendition of how she had been treated by himself, his siblings and his parents, was indeed valid. He also told me that he knew full well that as long as his wife was taking her antidepressants she was less inclined to confront him about his family's treatment of her.

At my suggestion Alba inquired of her physician if she could gradually reduce her intake of antidepressant medication, partly to enable her to think more clearly and be more consciously in touch with her feelings. He agreed, and over the succeeding weeks Alba stated that her thinking was becoming much less 'clouded' and she began openly expressing her thoughts and feelings more often and more effectively. During a joint session with her husband she told him, "I have not been myself for many, many years. I have been like a walking dead person. I love you but you are going to have to accept the fact that I am not willing to be your family's 'slave' any longer. And I don't want to holiday with your sisters and their families this summer. Those days are over! I deserve to have a holiday myself."

Rather sheepishly, Fritz agreed that his family had taken advantage of her over the years and that even though things were easier for him when she was medicated, he loved his wife and understood that he would have to treat her much better in the future. It can be noted that once Alba began to express herself more openly and more often to her husband, and given that he acknowledged and accepted the validity of her concerns, and acted upon them, her desire to shoplift entirely vanished.

****

Undoubtedly, the reader has been exposed to television commercials for one or other antidepressant and may have noted that when the accompanying lists of side effects are read aloud by an unseen narrator (usually with a reassuring voice), a rather hypnotic, repetitive and often loud 'melody' is played in the background, perhaps at between 40% to 85% of the loudness of the spoken words. These commercials almost always show an initially supposedly depressed person, and then within seconds, the same, now much happier person, perhaps enjoying an outing with his or her family.

While it is admittedly difficult to concentrate primarily on the spoken words while all the distracting visual images and accompanying music/sounds are being bombarding the viewer at the same time (Could that be the very reason they are used?), it is worthwhile attempting to do so. If one *does* really listen to the spoken words, one may well hear verbiage such as the following: *"In case of suicidal thoughts or actions... hostility or aggression... worsened depression... acting aggressive, being angry or violent... acting on dangerous impulses, etc...*" This verbiage may be offered as examples of the possible side effects of the antidepressant whose sale is being promoted. Note in particular the warning regarding any inclination towards "acting on dangerous impulses." That is exactly what Atypical Theft Offenders do; they act out the very dangerous impulse of taking something without paying for it and thereby risk getting arrested.

The reader may be aware of the debate raging in the professional community regarding the efficacy of prescribed antidepressants generally (a recent Google search using the term "doubtful efficacy of antidepressants" yielded over 2,470,000 results). While I do believe that antidepressants may be of assistance in some carefully selected and very severe cases, in my professional experience as a psychotherapist, I believe the evidence suggests strongly that most cases of depression can be relieved through psychotherapy augmented by regular physical exercise and changes in one's personal and/or working situations, and in changes in the ways one thinks, feels and behaves.

During a nearly half-century of conducting psychotherapy, one of the primary areas in which I have specialized is in treating clients who initially present with depression. Using a combination of rational-emotive, gestalt, cognitive-behavioural, mental imagery, existential and other therapeutic approaches, and with a direct focus on both the clients' inner cognitive (i.e., thinking) and affective (i.e., emotional) processes and their personal histories, while at the same time addressing current issues in their personal, social and/or working lives, most clients have reported markedly reduced feelings of depression within a relatively short time. During the therapy process they learn new, less neurotic and more mature ways of coping with the remnants of their past experiences, and better ways of dealing, at the time they emerge, with current or new potentially disturbing situations and circumstances.

****

Table Fourteen: Reported Use Of Antidepressants Among 29 Subjects in the 2013 Study   (data was available for 29 Ss)

Use of Antidepressants by Ss	# of Ss	% 0f 29 Ss
Ever used antidepressants	27	93.1%
Was using an antidepressant at the time of stealing	17	58.6%
Stole before ever using antidepressants	17	58.6%
Never stole before using antidepressants and were using them at the time they stole	7	24.1%
Frequency of stealing decreased while on antidepressants	0	0%

From the above Table it should be noted that more than half (17 or 58.6%) of the 29 Ss were using antidepressants at the time they stole. Furthermore, not a single one of the Ss stated that their stealing had *decreased* in frequency since beginning to take such a drug.

Furthermore, seven, or nearly a quarter of the persons in the 2013 study, reported that they had never stolen until *after* they began using an antidepressant. From the information provided above regarding the possible side effects associated with the use of these drugs, it is hardly surprising that Atypical Theft Offenders would not find their stealing curtailed by the use of antidepressants. One of the hallmarks of virtually all Atypical Theft Offenders is their marked anger and how poorly they tend to deal with disturbing emotions and events in their lives. Coupled with the possible side effects of (i) "new or worsened irritability", (ii) "becoming aggressive", iii) "becoming violent" and (iv) "acting on dangerous impulses", these drugs may have, in effect, added fuel to the fire raging inside these individuals and thereby possibly even promoted, via their disinhibitory side effects, the Ss acting out by stealing.

****

Table Fifteen: Classes of Antidepressants Used by Subjects in the 2013 Study (N=29)

Classes of Antidepressants Used by Ss	# of Ss	% of Ss
Number of Ss who used SSRIs (Selective Serotonin Reuptake Inhibitors)	19	65.5%
Number of Ss who used NRIs (Norepinephrine Reuptake Inhibitors)	4	13.8%
Number of Ss who used SNRIs (Serotonin-Norepinephrine Reuptake Inhibitors)	3	10.3%
Number of Ss who used SARIs (Serotonin Antagonist & Reuptake Inhibitors)	1	3.4%
Ss using antidepressants, of 29 Ss for which data was available	27	93%

Table Fifteen indicates that antidepressants of one or other of various types were used by 27 (or 93%) of the 29 Ss for whom the data regarding the use of antidepressants was available. It is worthwhile repeating the finding that <u>in not a single case did a subject report that the antidepressant being used had a positive effect in terms of actually reducing the frequency or the fact of stealing</u>.

****

Corroboration of our findings, by other investigators, of the presence of psychological reasons for atypical theft behaviour

In our original article titled *Shoplifting: An Occasional Crime of the Moral Majority*, published thirty years ago in a major peer-reviewed professional journal, we stated that, based upon the 34 cases we had reviewed for that study, we were able to articulate several possibly psychologically related reasons for the atypical theft behaviour of each and every one of these usually honest persons.

Twelve years after that 1983 study was published, an article titled *Considerations On The Dynamics Of Fraud And Shoplifting In Adult Female Offenders*, written by senior author and psychiatrist, Dr Renee

Fugere, of the Department of Psychiatry, McGill University and a member of the McGill Clinic in Forensic Psychiatry, was published in the *Canadian Journal of Psychiatry*, that largely corroborated our findings of psychological and psychodynamically based reasons for atypical theft behaviour. Their major finding concluded that "an unresolved mourning or loss in the context of high stress and depression" was one of the commonalities in the cases they examined.

In their paper, Fugere and colleagues also referred to the conclusions drawn by myself and my original co-investigator, psychiatrist Dr Don J Atcheson, in our 1983 article. They stated that, *"The mourning or loss (real or symbolic) in the context of high stress and depression is the basis for the loss substitution by shoplifting hypothesis of Cupchik and Atcheson (who)... were particularly struck by the extent of real or anticipated loss in the patient's life prior to the commission of the act... These losses usually involved one or more of the following categories: 1. loss of country, job, home, significant other because of separation or divorce; 2. life-threatening illness or death of a significant other, generally, and in particular; 3. the recurrence of cancer in a significant other or in the patient."* **Dr Fugere then stated, referring to their own independent clinical investigation, that "...(our) study _overwhelmingly supports (Cupchik's and Atcheson's) hypothesis_ not only in cases of shoplifting but also in those of fraud."**

[It is interesting that many studies that have reported upon the use of **antidepressant and other medications** to deal with cases of supposed 'kleptomania' have chosen to not refer to, or even reference, either our own 1983 article nor Dr Fugere's 1995 article, both of which were published in major peer reviewed psychiatric journals – specifically the *Bulletin of the American Academy of Psychiatry and the Law* and the *Canadian Journal of Psychiatry*, respectively.]

Since virtually all Atypical Theft Offenders initially present as depressed, it is understandable, *perhaps*, that their family physicians or psychiatrists have often speedily prescribed antidepressants. However, given the fact that they have been committing acts of theft that run counter to their usually high moral and ethical standards, it is prudent to inquire, *why* then prescribe a medication that, according to many of the antidepressant drug manufacturers themselves, may further disinhibit them and help precipitate acting out theft behaviour?

****

Special Note: Two personal accounts of possible powerful side effects of antidepressants
[I decided to add the next paragraphs to the end of this chapter a few days after the massacre of some 20 small children and their 6 staff members at Sandy Hook Elementary School in Connecticut in December of 2013. Incidentally, a Google search for "antidepressants and mass murders" done on the same day the following was written produced 149,000 entries.]

While this section does not deal in any *direct* way with the subject of atypical theft behaviour and the possible influence of the use of antidepressants upon such behaviour, I hope that by offering the following two stories, which were related to me by the individuals who I personally know and who were directly effected, may serve to contribute to a larger conversation that will hopefully take place regarding the use, safety and side effects of these drugs. You will also note that the first is actually a 'good news' story, of sorts.

A prominent musician reported to me that his concert performances evidently much improved after he began using an antidepressant.
It has been my pleasure to count as a friend for over 50 years a musician of world-class calibre. 'John' has played at concert halls and with major orchestras all over the world. Several years ago, when he was visiting Toronto for a series of performances later that week, we met and went for lunch 'to catch up' with each other's lives. During our time together he told me that several months earlier he had started using an antidepressant and to his surprise and delight, the reviews that appeared in the press shortly afterwards highlighted not only his technical expertise but raved about the sensitivity of his performances. He informed me that the reviews that praised the deep tonality of his playing were much like those he had received decades earlier but then had been absent for a long time – until he started on the antidepressant. It may also be noteworthy that *within minutes* of his having taken the first pill, he informed his wife that his personal angst had for the most part evaporated.

I have mentioned this case in part because I want to make clear that I have no desire to 'paint' the use of antidepressants as necessarily 'all bad in all cases and for every purpose'. Of course, at the same time, I certainly do not mean to imply that the use of such drugs will necessarily improve one's musical -or any other kind of- performance. Furthermore, whether the changes in my friend's performances were due to any genuine effects of the antidepressant or were the result of a placebo effect I am not in a position to speculate.

****

The next story is not such a positive one.

A prominent businessman attempted to kill his wife within 24 hours of the time he began using an antidepressant.
One day, more than a decade and a half ago, I received a call from a dear friend who lived in New England at the time and from whom I had not heard for several weeks. This friend, a professor in the history department of a major university, informed me that she was calling from her hospital bed where she was recovering from, literally, a near-death experience. She said that her husband had begun taking an antidepressant several days earlier and that, only a few hours after taking the first pills, he had physically attacked her during what started out as a minor argument, and that he had choked her, nearly fatally. In fact, she informed me that the police and paramedics doubted that she would survive the attack. A few weeks after she was released from the hospital she showed me some of the Polaroid photos that the police had taken while she was in hospital; the black eyes and deep red remnants of finger marks that showed so clearly on her neck were testament to the ferocity of the attack she had suffered.

A month or so later my friend shared with me the inch-thick collection of materials her husband's very prominent criminal lawyer's researchers had collected, containing many newspaper and other accounts of homicidal and suicidal acts that had been committed by persons who had recently begun taking antidepressants. Her husband's lawyer evidently hoped that, after reading the materials he provided, my friend would drop the criminal charges that had been laid against her husband. Having known my friend and her husband for over two decades prior to that event I would say that his violent physical attack upon my friend was absolutely out of character.

I have mentioned the two stories above to point out that the *side effects* of antidepressants may be very powerful indeed and it is incumbent on all of us to be alert to the possible risks and benefits of these prescribed medications.

****

During the past five decades I have very often worked with clients who initially presented as depressed and I have been largely successful in assisting many of them to markedly reduce or even nearly entirely eliminate their chronic feelings of depression. As a result I am thoroughly convinced that the use of the therapeutic modalities that I have learned and/or developed and that I regularly employ, including Redecision, Gestalt, Rational-Emotive, Cognitive Behavioural, Reintrojection, and Interpersonal therapies, are fully capable of helping a great many persons who present with mild to moderate (and in some cases even severe) depression. And that certainly includes most of the Atypical Theft Offenders with whom I have worked and who have completed the prescribed course of treatment.

[My next writing project is a book that describes the assessment and therapeutic approaches that I have developed and honed over the past five decades and that deal directly with altering an individual's most important and problematic relationships.]

PART VI

Treatment Approaches

When Working With

Atypical Theft Offenders

Chapter 16

TREATMENT FOR ATYPICAL THEFT OFFENDERS

Over nearly four decades I have developed and refined suitable assessment and treatment approaches for Atypical Theft Offender clients. When I worked at the Clarke Institute of Psychiatry (from 1974-86), where I first began my clinical investigations of atypical theft behaviour, I treated clients in both *individual* and *group* psychotherapy formats. Both approaches have pros and cons; seen one-on-one, the more well-known and/or otherwise more vulnerable clients could feel assured that their disclosures would remain confidential; in the group therapy format, clients gained the support of other theft offenders and more readily realized that they were not alone or 'weird' or 'bad' persons.

While a member of both the American Group Psychotherapy Association and the Canadian Group Psychotherapy Association for more than three decades, I gained valuable therapeutic tools to use in the group versions of the treatment programs I developed. I would be remiss if I did not also give credit here to Neil Lamper PhD, gestalt therapist extraordinaire and to my mentors, psychiatrist Dr Robert and Mary Goulding. I also learned a great deal during my years working for psychiatrist Dr Henry Fenigstein, the head of the North York Group Psychotherapy Foundation, in Toronto.

While there is a good deal to recommend individual, couples and group therapy formats for many different kinds of personal and interpersonal problems, having now used the live-video-via-webcam format for several years, I have concluded that the assessment and therapeutic work that can be done while the client stays at home and we can schedule our sessions much more flexibly, is in ways even superior to the work that could be done if we are in the same room for a compressed period of time or by using a group therapy format. The reasons for this are simple: for a client who lives in, say, California, Florida or Hawaii (and I have worked with clients in more than 17 states in the USA, including these three), to take several days away from home and work, travel to my location, stay at a hotel and arrange for transportation and food, (as many of my clients from all over the U.S. and Canada did do for over 15 years), at a cost of thousands of dollars, in order to take part in the four-day, in-office Intensive Intervention Program I offered, is simply not practical, and certainly not preferable, for many potential clients.

Now, by using our respective webcam-enabled computers, a client not only saves a great deal of time and a lot of money, but that individual can continue to carry on his daily personal and working life, while we work within our respective schedules and hold sessions about once a week, or as mutually agreed upon. As well, I am able to offer 'focused homework assignments' for the client to carry out in his or her day-to-day life in between our sessions, so that the therapeutic progress can be reality-tested and validated in the client's real world and in 'real-time'.

Webcam-enabled Therapy gets the attention of The New York Times.
In its September 23, 2011 issue, the New York Times published an interesting article titled, *When Your Therapist Is Only a Click Away*, by writer Jan Hoffman, about the increasing prevalence of therapy carried out by therapists and patients when they are not in the same physical locale. Eric A. Harris, a lawyer and psychologist who consults with the American Psychological Association, was quoted in that article as saying about 'web therapy' that, *"In three years, this will take off like a rocket.... Everyone will have real-time audiovisual availability."* While there may be certain kinds of problems and some clients for whom this format might not be appropriate, for the vast majority of Atypical Theft Offenders, webcam-enabled therapy is exceptionally well suited.

As I have indicated previously, having now utilized Skype to provide assessment and treatment of Atypical Theft Offenders for the past five years, I am entirely satisfied that this new modality offers excellent capabilities through which to carry out the clinical requirements of working with these theft offenders and, when and as appropriate, their Significant Others.

For an even more complete exposition of my clinical work and findings with Atypical Theft Offenders you are invited to thoroughly read *both* this book and my previous one on the same subject.
In my earlier book, *Why Honest People Shoplift Or Commit Other Acts Of Theft,* I devoted five chapters to describing, in some detail, the therapeutic approaches I employ, including Redecision Therapy (as

originally developed by Dr. Bob and Mary Goulding) and Reintrojection Therapy as well as Clinical Imaginative Imagery (my own original tools for helping clients to deal with important *earlier,* as well as current, relationships in their lives). I have chosen to not repeat most of that information in this book. Instead, I invite the reader to read my earlier book as well as this one; to facilitate this, I have arranged for the costs of my earlier book, in both the paperback and ebook editions, to be very economical indeed.

So, which persons are most likely to benefit from the webcam-based 20-Session Atypical Theft Offender *Intensive Intervention Program* that I offer?

The individuals most likely to benefit (in the order of likely probability of success) are the following:
1. Atypical Theft Offenders
2. many Mixed-Types of theft offenders
3. very occasionally, even some Typical Theft Offenders, so long as they are *genuinely motivated* to cease their theft behaviour.

I have found that the probability of success in assessing and treating Atypical Theft Offenders is directly related to:
a. their openness about their life experiences as well as the extent of their theft behaviour, recognizing that what they share will not be revealed outside of our sessions without their permission;
b. the strength of their motivations in wanting to stop stealing, *and*
c. the extent to which they are willing to work, not only during, but also *between,* sessions, carrying out the 'homework' assignments I offer them (including reading recommended books and addressing interpersonal issues with Significant Others).

Who would definitely not benefit from the *Intensive Intervention Program* that I offer?

Any theft offenders, whether Atypical Theft Offenders, the Mixed-type, or Typical Theft Offenders who are mainly interested in obtaining some sort of letter or 'report' for court purposes in order to minimize the courts' disposition of their cases, *but who have minimal or no genuine interest in ceasing their theft behaviour,* will find the Intensive Intervention Program of little use to them. Since the personal work invariably involved is indeed intense and self-revealing, attempts to fabricate an appearance of wanting to stop the theft behaviour will almost certainly fail.

Among the reasons that I like working with Atypical Theft Offenders is the fact that, in addition to almost invariably being truly fine, ethical individuals, they are usually very eager to uncover the reasons for the atypical theft behaviour that they have been having so much difficulty stopping. In other words, after having perhaps experienced many months or even years of one or other of various kinds of ineffective 'treatments', often including prescribed medications, they realize that the supposed remedies they have been receiving have been less than effective in addressing their theft behaviour.

My contact with a prospective client usually begins when I receive an email to my *wcupchik@aol.com* address. I ask those who wish to contact me to place my initials in brackets, i.e., **(WC)**, in the subject line of their email to me, so that I will be alerted to the fact that the email is not spam but rather, is indeed a personal communication intended for me to read. (I am the only person who has access to, and reads, these emails.) If the individual is requesting the 30-minute Free Brief Screening Interview that I offer, and assuming that the person has included enough information about himself and his theft behaviour so that I can make an initial determination that it might be appropriate to proceed to the screening interview, I can usually speedily respond to the query so that we can begin our dialogue. I encourage all individuals who are considering participating in the Intensive Intervention Program to first thoroughly read the webpages on my *www.WhyHonestPeopleSteal.com* website.

As well, at the end of this book (Appendix C), I have provided the *Free Brief Screening Interview Questionnaire* for prospective Atypical Theft Offender clients to fill out and email to me at *wcupchik@aol.com* in the event that they are ready, willing and able (and obviously, can afford) to participate in the web-based Intensive Intervention Program that I offer. My *www.WhyHonestPeopleSteal.com* will usually have the most up-to-date information about the Intensive Intervention Program, including its cost.

How I work to ensure that we don't waste either a prospective client's money or both our times

I usually offer the *Free Brief Screening Interview* via phone or webcam (the preferred means), to serious prospective Program participants, once they have filled out the *Free Brief Screening Interview Questionnaire* that I usually send them after receiving their initial email, and once I have had an opportunity to review their responses.

During the *Free Brief Screening Interview* both the client and myself are able to gauge what it might be like to work together. Of course, at the same time we also review a good deal of preliminary information pertaining to the individual's personal and theft behaviour history, and where things stand at the moment vis-a-vis any current criminal charges or recent sentences that were received from the court.

In many (but not all) cases, I may ask that the prospective client's spouse or partner join us for the *Free Brief Screening Interview* as well, since I have learned that the caring, supportive and involved participation of a Significant Other can be very helpful to achieving a successful outcome to the Program. The reason for this is simple; I have learned that atypical theft behaviour is almost invariably related to the quality and dynamics of the client's primary relationship; the partner's willingness to become actively involved in both the assessment and therapeutic process is often also an at least partial predictor of therapeutic success. (In some cases, the prospective participant is not yet ready or willing to involve their 'intimate other', and in those cases we carry on the *Free Brief Screening Interview* just one-on-one.)

If I have been able to determine the likelihood that I could be of assistance to the individual, and assuming that we are both comfortable with the webcam-enabled process, either we decide at the end of the brief interview that we will proceed with the Intensive Intervention Program or I may suggest that the individual review our conversation and perhaps discuss the matter further with his or her partner (or parent or other Significant Other) and then email me if he or she wishes to proceed with the full Program.

Since we work from our respective homes via webcam, I am able to offer clients a very flexible arrangement for the timing of our sessions. Frequently we will 'meet' in the early morning, late afternoon, early evening, or sometimes perhaps on the weekend, so as to accommodate our respective other work and home responsibilities. As well, neither sleet nor snow nor rain nor most any other sort of weather is as likely to interfere with our scheduled meeting times.

The general format of my live, online 20-session Intensive Intervention Program

In the early sessions, of course, we are primarily focused on the *assessment* phase of the Program. As well, I usually offer a variety of mini-lessons and reading assignments to the client so that we can begin to use a 'common language' (including Transactional Analysis) and I can quickly help the client to gain some preliminary understanding of why it is that he or she has been stealing.

As our sessions progress, I introduce more psychotherapeutic elements to assist the client to make the changes in his or her thinking, feelings, and/or behaviour that may be essential in order that the individual comes to think more clearly and positively, feel better and act more appropriately in a variety of situations.

I have found that, during the 20-session long Intensive Intervention Program, the majority of Atypical Theft Offender clients are able to make many, and perhaps even most of the changes necessary in order that they may cease their atypical theft behaviour. Of course, and at the same time, I reinforce the notion that stopping their stealing long-term is an ongoing process that requires conscious and deliberate self-observation, and this is not achieved instantaneously. Like physical fitness or stopping any one of a variety of inappropriate behaviours (like excessive drinking or smoking), effort and awareness are the keywords.

In some instances clients may request additional follow-up appointments with me to take place at a later time, and I am usually open to that possibility. I may also suggest that the Atypical Theft Offender client continue or follow-up with a local therapist, as well as possibly obtain some marital therapy sessions with an appropriate mental health professional.

Chapter 17

SUMMARIZING THE MAIN ELEMENTS OF MY APPROACH TO WORKING WITH ATYPICAL THEFT OFFENDERS

The reader will likely appreciate, especially after having finished reading this book and my earlier one, *Why Honest People Shoplift Or Commit Other Acts Of Theft*, that it is simply impossible to apply a one-size-fits-all 'cookie-cutter' approach to working with Atypical Theft Offenders. You have learned that the possible causes of atypical theft behaviour are numerous and yet only some of these underlying reasons may apply in any particular case. Therefore, of course, the approach to treatment must be *tailor-made* for each client. However, that being said, it *is* possible to provide a *general* template to initially bring to the task when considering the assessment and treatment of any single client who exhibits atypical theft behaviour.

In point form, therefore, the approach to assessing and treating an Atypical Theft Offender will likely include the following elements:

1. **Welcoming the new client as one deserving of the same respect and courtesy as all other clinical clients.** This is particularly important when dealing with Atypical Theft Offenders, since many of them are already experiencing profound shame and embarrassment, and a few may even be close to suicidal, in response to the humiliation they have been experiencing. As well, some Atypical Theft Offenders have told me of the punitive responses of their partners, relatives, and/or friends, as well as from their lawyers and even their local therapists, once they disclosed their theft behaviours. Atypical Theft Offenders should keep in mind that they themselves are not the only ones who are disturbed by their atypical theft behaviours. It is understandable that their closest relatives and friends may also be confused and upset that they have acted out as they have, especially for no readily apparent reasons (e.g., not being able to afford food or clothing for their children).

2. **Invite the client to complete the pen-and-paper tasks provided in this book, the *Cupchik Theft Offender Questionnaire* and *Cupchik Theft Offender Spectrum*.** These two tools provide a good deal of information that offers the clinician an initial view into the theft offender's personal background, current life situation and some other possible factors that have led to his theft behaviour.

3. **Ask the client to provide a selection of family photographs that are drawn from the his or her entire lifetime.** For decades I have employed so-called 'photo-analysis-therapy to deduce some very important features of the client's family dynamics; sometimes such photographs may have considerable value to be utilized later on in the clinical work together.

4. **Ask the client to consider inviting to one or more clinical sessions, a 'Significant Other' in the client's life, one who might offer valuable information and insight into the possible reasons for the client's atypical theft behaviour.** (I have had the opportunity to meet and interview Significant Others in well over 90% of the cases I have dealt with over the years; the S.O.s have included primarily intimate partners, but siblings, parents and/or adult children. It is absolutely true to say that *in every single instance* I have garnered some vitally important information about my clients and *what* and *whom* they must deal with in their present lives. It is most unlikely I would have acquired at least some of that data without input from their Significant Others.

5. **In the first few clinical sessions the aim is to gain as much relevant information as possible about the client's life, past and present.** It is my firm clinical opinion that it is vital to learn details of the client's personal history in order to better understand their atypical theft behaviour. In many cases, instances of severe childhood abuse and/or trauma have been a part of my clients' lives, and these experiences and their repercussions have had lasting impact upon their lives as well as a direct influence upon their theft behaviours.

6. **Offer the client some highly valuable information in the form of mini-lessons, including an understanding of the basics of the Transactional Analysis model of personality and interpersonal interaction and of the Drama Triangle.** This material is particularly helpful to Atypical Theft Offenders, since it assists them to learn to identify in the future, circumstances and occasions when they might be inclined to repeat their theft behaviours, and how to avoid acting out at those times.

7. **Provide clients an opportunity to consider a three-part contract <u>to make with themselves</u>, with the therapist as witness.** This contract basically consists of the following elements: (a) the client promises to not steal again; (b) in the event that he *does* steal again, he is to *not* keep the item that has been stolen; nor is the item to be given away to anyone else or put in a charity box or sold, and (c) the client is to contact me, via email, as soon as possible after the theft, and state <u>what</u> was going on in his life just prior (by perhaps minutes, hours or days) to his having stolen the items. Clients have reported that simply making this contract with themselves had very positive effects. *First,* by merely having made the contract, some clients have reported that they did not want to go back on their word. *Second,* the fact that they had agreed, that if they did steal again, that they would not keep the item or give it away or sell it, made the idea of taking something seem to not only *not* have a positive benefit but would actually be emotionally distressing. Their common refrain was; *"Well, what's the use of doing it (stealing) if I can't gain any benefit from it? I actually would find it painful to not keep or give away what I had stolen?"* Some clients have also reported that as a result of making this contract, it was as if they had a tiny version of the therapist sitting on their shoulder, reminding them of the contract they had promised to keep.

8. **Quickly commence the therapeutic part of clinical work.** For example, if the client had experienced either a significant loss early in his or her life (such as the loss of a parent, of a sibling, etc…) or some other kind of trauma (perhaps early childhood sexual and/or physical and/or emotional abuse), we begin to

address such matters in a therapeutic manner to help provide for some expression and resolution of pent up feelings and perhaps, even some closure. As another example of starting the therapeutic aspect of the work in short order, if there are current primary relationship issues that they are experiencing, we commence addressing these in therapy, with or without the primary 'other' being present in the clinical sessions.

9. **Employ appropriate, efficient and effective therapeutic modalities in the therapeutic work.** I use techniques and approaches that tend to produce results relatively quickly. For those readers who might have some familiarity with these approaches I will mention some of them by name: Transactional Analysis, Gestalt therapy, Redecision therapy, Cognitive-Behavioural therapy, Clinical Imaginative Imagery and Reintrojection therapy. The last two approaches are my own clinical developments about which I have written over the years.

10. **Use a live audio-video tool (such as Skype) that permits work with clients to proceed without them having to leave their homes to travel to the therapist's office (quite possibly in another city or country).** Indeed, this approach has demonstrated itself to be so effective that, since June of 2011, I have worked with all theft offender clients <u>exclusively</u> via Skype. As a result, my out-of-town and out-of-country clients have saved literally thousands of dollars in travel, room and board expenses – and of course, they also saved a great many hours and days in travel and away-from-home time. I have found that, optimally, 20 clinical hours are required for us to complete most of our work together. If there remains additional work to be done I may offer to continue working with them or else I refer them back to their previous or current local therapists with specific suggestions of issues to consider dealing with.

11. **Most competent and conscientious therapists recognize that dealing with atypical theft behaviour is beyond their professional training and skill sets.** I have had many excellent,

highly skilled therapists refer their clients to me to work on theft-related issues, recognizing that they did not have much (or any) experience working in the area of atypical theft behaviour. When desirable, I may consult with the local therapist in regard to continuing to work on specifically identified areas with the client.

12. **In some cases clients' lawyers request that a more formal Psychological Report be provided to them for court purposes.** The Psychological Reports that I provide clients' lawyers for use in court are often between 7 and 14 pages in length and are very detailed, describing in laypersons' terms: (a) what I believe are the most probable reasons for their clients' atypical theft behaviour, (b) the psychotherapeutic and other work the clients have carried out that may be expected to minimize the likelihood of recidivism, and (c) any recommendations I have for the clients to pursue in order to reinforce their new ways of coping with potentially triggering issues.

13. **Over the past two decades I have found, *on rare occasions*, that formal psychological testing has been a useful adjunct to our clinical work together.** This has been particularly true in cases where I have detected what may be severe and/or specific cognitive (thinking) and/or affective (emotional) deficits in the client's mental and/or emotional processing and/or behaviour. In order to determine whether there are indeed such deficits and to learn more about their nature, I have sometimes recommended formal psychological and/or neuropsychological testing to be carried out. In a very few instances, organic cognitive deficits have been identified and this information has had great import for clinicians in deciding whether and how to work with the clients, and for the courts regarding suitable sentencing.

14. **I request that clients see a general practice physician to determine whether there exists any kind of disease or other incapacitating process that might interfere with, or in any way affect our work together.** In instances where the client may have serious heart or other major physical medical issues, I request that

they see the appropriate medical doctor and that I receive a
written note from that professional, stating that our mutual client
is medically able to participate in what is likely to be an
emotionally arousing, and occasionally intense, assessment and
treatment process.

15. **I usually remain available to former Atypical Theft Offender
clients for additional follow-up sessions if/when they desire
such,** if I concur that such sessions would be appropriate, and if
we are able to make suitable arrangements.

The above outline of my work with Atypical Theft Offenders is not
meant to be exhaustive. For instance, in some cases, clients or I myself
have requested that I interview *more* than one 'Significant Other' in order
to gain a broader perspective of my clients' earlier and/or current life
situations. In other instances we have needed to explore particular issues in
considerable depth and thoroughness. As each Atypical Theft Offender
case presents unique features, I always remain open to dealing with any
relevant issues that present themselves, in effective and efficient ways. The
above 15 elements have been offered as a general outline; in most cases,
depending upon the material that emerges, specific 'detours' and/or
'feedback loops' can take place during the assessment and/or therapeutic
processes. Indeed, it is true to say that the initial assessment phase may
involve various therapeutic elements, and that the later, more focused
therapy component of our work together is likely to yield additional
information that adds to the totality and vigorousness of the final
assessment and treatment.

Chapter 18

OPTIMAL TREATMENT FOR ATYPICAL THEFT OFFENDERS REQUIRES SUFFICIENT EXPERTISE AND TIME

I have found that there are really no shortcuts to thoroughly understanding and dealing with Atypical Theft Offender clients' theft behaviour. Decades of experience have demonstrated to me that ten to twenty clinical sessions (meaning 500 to 1000 minutes of direct, one-on-one clinician-client contact) are usually required to arrive at the point that, not only has the *assessment* provided worthwhile answers as to *why* the individual has acted out in such obviously self-destructive ways, but also so that we have been able to make good progress *therapeutically*, to the point that the likelihood of further acting out theft behaviour is markedly diminished. The twenty sessions that I have with a client who takes the full Intensive Intervention Program are often sufficient to help ensure that the likelihood of further theft behaviour is minimized. In other cases, I am at least usually able to inform the court that the direction for further treatment has been mapped out in some detail for the theft offender to pursue further with either myself or a local therapist.

Incidentally, it is understandable that some clients and their lawyers are primarily interested in acquiring a 'letter' or 'report' of some kind that will state that further theft behaviour is virtually guaranteed to not occur in the future. I have certainly seen far too many such letters that previously consulted clinicians have provided to the courts on behalf of theft offenders – and yet, here are the same persons now contacting me, once again facing yet another charge of theft. I have often found such letters, written by clinicians who have seen their clients for just one, two or at the most, a very few sessions, to be remarkably superficial, offering such weak and inadequate comments as the following: *"This client stole because she was depressed. This individual now reports that she is no longer depressed, is currently on prescribed antidepressants and therefore I am confident that she will not steal again in the future."*

Hum! This sort of 'report' usually indicates to me that the problems underlying the theft behaviour, as well as any accompanying depression, have very likely *not* been dealt within the very few sessions that were held, and so the next time the person gets distressed or depressed... *look out!*

[A few years ago I actually had a prominent psychiatrist contact me because she had been apprehended for shoplifting - and, she informed me - not for the first time. She said that she was certain that her theft behaviour was merely an aberration that was no longer an issue and asked if I would be willing to see her *for a single session* and then write a letter to the court stating that I did not believe she would steal again. You can readily guess my response to *that* request!]

In the treatment phase of our time together, a client will often be invited to do some *Gestalt Therapy* work in order to deal with specific intrapersonal and interpersonal issues. We also frequently use *Redecision Therapy* and *Reintrojection Therapy*. As indicated in the previous chapter, I also utilize a number of other treatment modalities, if and as I consider them to be appropriate. I explain to the client why I am suggesting that we employ the approaches I recommend and together we decide whether to work in the specific ways I have suggested.

The work that I do with clients is grounded in our professional relationship. I make clear to the client that he or she has the right, and indeed the responsibility, to help move our work together forward, as well as to let me know when he or she might *not* wish to pursue specific areas of interest. In the rare instances that a client has asked that we not engage in a particular line of investigation I may ask what we 'just bumped into', in order to gain some degree of awareness as to why the client is reluctant to discuss a certain area. For example, I have had a few clients who have experienced severe sexual abuse as children, and who were not ready to discuss these matters in any detail until we had established a more secure therapeutic relationship. I have usually left it to the client to let me know when he or she was ready to discuss theses matters, after letting the person know that experience has shown that such issues nearly always bear some significance in regard to atypical theft behaviour.

To learn more about the webcam-based Intensive Intervention Program that I offer, the reader is invited to go to the following webpage on my website:
www.WhyHonestPeopleSteal.com/live_interactive_video_enabled_Interv ention_Program.htm

****

In order to give the reader an enhanced sense of the Intensive Intervention Program process, let's consider the case of Brenda.

Case # 14: Brenda: A Californian who took the web-based, 20-session Webcam-enabled Intensive Intervention Program from her own home
Brenda and her husband, Barry, contacted me by email in 2008 after having been on my www.WhyHonestPeopleSteal.com website. Because of their work (running an extremely successful web-based business) and large family commitments, it would have been very inconvenient for them to take five or six consecutive days out of their hectic schedules in order to travel to my office in Toronto for the 4-day Intensive Intervention Program that I offered at the time. As an alternative, they extended a very generous invitation to fly my wife and I out to California to spend two weeks at a five-star, ocean area resort and spa, at their expense, if only I were willing to conduct the Intensive Intervention Program near their home.

Unfortunately, it would have been inconvenient at that time for me to take Barry and Brenda up on their tempting offer. However, we agreed to attempt to work via Skype.

Happily, both Brenda and Barry quickly became very comfortable meeting with me via Skype (as have most clients I have worked with in this manner) and I quickly found that operating in this fashion was not only feasible but actually had some distinct advantages. Aside from the obvious value of being able to arrange our sessions at mutually satisfactory times across time zones (e.g., in the early evening and/or on the weekend), I found that I could easily see the facial expressions and body movements of both Barry and Brenda, even to the extent that, when Brenda became very emotional at one point and I could make out that she was on the verge of crying, I was able to request that Barry not reach out to pat her arm, as it seemed to me that this action might well not only stem Brenda's tears, but her emotional experience and expression as well.

Brenda was the designated patient, of course. That is to say that she was the theft offender about whom they had contacted me. Evidently, after they had moved to California from the Northeast once their Internet-based business expanded, Brenda's shoplifting was threatening not only their new social life but their business as well since it was essential that both Barry and Brenda have entirely exemplary, 'squeaky clean' reputations – and certainly no criminal records!

I had both Brenda and Barry present in front of their home computer (while their children were away at school) for the first four sessions, once I determined that Barry was very supportive to Brenda and they both agreed that they had marital issues with which to deal. While she was initially somewhat anxious when discussing her theft behaviour, Brenda quickly became more comfortable during our sessions and I then made a determination that it was time for her and I to 'meet' one-on-one via our respective computers. Barry understood that this was an important part of the process and for most of our remaining sessions, I 'met' with Brenda alone. As I expected, when Barry was not present, Brenda became even more forthcoming in describing the extent and precise nature of her shoplifting activities.

Brenda also revealed to me in our 1:1 sessions that she had experienced a great deal of abuse as a child, only some of which her husband was then aware. We were subsequently able to have sessions where she dealt with the very upsetting memories and emotional residues from these early experiences. I found that, having established a supportive, trusting relationship in the earlier sessions, there were no noticeable disadvantages at all to the fact that I was, at the time, more than three thousand miles away. [Indeed, as has become clear to many therapists who work via video or telephone, some clients feel less vulnerable when they are not in the same physical location as the therapist.] Brenda reported that she knew I was 'present', caring and concerned for her as she worked through her thoughts, feelings and memories associated with the abuse she had experienced from her alcoholic parents and drug-using siblings in the past, as well as the ongoing verbal and emotional abuse and manipulation that her parents attempted to continue to perpetrate upon her from their own home in New England.

At one point during the Intensive Intervention Program, Brenda informed me that her parents were coming to visit her and her family in California and we were able to prepare her to deal with their visit in a more satisfactory fashion than she had in the past.

Among the things we uncovered during our work together was the fact that Brenda <u>was often inclined to go shoplifting within minutes of having endured another one of her parents' guilt-provoking and anger-eliciting telephone calls</u>. Having made that connection, Brenda worked to change her ways of interacting with her parents during their twice-monthly phone calls, and she became increasingly aware that she was inclined to go into the Rebellious Child [Cr] ego state whenever her mother or father started in on one of their verbal rampages. Brenda initially found it difficult to easily change ego states immediately after the upsetting phone calls were over, and we worked together to help her find ways of acquiring and maintaining a more self-supportive, Nurturing Parent [Pn] ego state as well as a more appropriate Adult [A] ego state, both during the phone calls and once they were over. In learning how to stay in more effective ego states Brenda also acquired a greater sense of control over the direction and length of the phone calls. For safety's sake she also made an 'executive decision' to go for a bike ride or a run after one of these phone calls rather than go to a shopping mall.

Barry was interviewed for two sessions on his own, during which he was able to share with me personal and business-related concerns that he was not ready to reveal to Brenda for fear that she would become even more anxious and upset if she were to know what he was having to deal with, partly because of the economy and partly because Brenda's theft behaviour had become public knowledge for some persons in their immediate and online communities.

Among the many relevant bits of information that Brenda was able to provide me were a number of family snapshots that yielded some very useful clues as to the nature of the interactions amongst the members of her first family. For example, we could clearly see that Brenda's mother was usually situated between Brenda and her father in a host of family get-together snapshots as well as in posed photographs. Brenda was able to describe the circumstances surrounding many of these photos and they seemed to support her contention that her mother was possibly extremely jealous of Brenda's relationship with her father. We later used a few of these photos as 'therapeutic props' or stimuli, to assist Brenda in expressing and at least partially resolving some of her lingering resentment and anger towards her frequently inebriated mother, her "weak" father and her often 'stoned' sisters and brothers.

One of the most rewarding features of our work together was Brenda's gradually taking the time to appropriately nurture herself – something that had been a definite 'no-no' when she lived at her parents' home. She had promised herself that when she, Barry and their children moved out to California, she would take up horseback riding once again, an activity in which she had shown great promise as a teenager, and one that her parents had put a stop to at the very point that Brenda was beginning to enter and place well in dressage competition. It took a good deal of therapeutic work for Brenda to deal with the hesitation she had in taking up this activity once again, but with her husband's support for her doing something he knew very well she had thoroughly enjoyed as a child, she eventually began riding again. The changes in her deportment and emotional expression were truly a pleasure to witness. And by making this one important change in her day-to-day life, i.e., by treating herself well by taking up riding lessons again, she extended her improved attitude towards herself, her children and her husband. All these relationships subsequently became markedly enhanced!

By having our 20 sessions spaced out over ten weeks while she lived her life (as opposed to having a highly compressed, 4-day Intensive Intervention Program in my office), Brenda and her husband were able to initiate and solidify a number of changes in their daily lives. As well, Brenda contacted me once the formal, 20 sessions of the Skype-based Intensive Intervention Program was over, and we did some 'therapeutic fine-tuning'. I have received occasional emails from Brenda over the past years, usually accompanied by photographs of her riding for pleasure as well as in competition. A while ago I received a photo from Brenda showing her astride the horse that Barry had bought for her on the occasion of their twentieth wedding anniversary. She wrote that she had lost all desire to shoplift and had not participated in that inappropriate activity since the end of the Intensive Intervention Program.

One of the main reasons that I continue to find working with Atypical Theft Offenders so professionally rewarding is that they offer a very wide variety of examples of the atypical theft behaviour that some usually honest and ethical individuals display when they have not yet recognized, let alone dealt with, major pressing underlying issues. My experiences with these clients have been most informative, in that they have shown the extent to which <u>un</u>conscious and <u>sub</u>conscious material can precipitate overt behaviour that is clearly at odds with individuals' usual ways of consciously operating in the world. And the vast majority of these folks are genuinely fine persons - flawed, of course; wounded, very often - but capable of gaining much insight and demonstrating, time and time again, the ability to learn and grow and change - the very qualities that helped make the majority of them the exceptionally good persons they are.

A FINAL WORD...

In this book I have provided you, the reader, with a great deal of practical information pertaining to the atypical theft behaviour of usually honest persons.

I have also hopefully made it abundantly clear that the use of the term 'kleptomania', as it pertains to atypical theft behaviour, is almost never appropriate, and that the move that may be afoot to remove the exclusionary criterion that 'the stealing is not committed to express anger or vengeance' is, in my clinical experience, also inappropriate. As well, I have alerted you to the very questionable practice of prescribing antidepressants to usually honest persons who are having difficulties with theft behaviour.

Optimistically, I choose to believe that this book may help influence at least some professionals who may have a financial interest in investigating the pharmaceutical drugs that they are recommending be prescribed to usually honest persons who steal, since such prescriptions may not only not be appropriate, but may actually be contraindicated. And further, I hope that this book has made the case that it is entirely wrong to remove the 'why' (i.e., the probable, precipitating psychological reasons) from the 'what' (i.e., the mere fact of stealing) in regard to *atypical* theft behaviour. **The 'why' is crucially important and unless it is uncovered and dealt with, there is a distinct likelihood that the Atypical Theft Offender may well continue to steal.**

I am always interested in learning about the personal experiences of usually honest persons who steal and *whether* and *when* they may have been prescribed *which* antidepressant or other medication as a proposed 'solution' to the problem of their theft behaviour, and how that has been working for them. I invite any readers who wish to share their personal stories to email me at *wcupchik@aol.com* . Please remember to include my initials (WC) in the subject line of your email.

To all those usually honest persons who have engaged in theft behaviour that violates their usual moral and ethical principles and beliefs: I want you to seriously consider that **there may well be identifiable reasons for your theft behaviour that may not be due in some kind of**

so-called 'chemical imbalance' in your brain or elsewhere in your body, but rather may be related to earlier and/or more recent events in your life. Uncovering and dealing with these reasons is of utmost importance.

****

If, after having carefully read this book and completed the *Cupchik Theft Offender Spectrum*, you have concluded that you *are* possibly an Atypical Theft Offender, *please* also keep in mind that you are not a 'bad' or 'undeserving' individual. Rather, it is most likely that you are a good person who may have personal, psychological and/or interpersonal issues that need to be appropriately addressed, and that your atypical theft behaviour is likely a symptom of these underlying issues and/or a signal that you should attend to those matters in your life that are causing you distress. And be assured that, if you are willing to do the full therapeutic work required with a suitably trained and experienced professional, you very likely can be helped to stop any further self-destructive theft behaviour.

--- end ---

REFERENCES

- Anderson, Robert, *I Never Sang For My Father*, Signet Books, 1970

- Baird, Patricia, *Getting It Right: Industry Sponsorship And Medical Research,* Canadian Medical Association Journal, May 13, 2003; 168 (10)

- Bowlby, John, *Attachment and Loss: Volume 3, Loss, Sadness and Depression*, Penguin Books, copyright 1980

- Breggin, Peter R., *Recent U.S., Canadian and British regulatory agency actions concerning antidepressant-induced harm to self and others: A review and analysis,* International Journal of Risk & Safety in Medicine: 16: (2004) 247-259; published simultaneously in Ethical Human Psychology and Psychiatry, the Journal of the International Center for the Study of Psychiatry and Psychology

- Carlat, Daniel J, *Unhinged: The Trouble With Psychiatry – A Doctor's Revelations About A Profession In Crisis,* Free Press, 2010

- Courtois, Christine, *Healing the Incest Wound: Adult Survivors in Therapy*, W.W. Norton, 1988

- Covey, Stephen R., *The 7 Habits of Highly Effective People*, Free Press, 2004

- Cupchik, Will. *Clinical Imaginative Imagery*, Unpublished Doctoral Dissertation, University of Toronto, 1979

- Cupchik, Will. *Reintrojection Therapy: A Procedure for Altering Parental Introjects*, Psychotherapy: Theory, Research and Practice, Vol. 21, Summer, 1984, #2

- Cupchik, W and Atcheson, D J *Shoplifting: An Occasional Crime of the Moral Majority*, Bulletin of the American Academy of Psychiatry and the Law, Vol.11: 343-354, 1983. This article, as of December

2012, was available for viewing, for free, on the webpage http://www.jaapl.org/content/11/4/343.full.pdf+html?sid=331bd4e2-bd09-431c-858b-38bd3e11cb9d

- Cupchik, W and Atcheson, D J *Shoplifting: An Occasional Crime of the Moral Majority*, Chapter 18, <u>Clinical Criminology: The Assessment and Treatment of Criminal Behaviour</u>, Ed., M H Ben Aron, S J Hucker, C D Webster, Clarke Institute of Psychiatry/University of Toronto, 1985

- Cupchik, W *Why Honest People Shoplift Or Commit Other Acts Of Theft* (*Revised Edition*), Tagami Communications, 2002

- Fournier, J.C., et al. "Antidepressant Drug Effects and Depression Severity." *JAMA* 2010, 303-47-53

- Fugere, R, D'Elia, A, and Philippe, *Considerations on the Dynamics of Fraud and Shoplifting in Adult Female Offenders*, Can J Psychiatry, Vol. 40, April 1995

- Food and Drug Administration (FDA), *FDA issues Public Health Advisory on cautions for use of antidepressants in adults and children,* Rockville, Maryland (2004, March 22). www.fda.gov

- Grant, Jon E., Kim, Suck Won, *Kleptomania,* Journal of Family Practice, Volume 1, No. 8 August 2002 online edition.

- Goulding, Mary and Bob, *Changing Lives Through Redecision Therapy*, Brunner/Mazel, N.Y., 1979

- Healy, David, *The Antidepressant Era,* Harvard University Press, 1997

- Healy, David, *Let Them Eat Prozac: The Unhealthy Relationship Between The Pharmaceutical Industry and Depression,* New York University Press, 2004

- Hoffman, Jan, *When Your Therapist Is Only a Click Away,* article in The New York Times, Jan 23, 2011

- James, Muriel and Jongeward, Dorothy, *Born to Win*, Addison Wesley, Reading, MA, 1971

- Jung, Carl, *The Collected Works of C. G. Jung, Vol. 18, The Symbolic Life,* 1975,

- Karpman, Stephen. *www.KarpmanDramaTriangle.com [retrieved from the Internet, December 17, 2012]*

- Kirsch, Irving, *The Emperor's New Drugs: An Analysis of Antidepressant Medication Data* Submitted to the U.S. Food and Drug Administration, 2002

- Kirsch, Irving, *The Emperor's New Drugs: Exploding the Antidepressant Myth,* Basic Books, Reprint Edition, 2011

- Lepkifker, E, Dannon PN, Ziv, R, Horesh N, Kotler M, *The Treatment of Kleptomania with Serotonin Reuptake Inhibitors,* Clinical Neuropharmacology 1999 Jan-Feb; 22 (1): 40-3

- Sismondo, Sergio, *How Pharmaceutical Industry Funding Affects Trial Outcomes: Causal structures and responses,* Social Science & Medicine, 66 (2008) 1909-1914

- Sismondo, Sergio, Department of Philosophy, Queen's University, Canada. *Pharmaceutical Company Sponsorship of Research: A Review*, July 27, 2006: an article

- Villareal, JD, *Kleptomania Symptom Assessment Scale (K-SAS),* Impulse Control Disorders Clinic, University of Minnesota, 2009

- Viorst, Judith Necessary Losses, Ballantyne Books, 1987

- Wikipedia (retrieved on October 26, 2012, from http://en.wikipedia.org/wiki/credit_default_swaps)

APPENDICES

APPENDIX A: WHAT YOU WILL FIND IN MY EARLIER BOOK THAT AUGMENTS THE ONE YOU ARE NOW READING

In my previous book, *Why Honest People Shoplift Or Commit Other Acts Of Theft*, written more than a decade ago, I presented the main findings of a study I had conducted of some 34 cases of atypical theft behaviour by usually honest persons. A very few of those cases have also been mentioned in the book you have been reading because they still offer some of the most illustrative examples of *classic* Atypical Theft Offenders. The earlier book was written in a more formal style that made it suitable for not only the theft offenders it describes, but for their clinicians, lawyers, probation and parole officers and the courts, as well.

The earlier book also includes a chapter that is written as a 'letter' to the theft offender's Significant Other. It remains very useful reading for those who are part of the theft offender's everyday life and who want to gain insight into the role they might play in helping their loved one heal and overcome the inclination to steal again at any time in the future.

Also in the first book is a somewhat lengthy <u>abridged transcript</u> of the first and only session that I held with a classic Atypical Theft Offender (Alice, Case # 5 in the earlier book; presented as Case # 9 in the book you are now reading). It offers an excellent example of the kinds of psychological issues that might precipitate atypical theft behaviour, and makes it very clear that labelling such an individual as suffering from 'kleptomania' would be not only erroneous, and a gross injustice, as well.

The earlier book offers a good deal of other information regarding the nature of Atypical Theft Offenders, their assessment and treatment that I have chosen to not duplicate here. As mentioned previously, some five chapters and more than 50 pages of the earlier book are specifically devoted to my clinical treatment of Atypical Theft Offenders. For the reader who wants to gain the most information about the atypical theft behaviour of Atypical Theft Offenders, I would encourage you to also read *Why Honest People Shoplift Or Commit Other Acts Of Theft*. In order to make its purchase more economical the prices for both the paperback and ebook editions of the earlier book have been substantially lowered from their original sale prices.

APPENDIX B: CUPCHIK BRIEF SCREENING INTERVIEW QUESTIONNAIRE

This questionnaire is intended to be completed by persons considering taking the full 20-session Skype-based Intensive Intervention Program and who wish to apply for the *Free Brief Screening Interview* (that is, as long as I still remain in practice) to help determine whether taking the Program at this time may be worthwhile. In order to be aware of <u>the current cost</u> of the Program, the individual should first read the webpage http://www.whyhonestpeoplesteal.com/live_interactive_video_enabled _Intervention Program.htm and make certain that the cost of the program is not a problem. Then, assuming that the cost is not an issue, please fill out the questionnaire and email it to *wcupchik@aol.com* . In the subject line please write the following: [(WC) My completed FBSI Questionnaire]. Alternately, the completed Questionnaire may be faxed to 416-489-8882 (again, as long as I remain in active practice). After reading the individual's responses I will reply via email and if I believe that taking the Intensive Intervention Program may be of assistance, I will email the person and suggest possible times for the proposed Free Brief Screening Interview to take place. If I do not think that the Program may be suitable, then I will so advise via email.

1. First name only (at this time): _____

2. Age/gender: _____ / _____

3. Marital Status: If married or living common-law, please state your spouse's first name. _____

4. Ages and genders of your children, if any.
-
-

-
-

5. Educational Background:

_____
_____

6. Your work/profession:

_____
_____

7. Have you ever stolen from your workplace, your co-workers, clients or customers? If yes, please describe to what extent you have done so.
-
-
-
-

8. Describe the sort(s) of theft behaviour: (i.e., shoplifting, fraud, etc...) that you have engaged in.
-
-
-
-
-

9. How many times in total you have committed these kinds of acts?

_____

10. From whom (relatives, friends, strangers, etc...) and where (kind of stores, elsewhere) have you stolen?

-
-
-

225

11. Over what period of time? _____ years

12. Have you ever been caught? _____ Charged? _____
    Convicted? _____ When, where and how many times,
    please:

    -
    -
    -
    -
    -

13. Your estimate of the total amount, in dollars, of the value of the
    items/money stolen: _____

14. Issues in your personal and/or working life that have been and
    still are of concern to you:

    -
    -
    -
    -
    -

15. Do you take prescribed antidepressants? _____ If so,
    which one? _____ Dosage? _____ For how
    long have you been taking this medication? _____
    What other prescribed medications are you taking?

    -
    -
    -
    -

16. Did you ever steal <u>before</u> being on an antidepressant?

_____

17. Did you steal only <u>after</u> you began using an antidepressant?

_____

18. Did/do you have a problem with alcohol? ____ ___ Street drugs (which ones)? _____

19. Do you have a considerable amount of anger? _____ If so, towards whom?

-
-
-
-

20. Do you tend to be depressed a good deal of the time?

_____

21. Who in your personal life knows about your problem with stealing?

-
-
-
-

22. Does that person truly know the *full* extent of the problem?

_____

23. What else can you relate about yourself and the goings on in your personal life, that you think may be relevant to your stealing behaviour?

-
-
-

24. What (other) personal issues are of concern to you at the present time?

-
-
-
-

25. When did you last steal? _____

26. When did you last get caught and/or were charged?

_____

27. Do you currently have a charge pending before the courts?
_____ If yes, then in what jurisdiction (country, state or province)? Details of the charge, please...

-
-
-
-

28. How many times have you been charged? _____ Convicted?
_____ Have you ever spent any time in jail for stealing offences? _____ How many separate times, and for how much time in total?

29. Have you been convicted of <u>any</u> other offences? Please describe…
    -
    -

30. Do you genuinely wish to stop your theft behaviour once and for all <u>or</u> are you primarily or only interested in simply dealing with any current charge? _____ [If the latter, then working with Dr Cupchik is <u>definitely not</u> recommended]

31. Have you had any previous psychotherapy? _____ Are you currently in therapy? _____ What kind, when, with whom, and what was/has been the duration of the treatment?
    -
    -
    -
    -

   What did you learn and how has it helped you in any area(s) of your life?
    -
    -
    -

32. Please add below <u>any other information that you care to and/or that you think Dr Cupchik should probably be aware of</u>, when considering your request for the Free Brief Screening Interview.
    -
    -
    -
    -
    -

33. <u>Since</u> you have been using a prescribed antidepressant, has your stealing markedly increased, lessened or stayed about the same?

_____

Please elaborate.

-
-
-
-
-

34. How would you describe the state of your primary relationship? (Strained, supportive, in trouble, etc...)

-
-
-

35. How supportive do you think your partner would be if he/she knew the full extent of your stealing?

_____ *Does* he/she really know the FULL extent of your theft behaviour? _____

36. Are you seriously considering the possibility of taking the 20-session Skype-based Intensive Intervention Program with Dr Cupchik? _____ If your answer is 'Yes', what are your primary concerns in relation to considering this possibility?

-
-
-
-

37. Where (in what country, state or province) do you live?

_____

38. Does the jurisdiction in which you live have a so-called 'three-strikes policy' for criminal behaviour, including shoplifting?

_____

39. I understand that the Free Brief Screening Interview may be offered *only* to persons who might benefit from taking the Intensive Intervention Program *and* who have the funds required for the professional fee involved, should we decide to proceed with the 20-session Intensive Intervention Program. I have read the relevant pages on the www.whyhonestpeoplesteal.com website, and I believe that I am aware of the current cost of the 20-session of the Intensive Intervention Program, and payment of that fee is not an issue for me.

I agree:_____   I do not agree: _____

APPENDIX C: A NOTE TO CLINICIANS AND ORGANIZATIONS WHO WISH TO USE THE CUPCHIK THEFT OFFENDER QUESTIONNAIRE, THE CUPCHIK THEFT OFFENDER SPECTRUM, THE CUPCHIK BRIEF SCREENING QUESTIONNAIRE, TABLE ELEVEN AND/OR TABLE TWELVE.

I devised the **Cupchik Theft Offender Questionnaire** as a practical pen-and-paper instrument that provides a rapid means of gathering potentially important basic information about a particular client and may hold important clues as to what factors may have precipitated that person's atypical theft behaviour.

The **Cupchik Theft Offender Spectrum** helps determine whether a client should be categorized as (1) an Atypical Theft Offender, (2) a Typical Theft Offender, or (3) of the Mixed Atypical/Typical Type.

[Please note that earlier versions of the Cupchik Theft Offender Questionnaire and Cupchik Theft Offender Spectrum were also included in my previous book, *Why Honest People Shoplift Or Commit Other Acts Of Theft*. However, the current versions of both these two tools have more items and have been further refined.]

The **Cupchik Brief Screening Interview Questionnaire** is basically a 'quick take' tool that offers an initial estimate of whether the prospective client would be suitable for the Intensive Intervention Program.

****

Table Eleven: Commonly Shared Clinical Findings Of The Cupchik 2013 Study, With Columns Provided For Your Own Personal Responses

Table Twelve: A _Rank-Ordered_ Summary Of Shared Personal History, Qualities And Experiences Of Atypical Theft Offenders (As Drawn From The Cupchik 2013 Study), With Columns Provided For Your Own Self-Evaluation.

Tables Eleven and Twelve provide organized summaries of the findings of the 2013 Study; the reader may confirm (or not) that he or she shares similar experiences or characteristics with many of the 30 Atypical Theft Offenders in the 2013 study.

Both Tables have columns on the right that allow the reader of the print edition of this book who is a theft offender, to check off each of the listed items according to whether he or she identifies with the item (obviously, the 'Me Too' column) or does not identify with the listed item (the 'Not Me' column). Reviewing the theft offender's responses to these two Tables, together with the responses to the Cupchik Theft Offender Spectrum and Cupchik Theft Offender Questionnaire, will provide both the theft offender and the clinician or other professional who proposes to help the theft offender to (i) make a potentially valuable initial determination of the likelihood that the individual is in fact an Atypical Theft Offender, and (ii) will likely offer clear directions as to the assessment and therapeutic work that the theft offender may need to do in order to stop stealing.

****

ON USING AND/OR PURCHASING THE RIGHTS TO DUPLICATE AND USE ANY OR ALL OF THE ABOVE QUESTIONNAIRES AND/OR TABLES INCLUDED IN THIS BOOK.

Any PAPERBACK purchaser of this book is hereby granted the right to use any of the three pen-and-paper instruments and/or Tables (including Tables Eleven and Twelve) <u>one time only</u>. The use of any of these tools by any other person or persons is prohibited except as outlined directly below.

For solo practice clinicians:

Independent solo practice clinician who has purchased a hardcopy version of this book and wishes to employ (**1**) the *Cupchik Theft Offender Spectrum*, and/or (**2**) the *Cupchik Theft Offender Questionnaire*, and/or (**3**) the *Cupchik Brief Screening Interview Questionnaire* and/or (**4**) *Table Eleven* and/or (**5**) *Table Twelve* is hereby granted permission to use these pen-and-paper instruments, for free, <u>with one client only</u>.

If the clinician wishes to use any or all of these pen-and-paper instruments with more than one client, he or she should note that the

Cupchik Theft Offender Spectrum, the *Cupchik Theft Offender Questionnaire*, the *Cupchik Free Brief Screening Interview Questionnaire* as well as *Table Eleven* and Table Twelve are the copyrighted materials of Dr Will Cupchik and arrangements can be made to purchase the rights to copy and use these tools, only as described below.

(i) For a one-time fee of $145.00 U.S. for any <u>one</u> of these pen-and-paper instruments/tables, or (ii) a one-time fee of $195.00 U.S. for any <u>two</u> of these instruments/tables, or (iii) a one-time fee of $235.00 U.S. for <u>any</u> <u>three</u> of these instruments/tables, or (iv) a one-time fee of $265 for <u>any</u> <u>four</u> of these instruments, or (v) $290 for <u>all five</u> of these instruments/tables, the independent solo clinical practitioner or other professional will be granted permission to reproduce **printed copies only** **(not digital)** <u>at his or her own cost</u>, an <u>unlimited</u> number of hardcopies only, for use by him or her *only*, with the understanding that these materials are not, and will not, to be given, loaned, gifted, sold or in any way transmitted to, or shared with, any *other* individual practitioner or organization for his/her/their use. The buyer agrees to <u>not</u> include any of these instruments in any brochures or publications (digital or hardcopy) that he or she may produce or contribute to, or give to his or her clients. The permission to use these instruments should be understood to mean that <u>they are be used on their own</u>, and not part of any other package or brochure that he or she may produce or distribute that would contain any other materials. The copies must clearly indicate that the copyrights for these instruments are retained by Dr Will Cupchik alone.

****

For clinicians who are employed by an organization or company:
If clinicians or other professionals who work for an organization - and/or if the organization itself - wishes to use any of these instruments more than once only, then (i) For a one-time fee of $195.00 U.S. for any <u>one</u> of these pen-and-paper instruments/tables, or (ii) a one-time fee of $265.00 U.S. for any <u>two</u> of these instruments/tables, or (iii) a one-time fee of $295.00 U.S. for <u>any three</u> of these instruments/tables, or (iv) a one-time fee of $325 U.S. for <u>any four</u> of these instruments, or (v) $350 U.S. for <u>all</u> <u>five</u> of these instruments/tables, permission is hereby granted permission for the organization to print, at its own expense, an unlimited number of **hardcopies** (not in digital form), for use by the purchasing organization only and these materials are not to be given, loaned, gifted, sold or in any

way transmitted to, or shared with, any other individual practitioner or organization.

The organization-buyer also agrees to not include any of these instruments in any publications (digital or hardcopy) that the organization may produce or contribute to, or give to its clients. The permission to use these instruments should be understood to mean that they are to be used on their own, and not as part of any other package or brochure that the organization may produce or distribute that would contain any other materials. The copies must clearly indicate that the copyrights for these instruments are retained by Dr Will Cupchik alone.

All fees are to be paid only via cashier's checks or bank drafts drawn from a major bank, in U.S. dollars, payable to Dr Will Cupchik and snail mailed to *Dr Will Cupchik, 2528 Bayview Avenue, P.O. Box 35532, Toronto, Ontario, Canada M2L 2Y4.* An email should be sent to Dr Cupchik at wcupchik@aol.com stating that the fees have been sent, together with the name and title of the purchaser and/or organization that is making the purchase. Upon receipt of the funds Dr Cupchik will send an email to the purchaser stating that the individual or organization has paid the required fee for the unlimited hardcopy use by that individual or organization only. It will be understood that the purchaser is responsible for making any copies of these tools at his/her/their own expense.

Please note that any and all fees for the use of these instruments must be sent in the form of a bank draft or certified check or comparable form drawn from a major US or other major bank, and in U.S. funds. (Please do not send a regular check.)

Purchasers from countries *other* than the USA and Canada should send the fees, in US funds, via a bank draft or certified check payable to Dr Will Cupchik and drawn from a major bank in their country. An email should be sent to Dr Cupchik at wcupchik@aol.com stating that the fees have been sent, together with the name and title of the practitioner and/or organization that is making the purchase. When Dr Cupchik receives full and suitable payment for any of the pen-and-paper instruments/tables referred to above, he will reply with an email confirmation that states that the buyer is permitted to use the instrument(s)/table(s) in accordance with the conditions referred to above.

These pen-and-paper instruments are not to be copied, used by, or transmitted to any other person(s) or organization(s) aside from those specified above who have paid the stated fee(s), and permission is specifically **not** granted for the *electronic* duplication or distribution of these pen-and-paper instruments for any purpose or reason whatsoever.

Dr Will Cupchik alone retains the copyrights of these instruments and his name and copyright designations must not be removed from them when they are copied, distributed and/or used. Permission is also specifically **not** granted for their inclusion in any brochure, book or other publication of the solo practitioner or organization. Only loose, single copies of these instruments are to be used by the purchasers for their clients.

****

Cautionary notice:

The *Cupchik Theft Offender Spectrum, Cupchik Theft Offender Questionnaire, Cupchik Brief Screening Questionnaire* and *Tables Eleven* and/or *Twelve* may be used to assist the client at home, in the therapist's office, and/or for court purposes. Their use should be approached with considerable thought and caution. Theft offenders should preferably utilize the services of a competent professional when completing the *Cupchik Theft Offender Spectrum*.

No representation is being made or offered for the level of reliability or validity of these pen-and-paper instruments and/or tables. Rather, please be advised that Dr Cupchik developed them and has found them to usually be very helpful (i) in estimating where the theft offender belongs along the Spectrum and (ii) in providing often relevant information regarding the theft offender's personal history, recent and current life and legal situation.

****

[The decision to include the short paragraph that follows was made after it was deduced that some solo practitioners and/or organizations may have chosen to either not seek or not obtain written permission to use any of the five pen-and-paper instruments referred to in this Appendix.]

<u>Any unauthorized use of any of these tools</u> (that are the *copyrighted properties* of Dr Will Cupchik alone) <u>might perhaps be considered acts of theft</u> and needless to say, are hardly the behaviours that responsible practitioners and organizations would employ when dealing with their theft offender clientele.

APPENDIX D: TRAINING PROGRAMS FOR MENTAL HEALTH PROFESSIONALS WHO WISH TO LEARN TO WORK WITH ATYPICAL THEFT OFFENDERS

I have developed training programs for suitable professionals, including Clinical Social Workers, Psychologists and Psychiatrists, each of whom must have at least 10,000 clinical hours of post-certification practise in conducting psychotherapy.

Aims of the Programs

The programs involve distinct levels of training specifically aimed at producing skilled and experienced clinicians who will be able to carry out assessment and treatment of Atypical Theft Offenders.

The programs aim to train individual practitioners as well as those working in appropriate institutions or organizations. Some of the work may be conducted via live, webcam-enabled communications.

I may also be available to provide on-site training to therapists who are in the employ of suitable retreat and/or rehabilitation organizations.

For more information about the Training Programs, by all means contact me via email at _wcupchik@aol.com_ .

APPENDIX E: A NOTE ABOUT <u>INFORMATIONAL INTERVIEWS</u>* FOR FAMILY MEMBERS (FMs) OF A POSSIBLE ATYPICAL THEFT OFFENDER

I sometimes receive emails from family members of possible Atypical Theft Offenders in which they often write, in essence, the following: *"Do you conduct any sessions or seminars for family members? It has been very difficult dealing with this issue and it affects me and the entire family."* I have also received inquiries as to whether I would be willing to consult with a local therapist whom the individual is already seeing.

The answer is, yes, I do offer 'Informational Interviews' for family members (and/or qualified psychotherapists). The main purpose of such sessions is to assist the family members and/or their therapists to better understand and deal with the suspected Atypical Theft Offender.

I have had FM sessions, via Skype, with up to three persons at a time. As you will understand, a part of our time is taken up with learning about the theft offender, his or her family relationships (especially his/her primary relationship), the family members' own personal situations and details of the theft behaviour of the family member they care about.

Experience has shown that a double-session (i.e., 100 minutes long) Informational Interview is almost invariably required in order to afford us enough time to review key aspects of the history and issues of the theft offender and the family member(s), and to discuss those matters that are of most concern to the latter. Often family members want to address the best ways to confront - and at the same time support - their loved ones about the theft behaviour, to learn how to help minimize the theft offender's impact on the rest of the family, including especially children and/or grandchildren. These Informational Interviews are carried out within a supportive and educational framework so as to assist the family member to better understand and cope with the atypical theft behaviour of their loved ones.

You will understand that I could only speak *in general terms* about matters that may pertain to the possible Atypical Theft Offender; since I will not have met the possible ATO I could not possibly make any definitive or specific statements about that individual. Also, of course, if I *had* met the possible Atypical Theft Offender, I would not be able, out of the need to maintain confidentiality, to discuss *anything* pertaining to that person and our sessions without his/her explicit written permission (and preferably, his/her presence as well).

Having stated the above, I know that family members often gain a good deal from these Informational Interviews and I have also learned important information about my prospective client from those who presumably know a great deal about the individual.

* To find the current professional fee for the double-session (100 minutes long) please go to the
http://www.whyhonestpeoplesteal.com/live_interactive_video_enabled_Int ervention_Program.htm webpage;
the fee will be indicated at the appropriate place on the webpage; alternately just email me at wcupchik@aol.com and inquire about the current cost of the Informational Interview for Family Members or local therapists.

---

i Cupchik, W, Atcheson, D.J. *Shoplifting: An Occasional Crime of the Moral Majority,* Bulletin of the American Academy of Psychiatry and the Law, Vol.11: 4-343, 1983

ii *Clinical Criminology: The Assessment and Treatment of Criminal Behaviour,* Edited by Ben-Aron, M.H., Hucker,S.J., and Webster,C.D., Clarke Institute of Psychiatry/University of Toronto, 1985, Chapter 18. Cupchik, W, Atcheson, D.J. *Shoplifting: An Occasional Crime of the Moral Majority.*